PHOTOSHOP®

STUDIO SKILLS

Steven Moniz

Hayden
Books

President
Richard Swadley

Associate Publisher
John Pierce

Publishing Manager
Laurie Petrycki

Managing Editor
Lisa Wilson

Marketing Manager
Stacey Oldham

Acquisitions Editor
Rachel Byers

Development Editor
Bront Davis

Copy/Production Editors
Erik Dafforn, Kevin Laseau,
John Sleeva

Technical Editors
Kate Binder

Publishing Coordinator
Karen Flowers

Book and Cover Designer
Sandra Schroeder

Cover Illustration
Aren Howell

Manufacturing Coordinator
Brook Farling

Production Team Supervisors
Laurie Casey, Joe Millay

Production Team
Trina Brown, Kim Cofer,
Rowena Rappaport, Scott Tullis

Indexer
Bront Davis

Photoshop Studio Skills

©1997 Steven Moniz

Library of Congress Catalog Number: 96-80340
ISBN: 1-56830-356-4

Copyright © 1997 Hayden Books

Printed in the United States of America 1 2 3 4 5 6 7 8 9 0

Warning and Disclaimer

Trademark Acknowledgments

All terms mentioned in this book that are known to be trademarks or service marks have been appropriately capitalized. Hayden Books cannot attest to the accuracy of this information. Use of a term in this book should not be regarded as affecting the validity of any trademark or service mark. **Photoshop** is a trademark of **Adobe, Inc**.

About the Author

Steven Moniz is the Director of Training at Graphics Express in Boston and teaches regularly scheduled courses in everything from Macintosh Basics to Advanced Photoshop, QuarkXPress, HTML programming, and Web Design. On the cutting edge of desktop publishing and electronic prepress technology since its inception in the early '80s, Steve's background includes traditional offset printing, prepress, and typesetting. Steve often lectures on Digital Prepress topics and provides customized training for corporate clients on both Macintosh and Windows computers.

Steve was also one of the authors for *Photoshop 4 Complete*, from Hayden books. He wrote the chapters on scanning, painting, working with color images, and custom colorization.

Dedication

Dedicated to my parents Charles and Pauline, whose ic in my accomplishments has always been my inspiration.

Acknowledgments

Thank you to my family, Ann Mahoney, and Paul Daverio for their help and support. Special thanks to Rachel Byers, Bront Davis, Kevin Laseau, and all the folks at Hayden Books who helped get this book together, especially those who contributed photographs for use in the tutorials.

Hayden Books

The staff of Hayden Books is committed to bringing you the best computer books. What our readers think of Hayden is important to our ability to serve our customers. If you have any comments, no matter how great or how small, we'd appreciate your taking the time to send us a note.

You can reach Hayden Books at the following:

Hayden Books
201 West 103rd Street
Indianapolis, IN 46290
317-581-3833

Email addresses:

America Online: Hayden Bks
Internet: hayden@hayden.com

Visit the Hayden Books Web site at http://www.hayden.com

Contents at a Glance

Table of Contents

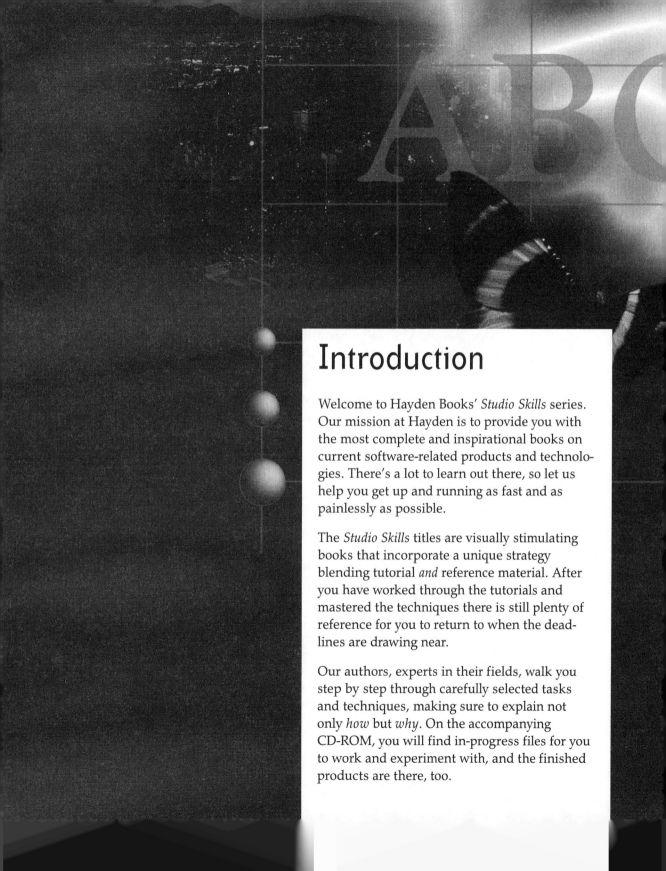

Introduction

Welcome to Hayden Books' *Studio Skills* series. Our mission at Hayden is to provide you with the most complete and inspirational books on current software-related products and technologies. There's a lot to learn out there, so let us help you get up and running as fast and as painlessly as possible.

The *Studio Skills* titles are visually stimulating books that incorporate a unique strategy blending tutorial *and* reference material. After you have worked through the tutorials and mastered the techniques there is still plenty of reference for you to return to when the deadlines are drawing near.

Our authors, experts in their fields, walk you step by step through carefully selected tasks and techniques, making sure to explain not only *how* but *why*. On the accompanying CD-ROM, you will find in-progress files for you to work and experiment with, and the finished products are there, too.

Or, if you have work to do, feel free to extrapolate from our steps using your own materials and files.

Conventions

Throughout this book you will see names of menus separated by arrows, such as Filter➡Stylize➡Emboss. This is a directive to choose the Filter menu from the menu bar, choose Stylize from the Filter menu, and choose Emboss from the Stylize submenu.

You will also note that CD-ROM icons are used throughout this book. This means an image on the CD-ROM is required to perform the tutorial. You can find the file by following the folder path given in the text. "Open lessons/chap16/village.psd," for example, is a directive to open the village.psd image located in the chap16 folder that is in the lessons folder.

Thanks for purchasing this title. We strive to make the best and most useful books. We hope that you learn as much from reading this and other Hayden titles as we did—and maybe have a little fun along the way.

Hayden Books

Photoshop Basics

Photoshop is the application of choice for most computer users involved in the graphic arts and photography today, and it is widely used by those designing Web pages for the Internet. Whether you are a designer, graphic artist, layout technician, or Web designer, you will benefit from the information contained in this book.

This book begins with an overview of the Photoshop interface, tools, menus, and palettes, creating a comprehensive reference source for the chapters that provide step-by-step instructions to achieve the "real world" results you need to be productive.

In the tutorial chapters you learn how to use Photoshop to create high quality graphics using practical examples and plenty of photographs, illustrations, and screen captures. Tips and tricks are included throughout the book, along with notes on labor-saving techniques.

Deleting the Preferences File

There are a few reasons why you might want to delete the Photoshop preferences file to restore the factory default settings. If Photoshop starts to act up, as all applications are apt to do at times, chances are that the preferences file on your hard disk is corrupt. Deleting the preferences file in this case will more than likely remedy the problems you're encountering. You may also want to restore the default settings simply as a matter of course to clean house. When you delete the preferences file from your hard disk, Photoshop creates a brand new Preferences file with all of the factory default settings in place. After you have used Photoshop for a while you will more than likely have preferences settings defined to suit your needs. In this case you may want to back up the preferences file on your hard disk when Photoshop is working smoothly so you can restore them if you have to delete the preferences file in the future.

The preferences settings on MacOS are stored in the file named "Adobe Photoshop 4.0 Prefs" located in the Preferences folder within the System folder. The preferences settings for Windows are stored in the file named "Photos40.PPS" in the Prefs directory within the Photoshop directory.

All the images used in this book are provided on the accompanying CD-ROM for your convenience, although all the exercises can be applied to your own images as well.

As you work with the techniques presented in this book, your skill set will become larger, and you will acquire all kinds of residual knowledge without even realizing it. Features that are new to Photoshop 4.0 are introduced in the first three chapters and indicated throughout the text.

This book is not just a reference source on how to use the tools in Photoshop, but rather a reference for results.

Setting Preferences

When you first launch Photoshop, all the preferences are set to what is referred to as the default preferences. Photoshop maintains a preferences file on your hard drive that records changes you make to the preferences so that they will be set the same way when you quit and relaunch Photoshop.

Setting the General Preferences

The General Preferences is where you set some general information about how you want things to work in Photoshop. Choose File➡Preferences➡General or type (Command-K)[Control-K] to display the Preferences dialog box (see Figure 1.1).

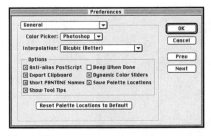

Figure 1.1

The General preferences.

Color Picker

Choose the color picker you want to use to specify color. On the Macintosh you can choose from Photoshop or Apple; in Windows the choices are Photoshop or Windows. In most cases, the Photoshop color picker is the best choice, although you may be more comfortable using the color picker for your particular system.

Interpolation

When Photoshop has to invent new pixels to enlarge a file, it uses a method called interpolation to accomplish this. The three choices for interpolation are Bicubic, Bilinear, and Nearest Neighbor. For best results, choose Bicubic; for the fastest interpolation times, choose Nearest Neighbor.

Options

▶ Select Anti-alias PostScript when you want to remove jagged edges from a pasted or placed element created in a PostScript drawing program such as Illustrator. If you are pasting or placing line art, this option should be off to preserve the sharp lines.

▶ Select Export Clipboard to save the contents of the Clipboard when quitting Photoshop on the Macintosh. Export Clipboard displays a prompt when quitting Photoshop in Windows, asking you whether you want to make the contents of the Clipboard available to other applications. When the Clipboard is exported, you can open another application and paste something you copied or cut in Photoshop.

▶ Select Short Pantone Names so the names assigned to the Pantone inks in Photoshop conform with the naming convention in programs such as Adobe Illustrator, Adobe PageMaker, and QuarkXPress.

▶ Select Show Tool Tips to display information about the tools and palette options when you position the cursor over them.

▶ Select Beep When Done if you want Photoshop to beep every time it completes a command or function.

▶ Select Dynamic Color Sliders to make the sliders in the Color palette display the colors in the Foreground or Background swatch as you drag.

▶ Select Save Palette Locations if you want the palettes to be in the same place they were the last time you used Photoshop.

▶ Click the Reset Palette Locations to Default to return the palettes to their original palette groups and display position.

Setting the Saving Files Preferences

The Saving Files preferences enable you to specify details about how you want your files to be saved, and whether you want them to have certain properties that may affect the file size. Choose File➡Preferences➡Saving Files to display the Preferences dialog box (see Figure 1.2).

Figure 1.2

The Saving Files preferences.

Image Previews

The Image Preview options often add size to your file and take longer to save in the case of large files.

▶ There are three choices in the Image Preview drop-down menu: Always Save, Never Save, and Ask When Saving. Choose Always Save to save the preview options you checked with every file. Choose Never Save to ignore the checked preview options and never save an image preview. Check Ask When Saving to have Photoshop prompt you to save the file with the checked preview options.

▶ For the MacOS, choose Icon to save a file icon of the image; choose Thumbnail to save a thumbnail preview to be displayed in file Open dialog boxes; choose Full Size only if you want to save a 72-ppi preview PICT with your file.

▶ In Windows you can choose whether to save images with a thumbnail preview to be displayed in Open dialog boxes. In Windows NT 4.0 and Windows 95, you also can create preview icons for files.

Append File Extension

You can choose to append a three-character file extension that adheres to DOS naming conventions so that the files are recognized by Windows applications and is only a choice for MacOS.

▶ Choose Never to never append file name extensions.

▶ Choose Always to always append a three character file name extension.

▶ Choose Ask When Saving to be prompted when saving the file to add a file name extension.

Options

▶ Select 2.5 Compatibility if you want files saved in Photoshop format to be available to users still using version 2.5. This option can add significant size to your file.

▶ Select Save Metric Color Tags if you use EFI color tables to create separation settings and want to save TIFF and EPS files that conform to the EfiColor standard used in QuarkXPress 3.3.x.

Setting Display & Cursors Preferences

The Display and Cursors preferences affect the way certain processes are displayed in Photoshop and enable you to set the type of cursors to use for painting and editing tools. Choose File➡ Preferences➡Display & Cursors to display the Preferences dialog box (see Figure 1.3).

CMYK Composites

Choose how you want the composite CMYK image to display on the screen. If you have an accelerated video card, choose Smoother rather than Faster.

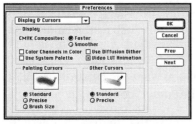

Figure 1.3

The Display & Cursors preferences.

Display Options

► Select Color Channels in Color to display the individual color channels in their respective colors.

► Select Use System Palette if you want all colors to be displayed using your systems 8-bit color palette. This option affords a maximum of only 256 colors and should be left unchecked unless you are using an 8-bit color or grayscale monitor. If you are using an 8-bit color monitor and you select Use Diffusion Dither, Photoshop smooths the appearance of the color on the screen by dithering.

► Select Video LUT (lookup table) Animation to see the changes you make when adjusting color on the whole screen. Selecting this option speeds up the process of updating the color onscreen when you are making color adjustments. If you check the Preview checkbox in the dialog boxes used for color adjustment when adjusting a selected area of the image, the Video LUT Animation is temporarily turned off and the color changes reflected in the selected area only.

Painting Cursors

The painting cursors affect the way the cursor appears for the painting tools such as the Paintbrush, Pencil, and Airbrush.

► Select Standard if you want the cursor to display the tool icon as the cursor icon.

► Select Precise to display the cursor as a crosshair.

► Select Brush Size to display the cursor as a round cursor the size of the active brush.

Other Cursors

To change the way the cursor appears for tools other than the painting tools, choose Standard to display the tool icon as the cursor icon or Precise to display the tool as a crosshair icon.

Setting the Transparency & Gamut Preferences

The Transparency & Gamut preferences are used to set the way the transparent layers are displayed and to choose a color and opacity for out-of-gamut colors when Gamut Warning is turned on. The Gamut Warning is used by Photoshop to help the user identify colors outside the range of colors (gamut) available for CMYK printing when working with other color modes. See Chapter 13, "Adjusting Focus & Tone" for information on using the Gamut Warning in Photoshop. Choose File➡Preferences➡ Transparency & Gamut to display the Preferences dialog box (see Figure 1.4).

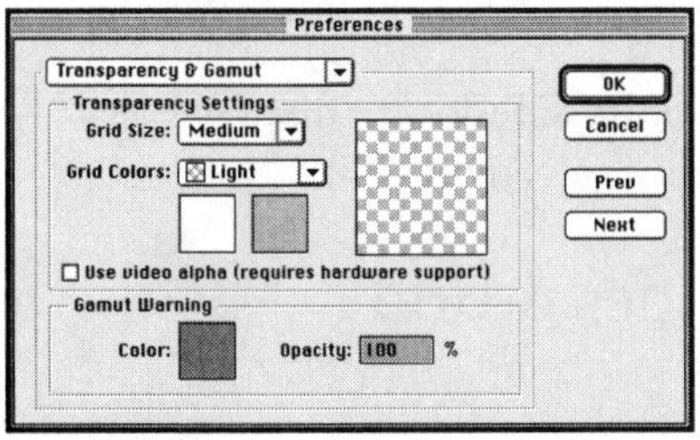

Figure 1.4

The Transparency & Gamut preferences.

Transparency Settings

▶ Choose a grid size and color from the drop-down menus to set how transparency is indicated on layers when they are viewed alone. You can click the color swatches to set the colors of the checkerboard if you can't find a suitable color in the drop-down menu.

▶ The Use video alpha option requires that you have the proper hardware installed. Do not select this option unless you have a 32-bit graphics card installed such as the TrueVision NuVista or Raster-Ops ProVideo32. If you have the proper hardware installed, you can capture the 8-bit alpha channels in Photoshop and use them in video editing software packages that support this option to mask video segments.

Gamut Warning

The gamut warning is the way Photoshop informs you that colors specified in RGB, LAB, or HSB cannot be converted accurately to CMYK for printing. When you turn on Gamut Warning in the View menu, a color mask is overlaid on the image to indicate where in the image colors are out-of-gamut.

► Click the color swatch in the Transparency & Gamut preferences dialog to choose a color for this overlay mask.

► If you choose a dark color, choose an opacity so you can see the image underneath.

Setting the Units & Rulers Preferences

The Units & Rulers preferences are simply the preferences that define what ruler units to use. The Column Size options refer to the Columns choice in the Image Size and Canvas Size dialog boxes. If you are going to be printing to a PostScript imaging device, choose PostScript (72 points/inch) when working with picas and points. Choose File➡Preferences➡Units & Rulers to display the Preferences dialog box (see Figure 1.5).

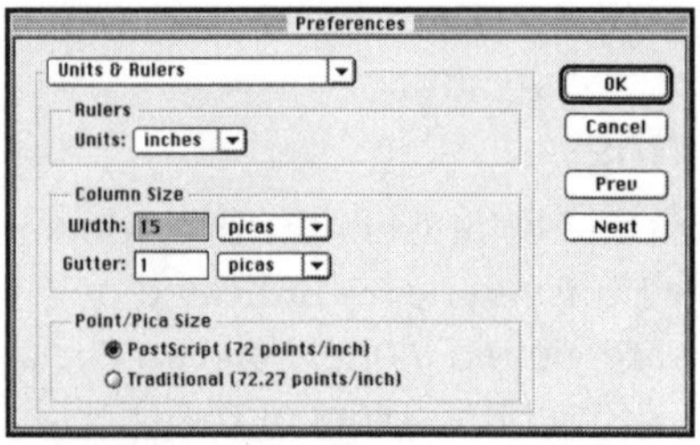

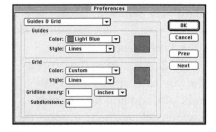

Figure 1.5

The Units & Rulers preferences.

Setting the Guides & Grid Preferences

The Guides and Grids are new in Photoshop 4.0. Choose a color and style for guides and grids and specify the size of the grid. You can click the color swatches to choose a color using the color picker. Choose File➡Preferences➡Guides & Grid to display the Preferences dialog box (see Figure 1.6).

Figure 1.6

The Guides & Grid preferences.

Setting the Plug-ins & Scratch Disk Preferences

The Plug-Ins Folder is where Photoshop's plug-ins are stored on the hard disk. In order for Photoshop to find installed plug-ins, you must specify the location of the Plug-Ins folder by clicking the Choose button and navigating to the folder or directory. Scratch Disks is hard drive space that Photoshop uses to perform processing operations when it runs out of RAM (memory) space. You can choose two separate hard disks for scratch disk space. If you want to use a removable drive like a Bernoulli or Syquest drive, keep in mind that the performance of Photoshop will be greatly hindered because removable drives have much slower access times than a hard disk. Choose File➡Preferences➡Plug-ins & Scratch Disk to display the Preferences dialog box (see Figure 1.7).

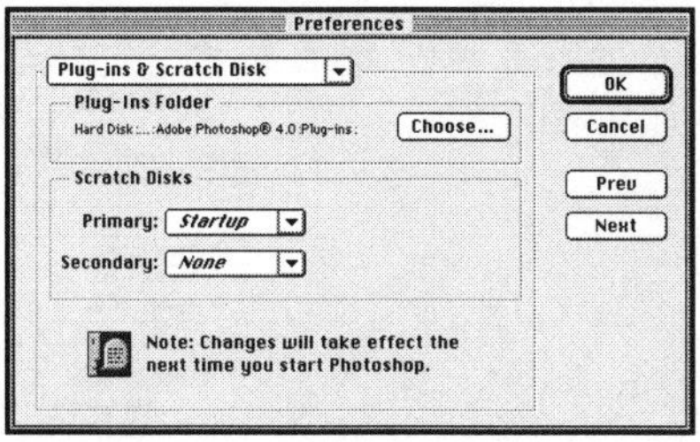

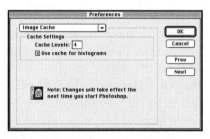

Figure 1.7

The Plug-ins & Scratch Disk preferences.

Setting the Image Cache Preferences

The Image Cache preferences determine how Photoshop caches the images it uses for screen display when performing certain functions. The higher the cache level, the faster Photoshop displays changes. You can choose a Cache Level between 1 and 8. If you choose Use cache for histograms, Photoshop displays the histograms in Levels and Histogram faster, but less accurately. You must quit and restart Photoshop for these changes to take effect. Choose (File➡Preferences➡Image Cache) [File➡Preferences➡Memory & Image Cache] to display the Preferences dialog box (see Figure 1.8).

Figure 1.8

The Image Cache (Macintosh) preferences.

The Photoshop Default Display

The Photoshop interface is designed to provide you with the tools and information you need in a highly organized fashion, utilizing tool selections, menu commands, and floating palettes. When you launch

Photoshop for the first time, the Toolbox and menu bar are displayed, along with four palette groups that contain all ten palettes available under the Window menu (see Figure 1.9).

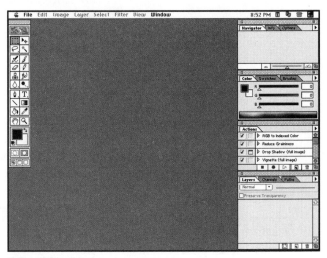

Figure 1.9

The default Photoshop interface.

The Toolbox

The Toolbox contains all the tools necessary to manipulate an image. Click the tools in the Toolbox to activate them or type the shortcut key indicated in bold in Figure 1.10. Some of the cells in the Toolbox contain more than one tool. Click and hold the tools that have a tiny triangle in the lower-right corner to choose from the available tools. If you have used previous versions of Photoshop, you notice that some of the tools have been rearranged in the Toolbox and some of the tools have been designated new shortcut keys.

TIP

(Option-click)[Alt-click] the tools to toggle through the hidden tools, or simply type the shortcut key to change the tools. Double-clicking a tool displays that tool's Options palette.

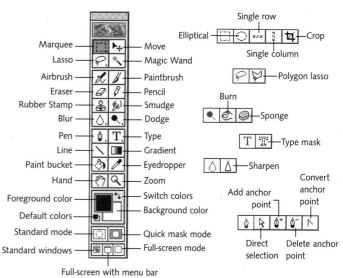

Figure 1.10

The Toolbox.

Note

At the very top of the Toolbox is a large button that displays the Photoshop splash screen (see Figure 1.11). The splash screen contains a rather humorous scrolling list of credits, and if you wait long enough you may see your name with a special message.

Figure 1.11

The Photoshop splash screen.

Click the Adobe logo in the upper-left corner of the splash screen to access Adobe's home page on the World Wide Web. If you have access to the Web and a Web browser such as Netscape Navigator or Microsoft Internet Explorer installed on your system, Photoshop launches the browser and displays a Web page that was installed on your hard drive during the Photoshop installation (see Figure 1.12). Click any of the hypertext links or buttons to go to Adobe's Web pages.

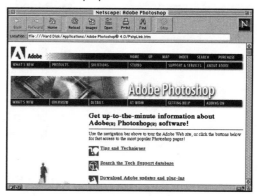

Figure 1.12

The Web page installed on your hard drive during installation of Photoshop.

The Tool Cursors

When you choose most of the tools in the Toolbox and position your cursor over the image area, the default setting is for the cursor to match the tool's icon with the exception of the Marquee, Line, and Gradient tools, which display a crosshair cursor. Making accurate changes to your image when the cursor displays the tool's icon is sometimes difficult because the hot spot of the cursor is difficult to position. The hot spot is the spot on the cursor that performs the tool's function. The hot spot on the Lasso tool's cursor, for example, is right at the tip of the end of the rope. Photoshop offers two other options for tool cursor display: precise pointers, which display a crosshair for all tools, and a brush shape for the painting tools, which displays the cursor in the size of the current brush. To set the cursor appearance, follow these steps:

1. Choose File➡Preferences➡Display & Cursors to display the Preferences dialog box for Display & Cursors (see Figure 1.13).

2. Choose the type of Painting Cursor to use with the painting tools such as the paintbrush, airbrush, and pencil.

   ▶ Standard displays the cursor for the tool with the tool's icon (default).

   ▶ Precise displays the cursor for the painting tools as a crosshair for more precise positioning.

   ▶ Brush Size displays the cursor for the paining tools as an open circle the size of the brush chosen in the Brushes palette.

3. Choose the type of cursor to use for tools other than the painting tools, such as the Magic Wand, Paint Bucket, and Eyedropper tool, in the "Other Cursors" section.

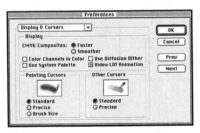

Figure 1.13

The Display & Cursors preferences.

► Standard displays the cursor using the tools icon.

► Precise displays the cursor as a crosshair.

4. Click OK for your changes to take effect.

The Image Window

When you open a document in Photoshop, it appears in a window that Photoshop refers to as the Canvas area. The canvas window contains scrollbars on the right and bottom to navigate when the image is larger than the window (see Figure 1.14). The name of the file and the view percentage both appear in the top bar of the image window. The view percentage also appears in the lower-left corner of the image window, where you can click and enter a new view percentage. Statistics about the image appear to the right of the view percentage box in the lower-left corner. Click the triangle to the right of the image statistics to display a menu in which you can choose which statistics to display (see Figure 1.15). Photoshop offers four choices for image statistics:

Figure 1.14

The Image Window.

✓Document Sizes
  Scratch Sizes
  Efficiency
  Timing

Figure 1.15

The image statistics choices.

► **Document Sizes.** This choice displays the document sizes in Kilobytes (K) or Megabytes (M). Two values are displayed. The first value to the left of the slash represents the printing size of the file—the amount of data that will be sent to a printer when you print the file. This printing size is often close the actual size of the flattened file when saved to disk, although the size of the file saved to disk may be smaller if the image is saved in a compressed format such as JPEG. The number to the right of the slash represents the file size including layers and alpha channels and is often larger than the saved file size as well, because Photoshop automatically compresses some data, such as alpha channels, when saving the file.

▶ **Scratch Sizes.** The Scratch Sizes choice displays the amount of memory Photoshop is currently using to work on your file. The number to the right of the slash indicates the total amount of memory currently available to Photoshop. When the number on the left is larger than the number on the right, Photoshop is using your hard disk to swap information and performance declines because the reading and writing to disk takes significantly longer than working in memory (RAM).

▶ **Efficiency.** The efficiency setting tells you what percentage of Photoshop operations are being performed in memory. If the number is less than 100 percent, Photoshop is using scratch disk space for some operations. Photoshop routinely uses the scratch disk space you set aside in the Plug-Ins and Scratch Disks preferences during idle times to save changes made, but this does not affect the efficiency setting. When Photoshop runs out of RAM to perform operations, it starts to use the available space on the hard disk you specify as the scratch disk and decreases the efficiency rating to reflect this.

▶ **Timing.** Timing displays the amount of time it took to perform the last operation. This setting is handy for benchmarking purposes or to evaluate project time for large projects.

Navigating

Photoshop provides an array of methods to navigate around your image inside the image window, aside from the scrollbars on the right and bottom of the image window.

Using the Zoom Tool

The Zoom tool is used to zoom in closer, enlarging the image in the image window or to zoom out, reducing the size of the image in the image window. To use the Zoom tool:

1. Open any file to try the following functions.

2. Select the Zoom tool in the Toolbox.

3. To Zoom In, position the cursor over your image and click once to zoom in to the next preset percentage. You can also choose View➡Zoom In or type (Command +)[Control +].

   ▶ To enlarge a specific area of your image, click and drag with the Zoom tool to select a rectangular area.

   ▶ When you have a tool other than the Zoom tool active, hold down (Command-Spacebar)[Control-Spacebar] to temporarily access the Zoom tool.

   ▶ Press (Command-0 "zero")[Control-0 "zero"] to fit the image to the screen or choose View➡Fit on Screen.

   ▶ Press (Command-Option-0 "zero")[Control-Alt-0 "zero"] to display the image at 100 percent or choose View➡Actual Pixels.

   ▶ Double-click the Zoom tool in the Toolbox to display the image at 100 percent.

   ▶ Double-click the Hand tool in the Toolbox to fit the image to the screen.

   ▶ Display the Zoom Tool Options palette by choosing Window➡Show Options and click the Fit on Screen button to resize the image and image window to fit your screen.

   ▶ In the Zoom Tool Options palette, click the Actual Pixels button to magnify the image to 100 percent.

   ▶ If you check the Resize Windows To Fit checkbox in the Zoom Tool Options palette, the window size stays the same when you zoom in or out.

4. To Zoom Out, with the Zoom tool active, position the cursor over the image and (Option-click)[Alt-click] on the image to zoom out. You can also choose View➡Zoom Out or type (Command –) [Control –].

   When you have a tool other than the Zoom tool active, hold down (Command-Option-Spacebar)[Control-Alt-Spacebar] to temporarily access the Zoom tool and zoom out.

Using the Hand Tool

The Hand tool is used to move the image around inside the image window when the image is magnified larger than the image window. The Hand tool works like putting your hand down on a piece of paper and moving the piece of paper around by dragging.

1. Zoom in so that the image is larger than the image window.

2. Select the Hand tool from the Toolbox.

3. Position the cursor over the image and click and drag with the Hand tool to position the image in the image window.

   ► When you have any tool besides the Hand tool active, hold down the Spacebar to temporarily access the hand tool.

   ► Double-click the Hand tool to size the image and image window to a dimension that will fit your screen.

Using the Navigator Palette

The Navigator palette (see Figure 1.16) displays a preview of the image with a colored square indicating the part of the image currently displayed in the image window.

► Click inside the colored box and drag to move the image inside the image window.

► Click the lower-left corner of the Navigator palette to type a magnification value. Type Return or Enter after entering a value to change the magnification.

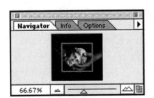

Figure 1.16

The Navigator palette.

TIP

After you type a magnification value in the percentage box in the lower-left corner of the Navigator palette, hold down the Shift key when pressing Return or Enter to keep the percentage box highlighted so you can switch to another magnification value.

► Clicking the icon to the right of the magnification percentage in the lower-right corner of the Navigator palette is like clicking the image with the Zoom tool.

► Clicking the icon in the lower-right corner of the Navigator palette is like (Option-clicking)[Alt-clicking] with the Zoom tool.

► Drag the triangle slider at the bottom of the Navigator palette to the right to zoom in and to the left to zoom out.

► Choose Palette Options from the palette menu by clicking the triangle in the upper-right corner of the Navigator palette to change the color of the View Box in the Navigator palette.

► If you click outside the View Box in the Navigator palette, but still on the image, the View Box will move to the area you click.

Palettes

The ten floating palettes contain the tools necessary to create masks, layers, and channels as well as quick methods for choosing color and brush shapes (see Figure 1.17). Each tool in the Toolbox, with the exception of the Type tool, has a corresponding Options palette in which the features of the tool are set. All the palettes, including the Toolbox, are available under the Window menu.

► The palettes can be grouped together or separated from their groups by dragging the tabs that contain the palette name.

► Double-click the palette tab to reduce the palette group to a bar that displays the tabs only. Double click again on the tab to restore the full palette.

Option-click the zoom box in the upper-right corner of the palette group to collapse the group on Macintosh. Alt-click the minimize/maximize box in Windows to collapse a palette group.

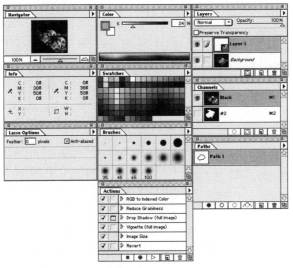

Figure 1.17

The ten floating palettes available in Photoshop.

▶ Click the (zoom box)[minimize/maximize box] in the upper-right corner of the palette group to reduce the palette to a minimum settings display. Click the (zoom box)[minimize/maximize box] again to restore the full palette.

▶ Reposition a palette group on the screen by clicking and dragging the title bar (gray bar at top of palette group).

▶ Resize the palette by dragging the size box in the lower-right corner (Macintosh) or drag the lower-right corner (Windows). To return the palette to the default size click the (zoom box)[minimize/maximize box].

▶ Close a palette group by clicking the close box in the upper-left corner (Macintosh only) or choose Window➡Hide.

TIP

To hide all the onscreen palettes, including the Toolbox, press Tab. Press Tab again to display the palettes. To hide all the palettes, except the Toolbox, press Shift-Tab. Press Shift-Tab again to display the palettes.

Figure 1.18

The Info palette.

Figure 1.19

Select a color mode from the drop-down menu in the Info palette.

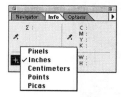

Figure 1.20

Change the x and y measurement units from the drop-down menu.

Using the Info Palette

The Info palette displays information about your file based on the location of the cursor and the state of your selections. The Info palette displays the color breakdown of pixels as you drag over them with the cursor, as well as the x and y coordinates of the cursor and the width and height of selections. Choose Window➡ Show Info to display the Info palette (see Figure 1.18).

► Two sections of the Info palette display color breakdowns, which means you can view the color breakdown of a pixel in two color modes, for example, RGB and CMYK. To change the color mode displayed, click the eyedropper icon in the Info palette (see Figure 1.19). You can choose from any of Photoshop's available color modes, as well as Total Ink and Opacity. Total Ink displays the total ink density when the image is printed using CMYK inks, and is the sum of the Cyan, Magenta, Yellow, and Black percentages. The Opacity choice displays the layer's opacity (percentage of transparency). This option does not apply to the background layer.

► The lower-left quadrant of the Info palette displays the x and y coordinates of the cursor when you drag the cursor over the image. To change the units of measurement used for the x and y coordinates, click the crosshair icon in the Info palette and choose a measurement unit from the drop-down menu (see Figure 1.20).

► When you click and drag a marquee selection on the image, the lower-right quadrant of the Info palette displays the width and height of the selection area using the measurement units chosen for the x and y coordinates. When you create a marquee selection, the upper-right quadrant information changes to reflect the x and y anchor points (where you started drawing

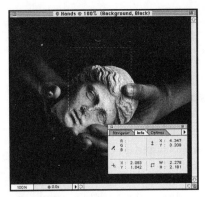

Figure 1.21

When you drag a selection, the Info palette information displays the anchor point, x and y coordinates of the cursor, and the width and height of the selection.

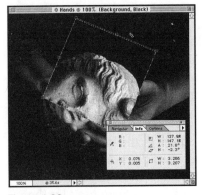

Figure 1.22

Transformation dimensions appear in the place of the color breakdown in the upper-right quadrant of the Info palette.

the marquee) while you are dragging to create the selection (see Figure 1.21). When you release the mouse button, this information returns to its original color mode display.

► When you use any of Photoshop's transformation tools, such as rotate, scale, skew, or distort, the upper-right quadrant of the Info palette displays the Width enlargement or reduction percentage, Height enlargement or reduction percentage, Angle of the rotation, and either the Horizontal or Vertical skew angle (see Figure 1.22).

► When you use the Move tool to move an image on a layer, a selected area of the layer, or when you move a selection marquee, the Info palette displays information about the move in the upper-right quadrant of the Info palette (see Figure 1.23). The values displayed represent the distance the selection is moved to the left or right (Δ X), the distance the selection is moved up or down (Δ Y), the Angle the selection is moved in, and the total Distance the selection is moved.

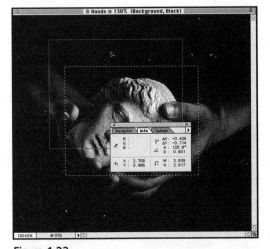

Figure 1.23

When you drag a selected area with the move tool or a selection marquee with a selection tool, the upper-right quadrant displays information about the move.

Using the Tool Options Palettes

Every tool in the Toolbox has a corresponding options palette except the Type tool. To display the options palette for any tool, except the Hand and Zoom tools, double-click the tool in the Toolbox. If the Options palette is already displayed on the screen, you can click once on the tools to view the tool's options. You can access the Hand and Zoom tool options by choosing the tool in the Toolbox and choosing Window➡Show Options if the Options palette is not already displayed on the screen. Each tool has its own specific settings that, after changed in the Options palette, remain in effect until you change them again.

To reset the tools, click the triangle in the upper-right corner of the Tool Options palette to display the palette menu and choose Reset Tool to reset only the tool in use, or Reset All Tools to reset all the tools in the Toolbox to the default settings.

Using the Color Palette

The Color palette is used to create the foreground and background colors. To change the foreground and background colors using the Color palette:

1. Choose Window➡Show Color to display the Color palette (see Figure 1.24).

2. The Color palette contains foreground and background swatches. If you click the active color swatch (outlined in black), the color picker dialog box is displayed. Click the inactive color swatch (not outlined in black) to make it active.

3. Select the color model for the Color palette by clicking the triangle in the upper-right corner of the Color palette and choosing an option from the palette menu (see Figure 1.25).

Foreground Color

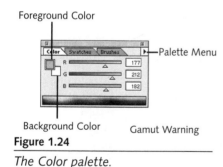

Palette Menu

Background Color   Gamut Warning

Figure 1.24

The Color palette.

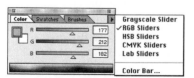

Figure 1.25

Choose a color model for the sliders in the Color palette.

4. The color bar at the bottom of the Color palette enables you to choose a color from the color model's spectrum. Click the triangle in the upper-right corner of the Color palette to display the palette menu choices and choose Color Bar to choose which color ramp is displayed at the bottom of the Color palette.

5. Drag the triangle sliders to mix a color.

Using the Swatches Palette

The Swatches palette enables you to save the foreground or background color into a palette of colors for use later on. The colors in the Swatches palette can be chosen as the foreground or background color. You can create a color palette from scratch, add to the palette displayed, save the color palette, and load previously saved color palettes. The default swatches contain the current palette.

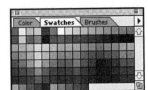

Figure 1.26

The Swatches palette.

► Choose Window➡Show Swatches to display the Swatches palette (see Figure 1.26).

► Position your cursor over one of the color swatches in the Swatches palette. The cursor changes to an eyedropper cursor.

► Click a swatch to load that color as the foreground Color.

► Hold down (Option)[Alt] and click a color swatch to load that color as the background Color.

► To add a color, position your cursor over an empty space in the Swatches palette. If no empty spaces are available, click and drag the lower-right corner of the Swatches palette to change the height and reveal empty spaces. The cursor changes to a paint bucket. Click the empty space to add the foreground color to the palette.

▶ To replace a color in the Swatches palette, hold down the Shift key (the cursor changes to a paint bucket) and click the swatch to change the swatch color to the foreground color.

▶ To insert a color swatch, position the cursor over a color swatch in the palette. Hold down (Shift-Option)[Shift-Alt] (the cursor changes to a paint bucket) and click the swatch to insert a new swatch in the foreground color.

▶ To delete a color swatch in the Swatches palette hold down (Command)[Control]. When the cursor changes to the scissors, click a swatch to delete it.

▶ To reset the Swatches palette to the default swatch colors click the triangle in the upper-right corner of the Swatches palette to display the palette menu and choose Reset Swatches. A dialog box appears in which you can choose whether to replace all the current swatches with the default color swatches or append the default color swatches to the current swatches.

▶ To save a custom set of color swatches, click the triangle in the upper-right corner of the Swatches palette and choose Save Swatches from the palette menu. Navigate to the folder or directory you want to save the swatches in and click the Save button. Save your swatches if you want to use them on another image at a later date. Opening an indexed color image or converting an image to indexed color replaces the custom color palette with the indexed colors. Refer to Chapter 7, "Specifying Color" for more information on indexed color.

▶ To replace the current swatches with swatches previously saved, click the triangle in the upper-right corner of the Swatches palette and choose Replace Swatches from the palette menu. Navigate to the folder or directory containing the saved swatches and click the Open button. The current swatches are replaced with this new set.

▶ To append swatches previously saved, click the triangle in the upper-right corner of the Swatches palette and choose Load Swatches from the palette menu. Navigate to the folder or directory containing the saved swatches and click the Open button. The loaded swatches are appended to the current set.

► To sample colors from your image to add to the swatches palette, use the Eyedropper tool and click the image to load the colors of that pixel as the foreground color. Click an empty space in the Swatches palette to add it.

Using the Brushes Palette

All the painting tools in Photoshop use brushes whose size and style are defined and chosen from the Brushes palette. The default brushes are round brushes with hard or soft edges. The brush shape and size is entirely user-definable, however, enabling you to be as creative as you like when applying color to the image.

► To choose a brush, choose Window➡Show Brushes to display the Brushes palette (see Figure 1.27) and click a brush to choose it.

► The brush you choose is used for the particular tool that is active, which means you must choose a brush type for each tool you use.

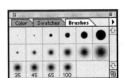

Figure 1.27

The Brushes palette.

► The brushes in the Brushes palette are displayed in their actual size unless the brush is larger than the palette's cell size. In this case, the diameter of the brush in pixels in indicated below the brush, as is the case with the four brushes along the bottom row of the default Brushes palette.

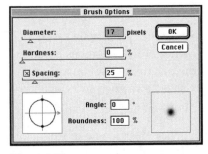

Figure 1.28

Modify the attributes of an existing brush.

► To modify Brush options, double-click the brush in the Brushes palette or choose Brush Options from the palette menu. The Brush Options dialog box appears (see Figure 1.28), enabling you to specify the Diameter, Hardness, Spacing, Angle, and Roundness of the brush.

► To create a new brush, click any of the empty spaces in the Brushes palette to display the New Brush dialog box or click the triangle in the upper-right corner of the Brushes palette to display the palette menu and choose New Brush. If you don't see any empty spaces, click and drag the lower-right corner of the Brushes palette to change the height and reveal the empty spaces. The Brush Options dialog box is displayed (see Figure 1.28), enabling you to specify the Diameter, Hardness, Spacing, Angle, and Roundness of the brush.

▶ To delete brushes, hold down the (Command)[Control] key and position the cursor over the brush you want to delete to display the scissors cursor and click the brush to delete it. You can also choose the brush you want to delete and choose Delete Brush from the palette menu.

▶ To import and export brushes, choose Save Brushes from the palette menu of the Brushes palette to save the current set of brushes. Choose Replace Brushes from the palette menu to replace the current set of brushes with a previously saved set. Choose Load Brushes from the palette menu to append a saved set of brushes to the current set of brushes.

▶ To reset the brushes to the default brushes, choose Reset Brushes from the Brushes palette menu.

Using the Layers Palette

The Layers palette enables you to create or place images on separate transparent layers, juggle the layers around, and affect the way the layers interact with each other. The Layers palette can also contains adjustment layers, which enable you to make color adjustments that are non-destructive and overlay them with layers and other adjustment layers. Non-destructive means the original image and images on layers will remain unchanged until the adjustment layer is merged with the image layers. Most images in Photoshop start out with only one layer, the Background layer. The Background layer is always at the bottom of the layers and cannot be moved between other layers. The available options for the Layers palette are located in two places: in the drop-down palette menu and from the Layer menu in the menu bar.

▶ Choose Window➡Show Layers to display the Layers palette (see Figure 1.29).

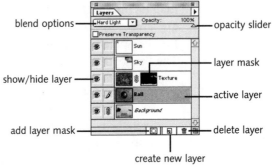

Figure 1.29

The Layers palette.

▶ To create a new layer, click the New Layer icon in the Layers palette, choose New Layer from the Layers palette menu, or choose Layer➥New➥ Layer.

▶ To delete a layer, select the layer you want to delete in the Layers palette and click the Trash Can icon in the lower-right corner of the Layers palette. You can also choose Delete Layer from the palette menu or from the Layer menu in the menu bar.

▶ To move a layer, drag any layer, except the Background layer, up or down in the Layers palette. When the dividing line between two layers is highlighted, release the mouse button to insert the layer you are moving between the two layers (see Figure 1.30). You can also choose Send Backward, Bring Forward, Send to Back, and Bring to Front from the Layer➥Arrange menu.

Figure 1.30

Drag the layer until the divider line is highlighted to insert it between two layers.

▶ To hide/show layers, click the Eye icon to the left of the layer thumbnail to hide a layer. Click the same spot again to make the layer visible. (Option-click)[Alt-click] the eye icon to hide all layers except the one you clicked. (Option-click) [Alt-click] again to make all layers visible.

TIP

To move layers using the keyboard, type (Command-"]") [Control-"]"] to move a layer up or (Command-"["][Control-"["] to move a layer down. To move a layer to the top position, type (Command-Shift-])[Control-Shift-]]. To move a layer to the bottom position, type (Command-Shift-[) [Control-Shift-[].

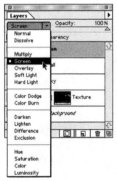

Figure 1.31

The blending modes in the Layers palette.

TIP

You can quickly set the opacity for the active layer by typing single digit numbers from 0 to 9. For example: typing 0 (zero) sets the opacity to 100 percent; typing 5 sets the opacity to 50 percent. To set the opacity to a value other than increments of 10 percent, type a two digit number quickly using the numeric keypad. For example: type 43 to set the opacity to 43 percent.

▶ To group layers together, select the first layer you want to group. Click between the eye icon and the layer's thumbnail picture of another layer to group that layer with the active layer. When you group two or more layers, you can move them together as a unit.

▶ To choose a blending mode, click the Blending Mode drop-down menu in the upper-left corner of the Layers palette to choose a blending mode for the current layer (see Figure 1.31). The blending modes are explained in Chapter 2, "Color and Resolution in Photoshop."

▶ To set the opacity for the current layer, drag the Opacity triangle slider in the upper-right corner of the Layers palette. You can set an opacity value from 1% to 100%.

▶ Turn on Preserve Transparency to protect the transparent pixels (0 percent opacity) on the active layer from change. Changes you make to the image on the layer affect only the non-transparent pixels.

▶ Double-click the Background layer to make it a transparent layer like all the other layers. A dialog box appears in which you can enter a name for the layer. After you make the Background layer a transparent layer, you can move it between other layers.

▶ To add a layer mask, click the Add Layer Mask icon at the bottom of the Layers palette. The layer mask affects the opacity of the pixels on the layer. You also can choose Layer➡ Add Layer Mask from the menu bar, in which case you can choose Reveal All (100% Opacity) or Hide All (0% Opacity) for the initial mask. The layer mask thumbnail is added to the right of the layer thumbnail and is made active.

TIP 🔍

To create an inverted new layer mask (Hide All), (Option-click)[Alt-click] the Add Layer Mask icon at the bottom of the Layers palette.

► To edit the layer mask: When the layer mask is active, the layer mask icon appears to the right of the eye icon instead of the paintbrush icon in the Layers palette, and the layer mask thumbnail is outlined in black. Paint over the image with 100 percent black to delete parts of the image (change the opacity to 0 percent). Paint over the image with white to restore the image (100 percent opacity). Paint with a percentage of black to change the image opacity. For example: paint with 50 percent black to change the image opacity to 50 percent in the painted areas; paint with 80 percent black to change the image opacity to 20 percent in the painted areas (see Figure 1.32).

Figure 1.32

Before changes are made to the layer mask for the "Couple on Beach" layer.

After changes to the layer mask are made.

► To view the layer mask, (Option-click)[Alt-click] the layer mask thumbnail in the Layers palette to toggle the layer mask view on and off (see Figure 1.33).

Figure 1.33

The layer mask view.

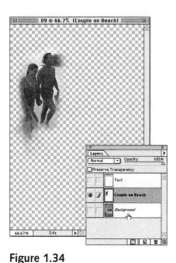

Figure 1.34

The layer after the layer mask is applied.

► To hide the layer mask, shift-click the layer mask thumbnail in the Layers palette to toggle the layer mask on and off.

► To load the transparency mask: When you load the transparency mask, a selection is created in the shape of the non-transparent pixels. (Command-click)[Control-click] the layer thumbnail to load the layer's transparency mask or (Command-click)[Control-click] the layer mask thumbnail to load the layer mask's transparency mask.

► To lock the layer mask to the layer so they cannot be moved independently, click between the layer thumbnail and the layer mask thumbnail in the Layers palette. The link icon indicates that the layer and layer mask are locked.

► To apply or discard the layer mask, click the layer mask thumbnail to activate the layer mask. Click the trash can icon in the lower-left corner of the Layers palette and choose whether to apply or discard the mask from the dialog box that pops up. Applying the mask makes the changes to the layer permanent. You also can choose Layer➥ Remove Layer Mask. See Figure 1.34.

► To merge the layers: Choose Layer➥Merge Visible to merge all visible layers into one layer. Choose Layer➥Merge Down or type (Command-E)[Control-E] to merge the current layer with the layer under it. Merge Down and Merge Visible are also available in the Layers palette menu. When layers are linked together, Merge Down becomes Merge Linked in the Layer menu and Layers palette menu.

Figure 1.35

The New Adjustment Layer dialog box.

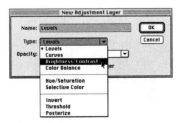

Figure 1.36

Select the type of adjustment layer to create from the Type drop-down menu.

▶ To Flatten the image, choose Layer➡Flatten Image. This merges all layers together into a single Background layer. Flatten Image is also available in the Layers palette menu.

Using Adjustment Layers

Adjustment layers are a new addition to the Layers palette in Photoshop 4.0 and are used to make non-destructive color changes to your image. Using adjustment layers enables you to apply many of the choices commonly found in the Image➡Adjust menu to a transparent layer so that the image adjustments affect the layers below the adjustment layer.

▶ To create an adjustment layer, choose New Adjustment Layer from the Layers palette menu or choose Layer➡New➡Adjustment Layer from the menu bar or (Command-click)(Control-click) on the New Layer button on the Layers palette to display the New Adjustment Layer dialog box (see Figure 1.35).

▶ To choose an adjustment type, click the Type drop-down menu in the New Adjustment Layer dialog box and choose the type of color adjustment you want to make (see Figure 1.36). Click OK to display the dialog box that corresponds to the choice you made for type. Make adjustments and click OK.

▶ The adjustment layer is inserted in the Layers palette above the active layer and only affects the layers beneath it (see Figure 1.37).

▶ You can stack adjustment layers on top of each other in the Layers palette to combine the effects of the adjustments.

▶ Choose an opacity setting by dragging the opacity triangle slider in the Layers palette or by

Figure 1.37

The adjustment layer affects only the layers beneath it.

Figure 1.38

The adjustment layer is a mask layer that you can paint to control the application of the adjustment.

typing an opacity percentage on the numeric keypad to reduce or increase the overall effect of the adjustment.

▶ The adjustment layer is actually a mask that you can paint to isolate the adjustment to parts of the underling layer images (see Figure 1.38) and is indicated by the layer mask icon to the left of the layer thumbnail. Paint with 100 percent black to mask areas. Paint with white to open the mask and apply the adjustment layer to the underlying layers. Use percentages of black to decrease the overall effect of the adjustment layer in specific areas.

▶ Treat the adjustment layer like any other layer in your image. You can apply the blending mode choices to this layer, move the adjustment layer up or down in the Layers palette, and merge the adjustment layer with underlying layers.

▶ To view the adjustment layer's mask, (Option-click)[Alt-click] the layer thumbnail.

▶ To force Photoshop to ignore the layer's built-in mask and apply the adjustment layer's effects to the whole image, Shift-click the layer thumbnail.

▶ To turn off the adjustment layer's effect, click the eye icon next to the layer thumbnail.

Using the Channels Palette

The Channels palette displays the individual channels for the particular color model you're working with along with a composite channel in the case of RGB, CMYK, and LAB color images. The Channels palette can contain mask channels called alpha channels that are used to save and load selections.

▶ Choose Window➡Show Channels to display the Channels palette (see Figure 1.39).

Figure 1.39

The Channels palette.

► To save a selection: When you have made a selection on your image, click the mask icon at the bottom of the Channels palette to save the selection as a channel or choose Select➜Save Selection. A new channel that displays the mask for the selection is inserted after the last channel (see Figure 1.40).

Figure 1.40

The selection saved to a mask channel.

► To load a selection, (Command-click)[Control-click] a mask channel to load the channel as a selection or drag the mask channel onto the selection icon at the bottom of the Channels palette.

► To edit the mask channel, click the channel name in the Channels palette to display the mask channel in the image window (see Figure 1.41). The selection area is displayed as white or percentages of black less than 100 percent. 100 percent black represents unselected areas. The mask channel is an 8-bit grayscale channel that can contain up to 256 levels of gray. Gray levels represent opacity when the mask is used to make a selection. To go back to editing the color image, Shift-click the mask channel or click the composite color channel.

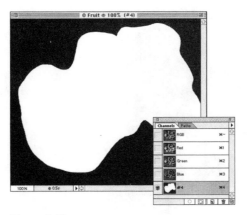

Figure 1.41

The mask channel can be edited in the image window.

► To apply a mask to an image, you must first load the mask as a selection, then either copy/cut the selected area and paste it somewhere else or paste an image from the clipboard into the selected area (see Figure 1.42).

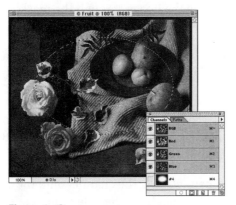
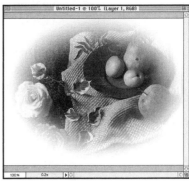

Figure 1.42

The mask is loaded to create the selection and the selection is copied (Command-C)[Control-C].	*The copied image is pasted onto a white background to see the effect of the mask selection.*

► The mask channel can be viewed with the image by clicking in the space to the left of the channel thumbnail to turn on the Eye icon. The mask is overlaid on the image in a mask color that you can specify; the default color is red at 50 percent opacity (see Figure 1.43).

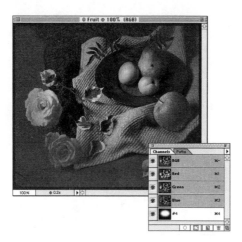

Figure 1.43

The mask channel is displayed as an overlay on the image.

► To change the mask color, double-click the mask layer to display the Channel Options dialog box and click the color swatch in the lower-left corner to change the mask color. Set the opacity to a level that enables you to see the image through the mask; 50 percent works best in most cases.

► To create a new blank channel, click the New Channel icon at the bottom of the Channels palette or choose New Channel from the palette menu.

► To duplicate a channel, drag an existing channel onto the New Channel icon at the bottom of the Channels palette or choose Duplicate Channel from the palette menu.

► To remove a channel, drag the channel onto the Trash Can icon or choose Delete Channel from the palette menu. If the channel you want to delete is the active channel, click the Trash Can icon in the Channels palette to delete it.

Using the Paths Palette

The Paths palette works in concert with the path tools in the Toolbox. Using a pen tool that creates vector curves and lines you can create paths that can be stroked, filled, and saved as part of a Photoshop EPS file as a clipping path to create silhouettes. The Paths palette is empty until you create a path using the Pen tool. Drawing paths is covered extensively in Chapter 6, "Creating Paths."

► Choose Window➡Show Paths to display the Paths palette (see Figure 1.44).

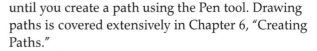

Load path as selection

Make selection into Work Path

Fill Path

Delete Path

Stroke Path   New Path

Figure 1.44

The Paths palette.

► When a path is first created using the Pen tool, it is represented in the Paths palette as a work path. The work path is a temporary path that will not be saved with the file. Double-click the work path to define it as a path. You can name the paths anything you like to help keep track of paths when you have a lot of them.

► To edit a path, click a path in the Paths palette. Click the white space below the paths in the Path palette to hide all paths.

► To create a new path, click the New Path icon at the bottom of the Paths palette or draw with the Pen tool to create a new work path and double-click the work path.

► To fill a path, choose Fill Path/Fill Subpath from the palette menu the first time you fill a path to define the fill settings. The Fill Path dialog box is displayed enabling you to set the fill options (see Figure 1.45). After you have defined the fill options, you can click the Fill Path icon at the bottom of the Paths palette to fill a path.

► To stroke a path, choose Stroke Path/Stroke Subpath from the palette menu. The Stroke Path dialog box is displayed enabling you to choose the tool you want to use to stroke the path (see Figure 1.46). You should set up the tool options by double-clicking the tool in the Toolbox before choosing the tool as the Stroke Path tool.

Figure 1.45

The Fill Path dialog box.

Figure 1.46

The Stroke Path dialog box offers a list of tools to choose from to stroke a path.

Figure 1.47

The Make Selection dialog box.

▶ To convert a path to a selection, select the path in the Palette and click the selection icon at the bottom of the Paths palette or drag the Path onto the selection icon. You can also choose Make Selection from the Paths palette menu to display a dialog box to control the way the selection is created (see Figure 1.47).

▶ To convert a selection to a path: When you have defined a selection marquee, click the Make Work Path icon at the bottom of the Paths palette. Choose Make Work Path from the palette menu to display the Make Work Path dialog box where you can set the tolerance level.

▶ To duplicate a path, drag the path onto the New Path icon at the bottom of the Paths palette or choose Duplicate Path from the palette menu to give the duplicate path a name while you create it.

▶ To define the clipping path, choose Clipping Path from the palette menu to choose which of the existing paths should be used as a clipping path when you save the file. The clipping path silhouettes the image when it is placed into a page layout application like QuarkXPress or PageMaker so only the area of the image within the path is displayed and printed.

▶ To delete a path, drag the path onto the Trash Can icon in the lower-right corner of the Paths palette or choose Delete Path from the palette menu.

Using the Actions Palette

The Actions palette enables you to record a series of actions, assign a name to them, and play them back. After actions are created they can be applied to a batch process that performs the actions on a folder or directory of files, as well as files that are input using a digital camera or scanner. Creating and playing actions is covered extensively in Chapter 15, "Using Actions."

► Choose Window➡Show Actions to display the Actions palette (see Figure 1.48).

► The Actions palette has two display modes: Button mode and List mode. Choose Button mode from the Actions palette menu by clicking the triangle in the upper-right corner of the palette to display the actions as clickable buttons (see Figure 1.49). When in Button mode, creating new actions is disabled. To switch back to List mode, choose Button mode from the palette menu again.

► Before you can record an action, you must first create a New Action or choose an action in the Actions palette to record to. To create a New Action choose New Action from the palette menu or click the New Action icon at the bottom of the Actions palette to display the New Action dialog box (see Figure 1.50). Type a name for the new action and choose a function key and color. Click the Record button to begin recording the new action.

► To stop recording, click the Stop icon at the bottom of the Actions palette or choose Stop Recording from the palette menu.

► To play an action: When in List mode, click the action in the Actions palette and click the Play icon at the bottom of the Actions palette or choose one of the play options in the palette menu. When in Button mode, simply click the action in the Actions palette.

► To record actions, select an action in the Actions palette and click the Record icon at the bottom of the Actions palette or choose Start Recording

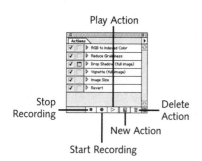

Play Action

Stop Recording

Delete Action

New Action

Start Recording

Figure 1.48

The Actions palette in List mode.

Figure 1.49

The Actions palette in Button mode.

Figure 1.50

The New Action dialog box.

from the palette menu. To re-record an action, choose Record Again from the palette menu.

▶ To toggle actions on and off, click in the check mark column in the Actions palette. When an action is toggled off, it cannot be played in either List mode or Button mode.

▶ To toggle dialog boxes on and off, click the column to the right of the check mark column. When dialogs are toggled on, the Action pauses at dialog boxes when running and require user input. If the dialog icon is displayed in black, dialogs are turned on for all parts of the action. When the dialog icon is red, it means that some parts of the action have dialogs turned on, while others do not.

▶ To display the action parts, click the triangles to the left of the action name to expand the list of commands used in the action. Click the triangles next to the commands to display the settings for the command (see Figure 1.51). Note that you can turn the dialogs on or off for each command in the list.

Using Context Menus

Context menus are floating menus that are available in various places in Photoshop. The context menus display choices for tools that are active or palettes that are displayed.

▶ To display the context menu: On the Macintosh, hold down the Control key and click the image to display the context menu for the active tool. In Windows, click the image with the right mouse button to display the context menu for the active tool (see Figure 1.52).

Figure 1.51

Click the triangles to expand the actions list.

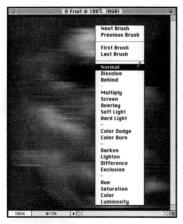

Figure 1.52

The context menu for the Paintbrush tool.

Figure 1.53

The context menu for the Brushes palette.

► Use the same technique to display the context menu for open palettes. (Control-click)[Right-click] the palette to display its context menu (see Figure 1.53). Not all palettes contain context menus.

Summary

This chapter covered the basics of the Photoshop application and its environment. Understanding where things are located in Photoshop and how to access them is the first step to working efficiently and successfully in the application. The chapters in this book will refer to this chapter often as a reference for things such as setting preferences and understanding palette options. In the next chapter you will learn about working in Photoshop and be introduced to the various image modes, methods for acquiring and creating imagery, essential terminology, and techniques for calibrating the monitor.

Color and Resolution in Photoshop

Photoshop is an application that works on bitmapped images made up of pixels. The number of pixels in an image determine its resolution. The resolution of an image is important because it directly affects the quality of the printed image and, in the case of screen images for presentations and Web pages, the quality of the display.

Defining the Photoshop Image

Image resolution is primarily decided when the original image is created. Most Photoshop images are created by digital scanners, which capture image data at varying resolutions depending on the capability of the scanner. Scanners have their own resolution, also referred to as dpi, which determines the maximum image resolution (ppi). A scanner must have a resolution (dpi) that is equal to or larger than the desired image resolution when the image is scanned at 100 percent. If the resolution of the scanner is too low, the scanned image lacks detail, appears flat, and is of poor overall quality. Aside from scanning your own images on a flatbed scanner, you can purchase high resolution scans from color prepress companies, service bureaus, and printers.

Screen captures are image files created by taking a snapshot of the computer screen using specialized software or, in the case of the MacOS, a built-in system function (Command-Shift-3). The screen captures in this book, for example, were created using Snapz Pro by Ambrosia Software, Inc. Screen captures are generated at the monitor resolution, which typically is 72 ppi for Macintosh and 96 ppi for Windows.

LPI, PPI, and DPI

The resolution of a Photoshop file is described in pixels per inch (ppi). You may have heard image resolution referred to as dpi (dots per inch), but a little further on you learn why this terminology is not quite correct. The resolution of the Photoshop image depends solely on where you intend to use the image. The resolution for graphics used on Web pages and in presentation graphics programs such as Adobe Persuasion and Microsoft Powerpoint, for example, is 72 pixels per inch; the resolution for images to be offset printed is significantly larger, typically twice the line screen.

Target resolution for an image that will ultimately be offset printed is determined by the size of the halftone dot. Halftone dots break down the gray levels of the image into dots of varying sizes, so the printing press can print the grayscale using a single solid ink color (see Figure 2.1). The size of the halftone dot is determined by the lpi—the number of lines of halftone dots in an inch—and is often referred to as the *screen frequency* or *line screen*. The line screen is determined by the printer; the folks with the printing press. The paper, pressroom conditions, and the particular printing press are some of the factors that decide the optimum screen frequency. There is no magic number that applies to all printing projects, so communication with the printer is necessary to learn the screen frequency.

Figure 2.1

Continuous tone images are broken down into halftone dots to be printed with solid inks.

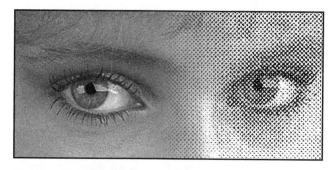

> ### Note
>
> Some 600 dpi laser printers and color output devices such as the Iris Inkjet printer use screening methods other than halftoning. Talk to your service bureau or printer before scanning images for use on these devices; most require a relatively low pixel-per-inch ratio compared to offset printing requirements.

The dpi is the resolution of the output device, such as a laser printer or high resolution imagesetter. The laser printer or imagesetter prints your pages using an array of dots whose size is determined by the printer's resolution. Halftone dots are also created using these dots, so the roundness of the halftone dot depends on the size of the laser printer or imagesetter dots used to create it (see Figure 2.2). Most desktop laser printers are either 300 or 600 dpi, whereas an imagesetter can print at 1200 dpi, 2400 dpi, and higher. Because the size of the printer's dot affects the roundness of the halftone dot, high screen rulings, 85 lpi and higher, reproduce better on higher resolution printers.

Figure 2.2

The halftone dots are created by the laser printer or imagesetter using spot sizes determined by the laser printer's or imagesetter's resolution.

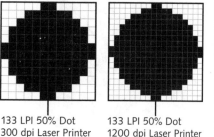

133 LPI 50% Dot
300 dpi Laser Printer

133 LPI 50% Dot
1200 dpi Laser Printer

133 LPI 50% Dot
2400 dpi Imagesetter

Determining Resolution

In order to determine the correct resolution for your Photoshop image, you must decide how the image is going to be used. In some cases, a target ppi is already determined for the output device or computer program. In the case of preparing files for offset printing, a simple formula determines the target resolution of the Photoshop image.

Determining Resolution for Bitmap Images

Bitmap images are created from original artwork that contains only solid black and solid white areas (no grays). Bitmap images require a high resolution to make curved areas appear smooth. A bitmap image can be colorized after it is scanned in and placed in a page layout application such as QuarkXPress or PageMaker. A bitmap image is desirable because the white areas can be made transparent or colorized separately in the page layout application. The file size of a bitmap image is significantly smaller than that of a grayscale image and line art images can be compressed to a remarkably small size using compression software such as StuffIt on the Macintosh or PKZip on PCs. When scanning line art or type, a resolution of 600 ppi or higher is recommended. The best resolution would actually be the same as the printer resolution; when scanning line art to print on a 1200 dpi imagesetter, a resolution of 1200 ppi produces optimal quality. Scanning at the printer resolution can produce very large file sizes, though, and 600 ppi is sufficient for most artwork (see Figure 2.3).

Figure 2.3

An example of line art, scanned at 600 ppi on the left and 72 ppi on the right.

Determining Resolution for Grayscale Images

Grayscale images are images that contain a full range of grays to closely approximate continuous tone black and white photographs. In Photoshop, grayscale images can contain up to 256 levels of gray. Each pixel in a grayscale image contains 8 binary bits of data to describe the pixel's brightness value. The individual gray levels are numbered 0 (zero) to 255. Black pixels have a value of 0 (zero) and white pixels have a value of 255. After a grayscale image is in Photoshop, the pixel's gray level can be viewed using the Info palette, as well as the equivalent ink percentage (0 percent to 100 percent) that is printed when the image is output with a halftone screen. The optimum resolution for grayscale images is 1.5 multiplied by the halftone screen frequency (line screen). If, for example, an image is to be printed with a 133 lpi screen frequency, it must be scanned at 200 pixels per inch (199.5 rounded) (see Figure 2.4).

133 lpi/72 ppi

133 lpi/200 ppi

Figure 2.4

The same image printed at 133 line screen.

Determining Resolution for RGB Images

RGB color images are full-color images created in three separate color channels: red, green, and blue. RGB color images are created using colored light at varying intensities. All digital scanners use RGB to capture color images because a scanner must use light to capture the image data. The same is true for computer monitors: Computer monitors display color by illuminating the individual screen pixels with varying intensities of red, green, and blue light. For this reason, RGB images are used for screen presentation in multimedia programs such as Macromedia Director and QuarkImmedia, presentation programs such as Persuasion and Power-point, and for some Web formats such as JPEG and PNG.

Some specialized output devices such as color slide/transparency imagesetters also require RGB data because they image color film using red, green, and blue light. The optimum resolution for RGB images that will ultimately be output to a printer or imagesetting device for offset printing is two times the line screen (lpi). RGB images cannot be color separated to imagesetters and printers. Because the scanner captures the image data in RGB, however, the RGB file is used to generate a CMYK image that ultimately becomes color separated to a printer or imagesetter. RGB images used in presentation programs such as those mentioned previously require only enough resolution to appear nicely onscreen and should be 72 ppi for Macintosh and 96 ppi for most Windows environments. A resolution of 72 ppi is often used for Windows presentations that will be displayed on both the Macintosh and Windows platforms. The same applies to RGB images for use on Web pages: screen resolution is all that is needed if the image is for display purposes only (see Figure 2.5).

In Photoshop, RGB images are represented by three individual grayscale channels for each of the colors (red, green, and blue) and one composite channel to display the composite image on the screen. Because each of the three color channels is an 8-bit grayscale channel, each pixel in an RGB image can be one of 256 levels of gray for each color: 256 red, 256 green, and 256 blue. If you calculate every combination of the 256 possibilities for each color (256^3), you get 16.7 million colors.

Figure 2.5

The resolution of an RGB image depends on the intended output.

2 × lpi for color separations

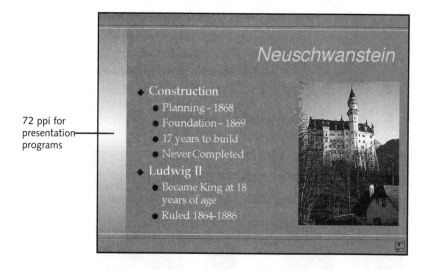

72 ppi for presentation programs

72 ppi for Web graphics

Determining Resolution for CMYK Images

CMYK Color images are used to print full color on an offset printing press using the four process color inks: cyan, magenta, yellow, and black (K represents black to avoid confusion with other colors that begin with "b"). Some color scanners claim to scan in CMYK, but what actually happens is the scanner scans the image data in RGB and converts the RGB data to CMYK using built-in color lookup tables (CLUTs). When a scanned image is brought into Photoshop as RGB color, Photoshop converts the RGB data to CMYK color data using a

CLUT built into Photoshop. The optimum resolution for CMYK images to be printed to color separated plates for offset printing is two times the line screen (lpi). In Photoshop, the CMYK image is represented on four 8-bit grayscale channels—one for each of the process colors: cyan, magenta, yellow, and black. A fifth composite channel displays the four color channels combined, but it is not output when the file is printed (see Figure 2.6).

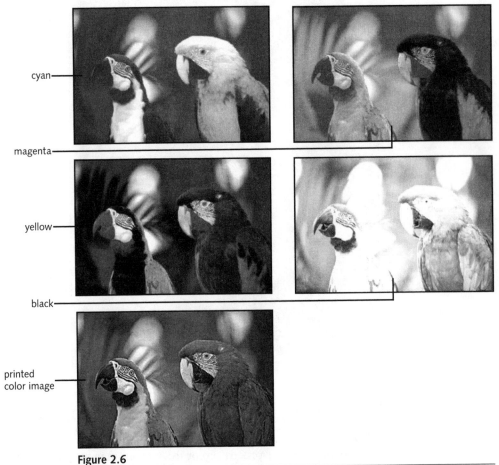

cyan

magenta

yellow

black

printed
color image

Figure 2.6

For offset printing, four colors combine to create a full-color picture.

Determining Resolution for Indexed Color Images

Indexed color images are used primarily for screen display and are single channel images that can contain up to 256 separate and distinct colors.

The colors in an indexed color file can be limited to only the colors used in the image, resulting in a much smaller color file for use on Web pages and in presentation programs. When a color image contains more than 256 individual colors, the image is dithered using 256 or fewer colors to create the illusion of more colors. Photoshop generates indexed color images from RGB color images and applies a color table that you specify. For example, if you scan a color picture that contains only black, degrees of gray, and degrees of red, you can convert the image to an indexed color file that contains only the colors used in the picture—256 colors maximum. Indexed color images are used to create GIF files as Web graphics. When you create a GIF file, you can assign one of the indexed colors transparency. Because indexed color images are used for screen display, the optimum resolution is 72 ppi.

Determine how you are going to use the Photoshop image, then select the resolution from Table 2.1.

Table 2.1

Target Resolutions for Photoshop Images		
Type of Printing	Description	Resolution
Line Art Printing	Black and White	600 ppi
Grayscale Printing	Grayscale	$1.5 \times$ lpi
Presentation Graphics	Persuasion, Powerpoint, Director	72 ppi
Web Graphics	GIF, PNG, JPEG, PDF	72 ppi
Color Printing	CMYK to generate color separated plates	$2 \times$ lpi

Enlarging and Reducing

Because resolution plays such an important part in the ultimate quality of a Photoshop image, enlarging or reducing the image after it is created can adversely affect that quality.

Enlarging in Photoshop

Enlarging an image in Photoshop, although preferable to enlarging in the page layout application, has its limitations. In Photoshop the image size can be modified as well as the resolution. Called resampling, Photoshop creates the needed pixels to increase the resolution based on the existing

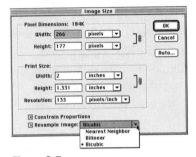

Figure 2.7

You can set the interpolation method in the Image Size dialog box independent of the default settings.

Note

Enlarging an image by resampling results in some blurring of the image. Applying the Unsharp Mask filter after resampling an image may help to improve overall sharpness.

---

pixels. The method Photoshop uses to enlarge an image while retaining its resolution is called interpolation. Three quality levels of interpolation can be specified as the default method in the General Preferences: Nearest Neighbor, Bilinear, and Bicubic.

The Image Size dialog box contains a drop-down menu to select the method of interpolation for a single instance. To resize the image and maintain the resolution, select Image Size from the Image menu. Check the Constrain Proportions checkbox to maintain the aspect ratio (horizontal and vertical proportions) of the image. Check the Resample Image checkbox to maintain the resolution while resizing (see Figure 2.7).

See Chapter 1, "Photoshop Basics," for more information on interpolation methods.

Reducing in Photoshop

Down-sampling in Photoshop is achieved by discarding the proper number of pixels to arrive at a target size and resolution. There is no interpolation involved here because Photoshop has to decide which pixels to throw away. To resize the image and maintain the resolution, select Image Size from the Image menu. Check the Constrain Proportions checkbox to maintain the aspect ratio of the image. Check the Resample Image checkbox to maintain the resolution while resizing. The quality of the resulting image is largely dependent on how high the resolution is to begin with. A 5×5-inch, 300-ppi image, for example, resampled down to 3×3-inch at 300 ppi only subtly affects the image quality, whereas a 5×5-inch, 72-ppi image resampled down to 3×3-inch at 72 ppi displays an apparent loss of quality. It's important to remember that Photoshop uses logic-based algorithms to determine which pixels to throw away, so sampling down too much can cause undesired results. If, for example, you have an image that contains a fine line that is 1 pixel wide, Photoshop may choose to remove some of the pixels that make up the 1 pixel wide line and keep adjacent pixels, thus breaking the line apart or eradicating it altogether. The Unsharp Mask filter can help improve quality after resampling, although I suggest examining the pixel structure before and after to observe the effect resampling has on the image.

Photoshop's Image Modes

Photoshop has eight Image modes available under the Image➡Mode menu:

- ► Bitmap

- ► Grayscale

- ► Duotone

- ► Indexed Color

- ► RGB Color

- ► CMYK Color

- ► LAB Color

- ► Multichannel

A Photoshop image can be converted to any of the available image modes.

Bitmap Mode

Bitmap images, also called 1-bit images, consist of pixels that contain one of two color values: black or white. For this reason, bitmap images require the least amount of memory and disk space. Line art is often scanned as a bitmap to preserve the sharpness of the lines. Because page layout applications such as PageMaker and QuarkXPress can make the white pixels of a bitmap image transparent, grayscale images are sometimes converted to bitmap images with a halftone screen or dithered pattern applied. Many of the image editing options are disabled in Bitmap mode, making it necessary to edit these images in grayscale mode before converting back to Bitmap mode.

In order to convert to Bitmap mode, the image mode must first be set to Grayscale. After you have converted color images to Grayscale mode, the Bitmap mode option is available under the Mode menu.

Figure 2.8

The Bitmap dialog box.

Figure 2.9

50% Threshold.

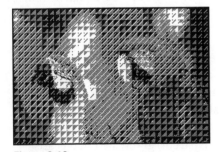

Figure 2.10

Pattern Dither.

1. Choose Bitmap from the Mode menu. The Bitmap dialog box appears (see Figure 2.8).

2. Select the units of measure from the drop-down menu.

3. Enter the output resolution. This defines the resolution of the resulting bitmap image. The current resolution is displayed automatically for output resolution.

4. Select one of the five options for bitmap conversion method.

   ► 50% Threshold converts all gray pixels at or above 128 (50 percent black) to white and all gray values below 128 to black. See Figure 2.9.

   ► Pattern Dither generates a dithered pattern of black and white pixels to represent the grayscale image. Bitmap images created using this method often print better than they appear onscreen. See Figure 2.10.

   ► Diffusion Dither is the best choice for generating grayscale images at 1 bit per pixel for display on computer screens. The diffused pattern creates the illusion of gray values using only black and white pixels. See Figure 2.11.

   ► Halftone Screen emulates the process of applying a halftone screen to a grayscale image. The resulting image is broken up into dots of various sizes to represent the grayscale tones in the image. See Figure 2.12.

   ► Custom Pattern enables you to apply another image as the pattern to create the bitmap image. You can create special screens (wood grain, mezzotint, or stipple pattern, for example) and apply them to the bitmap image. The pattern should be the same size as or larger than the image, because smaller

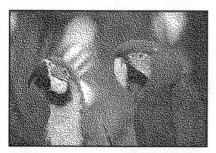

Figure 2.11

Diffusion Dither.

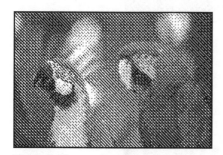

Figure 2.12

Halftone Screen.

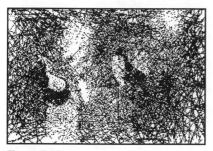

Figure 2.13

Custom Pattern.

Figure 2.14

The Halftone Screen dialog box.

patterns are tiled to create the screen. Custom patterns capture more of the detail in the grayscale image when they themselves contain gray areas. If you want to apply a pattern that is already bitmapped, convert it to grayscale first and apply the Gaussian Blur or Blur More filter to create some gray values. Keep in mind that patterns that are too tight might not print as you expect due to ink spread on press. See Figure 2.13.

If you select Halftone Screen as the method to create the Bitmap image, a dialog box opens (see Figure 2.14) and you must perform the following steps:

1. Select the units of measure from the drop-down menu.

2. Enter a Screen Frequency value. Remember that the screen frequency is the same as "line screen" and ranges from 1 to 999 lines per inch or 0.400 to 400 lines per centimeter (lines per inch is the U.S. standard). Decimal values are allowed here to accommodate matching advanced screening methods.

3. Enter the screen angle. The screen angle can range from -180 degrees to +180 degrees. The printer or service bureau also can tell you what value to use here, although images that are going to print in black ink or one color are generally at a 45-degree angle.

4. Choose a dot shape from the Shape pull-down menu. Most halftone screens are created using either elliptical or diamond-shaped dots.

5. Click OK to accept these settings and generate the bitmap image. Converting grayscale images to bitmap images using the Halftone Screen option enables you to override the halftone screen that is applied when the film is generated. The three

Typical Screen Frequencies

Screen frequency for newspapers and circulars is usually between 65 and 85 lines per inch; magazines are usually between 120 and 150 lines per inch, but check with your printer before indicating a screen frequency because only the printer can tell you what the best line screen for your project is.

Note

You can save your halftone screen settings to a file by clicking the Save button in the Halftone Screen dialog box and reload the settings by clicking the Load button.

images in Figure 2.15 were created using the Halftone Screen option to facilitate the use of multiple screen frequencies on the same page.

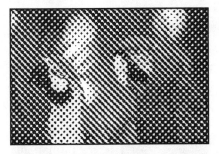

25 LPI

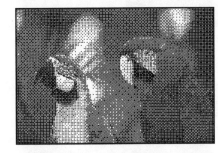

65 LPI

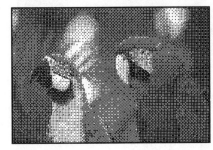

120 LPI

Figure 2.15

The Halftone Screen breaks up the grayscale image into dots. Examine the dots with a magnifying loupe to see the dot structure.

Grayscale Mode

Grayscale images are represented by up to 256 shades or levels of gray. Each pixel in a grayscale image contains 8 bits of data to describe the pixel's brightness value. Gray levels range from 0 (black) to 255 (white). The pixels in a grayscale image are also represented as percent of black where 0 percent is white and 100 percent is black. Bitmap and color images (RGB, LAB, or CMYK) can be converted to grayscale mode. When converting from color to grayscale, Photoshop discards all color information and generates the grayscale image from the luminosity values of the color image. When you convert grayscale images to RGB or CMYK, the gray pixel values are converted to their comparable values in the respective color space. In RGB, for example, grays are represented by combining equal parts of red, green, and blue, such as 230 red, 230 green, and 230 blue to represent 10% gray. In CMYK the gray values are created using varied combinations of cyan, magenta, yellow, and black; 45% cyan, 32% magenta, 32% yellow, and 10% black, for example, create 50% gray.

Converting Bitmap to Grayscale

Bitmap images are usually converted to grayscale to facilitate editing the image because many of the editing tools are not available in Bitmap mode. The resulting grayscale image contains just two gray levels, black (0) and white (255).

1. Choose Image➡Mode➡Grayscale to display the Grayscale dialog box (see Figure 2.16).

2. Enter a size ratio for the conversion. A ratio of 1 creates a grayscale image of the same size. A number higher than 1 creates a smaller sized image. For example, a ratio of 2 generates a grayscale image at 50 precent of the size; Photoshop averages two pixels to create 1 pixel in the grayscale image in this case. Choosing a ratio value less than 1 may cause the image to fall apart because Photoshop has to invent the needed data based on the existing bitmap.

Converting Color to Grayscale

When converting from RGB, CMYK, Lab, or Multichannel mode to Grayscale mode, Photoshop uses the luminance values of the pixels to generate the grayscale image. To convert a color image to grayscale mode, follow these steps:

1. Open any RGB, CMYK, Lab, or Multichannel image.

2. Choose Image➡Mode➡Grayscale.

Figure 2.16

The Grayscale dialog box.

3. A dialog box appears asking whether you want to discard the colors. Click OK to discard the color information. Note that after you discard the color information, converting back to a color mode from Grayscale mode does not restore the color information.

Converting Grayscale to Color

You can convert a grayscale image into any of the available color modes, enabling you to add color or colorize a grayscale image. You can also create a "4-color halftone" by converting grayscale directly to CMYK mode.

1. Open any grayscale image.

2. Choose Image➞Mode➞RGB. You can select CMYK or Lab as color modes, as well.

RGB Mode

The RGB mode in Photoshop uses the RGB color model and represents color by using varying degrees of light intensity in each of the Red, Green, and Blue channels (see Figure 2.17). The values for each color channel are created using 8 bits of data per pixel per color; therefore, each pixel in the RGB image contains a value from 0 to 255 for red, 0 to 255 for green, and 0 to 255 for blue. When all three color values are 255, the pixel appears white. When all three color values are zero (0), the pixel appears black. Equal proportions of the three colors results in a shade of gray.

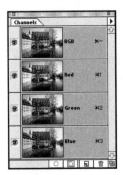

Figure 2.17

The RGB Channels.

CMYK Mode

CMYK images are used in the production of the four process color plates used in four-color printing. For the most part, CMYK images are generated by Photoshop and similar programs from RGB images. In CMYK mode, each pixel of the color image is assigned a value that represents percentages of cyan, magenta, yellow, and black ink. Light colors have low percentages of color; dark colors contain high percentages of ink. In CMYK mode, the lack of ink percentage is equivalent to the paper color (white for proofing). Black is often represented by a high percentage of black combined with some percentage of the other three process colors. When RGB images are converted to CMYK mode, the resulting color separation is generated using parameters in Photoshop's separation table.

The separation table is generated to the specific settings in the Monitor Setup, Printing Inks Setup, and Separation Setup dialog boxes. (See the following section, "Converting to CMYK," for further information.) You can make color and retouching adjustments in RGB before converting to CMYK and use the CMYK Preview command available under the Image menu to view the image in CMYK while working in RGB. If the images are already in CMYK mode when you receive them (from a service bureau, for example), edit the color images in CMYK mode. Converting to RGB from CMYK and then back again can cause some undesirable color shifts. For more information on color correcting images see Chapter 8, "Adjusting Color and Grayscale." CMYK mode contains four color channels for each of the four process colors and one composite channel (see Figure 2.18).

Converting to CMYK

A significant amount of preliminary work must be done in Photoshop before converting images to CMYK mode. Photoshop takes many factors into account when creating the separation table necessary to generate a CMYK image. When Photoshop converts an RGB image to CMYK, it first converts the image to Lab mode (internally; you don't see this). Photoshop uses the settings in the Monitor Setup to perform this interim conversion, so calibrating the monitor and entering the Monitor Setup information is necessary. Refer to your Photoshop user manual for information on calibrating the monitor. The image is then converted from Lab mode to CMYK mode. During this step, Photoshop uses the settings in Printing Inks Setup and Separation Setup to generate the separation table (see "Color Settings" later in this chapter). To convert to CMYK mode, follow these steps:

1. Open any Grayscale, RGB color, or Lab color image.

2. Choose Image➡Mode➡CMYK.

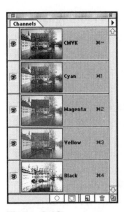

Figure 2.18

The CMYK Channels.

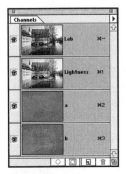

Figure 2.19

The LAB Channels.

Lab Mode

Lab mode uses the L*a*b color model to represent the color of pixels. Each of the three color channels in Lab mode contains 8 bits of data for each pixel, for a total of 24 bits (see Figure 2.19). "L" is the lightness component of the image; each pixel has a value in the range of 0 to 100. The "a" value (green to red) and the "b" value (blue to yellow) range from +120 to -120. Because the color specifications in the L*a*b color model are device independent, Lab mode is the best mode to use when transferring images from one system to another. Adobe recommends using Lab color to print to PostScript Level 2 devices, but check with your service bureau if it is doing the output. The Lab mode is the hardest to understand until you experiment with editing the lightness and color values separately.

Converting to Lab Mode

Grayscale, RGB, Duotone, and Indexed Color images can be converted to Lab mode. You can adjust the "L" (lightness) value in lab mode to adjust the brightness of the image or parts of the image without affecting the color. The image can then be converted back to RGB or Indexed Color without affecting the color values. Lab images can also be converted to CMYK for process color printing. Converting between Lab mode and other color modes or vice versa does not affect the original colors of the image in any way unless you adjust the "a" or "b" values in Lab mode. To convert to Lab mode, follow these steps:

1. Open any Grayscale, RGB, CMYK, Duotone, or Multichannel image. Bitmap images cannot be converted to Lab mode because Lab mode requires at least 8 bits of information per pixel; convert the bitmap image to grayscale first.

2. Choose Image➡Mode➡Lab.

Duotone Mode

When you choose Duotone from the Mode menu, the Duotone Options dialog box appears. A drop-down menu in this dialog box displays the four available modes: Monotone, Duotone, Tritone, and Quadtone. Monotones are 8-bits-per pixel, grayscale images printed with a non-black ink. Duotones are grayscale images printed with two colors, usually black and a spot color. Tritones and quadtones are grayscale images printed with three and four colors respectively. Printing presses are generally capable of printing up to 50 levels of gray for one color, a lot fewer than the 256 gray levels generated by Photoshop. Duotones, tritones, and quadtones are often used to extend the gray levels of the printing process. When creating a duotone, tritone, or quadtone, the gray values of the grayscale image are actually represented by the colors chosen, so the image is still an 8-bit-per-pixel image with the gray values mapped to two, three, or four colors. Unlike the RGB, CMYK, and Lab modes, the colors used in duotones, tritones, and quadtones are contained in a single 8-bit channel and are adjustable only using the curves in the Duotone Options dialog box.

Creating a Duotone

To create a duotone start with a grayscale image. If you are using a color image, you have to convert it to Grayscale mode before continuing.

1. Open any Grayscale image and choose Image➡Mode➡Duotone to display the Duotone Options dialog box (see Figure 2.20).

2. Select Duotone from the Type pull-down menu.

3. Select the colors for your Duotone by clicking the color box to the left of the color name. When the Photoshop Custom Color Picker appears, you can use any of the Custom Color models to select a color for your Duotone or click the Picker button to specify a color mix in one of Photoshop's color spaces. See "Selecting Custom Colors" later in this chapter for more information on specifying spot colors.

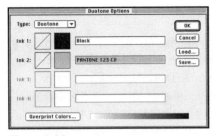

Figure 2.20

The Duotone Options dialog box.

Naming Duotone Spot Colors

If you choose a Custom spot color, be sure the color is named exactly as the color name in your page layout application (upper- and lowercase count, as well as spaces).

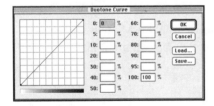

Figure 2.21

The Duotone Curve dialog box.

4. To modify the Duotone curve, click the curve box to the left of the ink swatch in the Duotone Options dialog box to display the Duotone Curve dialog box (see Figure 2.21). The default Duotone curve is a straight diagonal line across the entire grid. The default Duotone curve maps the printing ink percentages exactly to the grayscale values in the image; a 10 percent highlight pixel in the image, for example, prints with a 10 percent dot of the ink color and a 60 percent midtone value prints with a 60 percent dot of the ink color. See "Adjusting Duotone Curves" for information on how to adjust the Duotone curves.

5. After you have adjusted the Duotone curves, click OK in the Duotone Options dialog box. Duotones created with both colors having the same curve produce a Duotone that prints one ink entirely over the other, so make sure that you change the curve for at least one of the colors. If you want to readjust the color settings for your Duotone, type (Command-Z)[Control-Z] to undo the conversion and try again.

6. Save the file in Photoshop EPS format if you want to import the Duotone into a page layout application such as QuarkXPress or PageMaker.

Adjusting Duotone Curves

You should always adjust the Duotone curves to control the way the colors are applied to the image. If you leave the curves as a straight line for both colors, a true Duotone effect will not be achieved because one color will print directly on the other. To adjust the Duotone curves, click the curve box to the left of the ink swatch in the Duotone Options dialog box to display the Duotone Curve dialog box.

1. You can adjust the Duotone curve for each of the ink colors by dragging points on the graph or by

entering values for the printing ink percentages to correspond with the grayscale values in the image.

2. Click the diagonal line in the center of the graph and drag to the right to adjust the ink percentages toward the shadow areas. Drag the point down until the value in the 50% box becomes 30% (see Figure 2.22). With this setting the 50 percent grayscale values in the image print with a 30 percent printing ink dot. The values between 0 percent and 30 percent and the values between 30 percent and 100 percent are automatically recalculated by Photoshop, even though the numbers are not inserted in the corresponding boxes. This ink color maps the grayscale values in the image that are between 0 percent and 50 percent to print with the color ink between 0 percent and 30 percent, so the ink coverage is light in these areas. The ink coverage is highest for the midtone, 3/4 tone, and shadow areas because the largest proportion of ink percentage is distributed between the 50 percent and 100 percent grayscale values in the image.

3. Click the diagonal line in the center of the graph and drag to the left to adjust the ink percentages toward the highlight areas. Drag the point up until the value in the 50% box becomes 70% (see Figure 2.23). With this setting the 50 percent grayscale values in the image are printed with a 70 percent printing ink dot. The values between 0 percent and 70 percent and the values between 70 percent and 100 percent are automatically recalculated by Photoshop, even though the numbers are not inserted in the corresponding boxes. This ink color maps the grayscale values in the image that are between 0 percent and 50 percent to print with the color ink between 0 percent and 70 percent, so the ink coverage is heavy in the highlight and 1/4 tones. The ink coverage is lowest for the midtone, 3/4 tone, and shadow areas because the smallest proportion of ink percentage is distributed between the 50 percent and 100 percent grayscale values in the image.

4. You can click the diagonal line in the graph and add up to 13 points to set the values for the 13 boxes (see Figure 2.24). Note that the end points of the diagonal line can also be adjusted to set the 0 percent and 100 percent values. Photoshop calculates any intermediate ink percentages automatically.

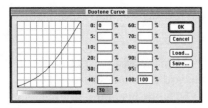

Figure 2.22

The Duotone Curve dialog box with the 50 percent grayscale pixel mapped to a 30 percent printing dot.

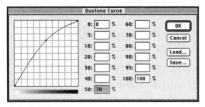

Figure 2.23

The Duotone Curve dialog box with the 50 percent grayscale pixel mapped to a 70 percent printing dot.

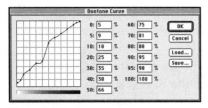

Figure 2.24

The Duotone Curve dialog box with all 13 values mapped on the diagonal line.

▶ Click and drag the points off the grid to remove them.

▶ Click the Save button in the Duotone Curve dialog box to save a particular curve setting.

▶ Click the Load button in the Duotone Curve dialog box to load a previously saved curve setting.

Setting Duotone Overprint Colors

When two or more unscreened colors (100 percent solid ink) overlap in a duotone, tritone, or quadtone, the overlapping colors create a new color (red and yellow produce orange, for example). You can adjust how these colors display on the screen only, which is helpful if you want to calibrate your screen display to accurately display the colors that will print in Duotone mode. Adjusting the colors for overprint does not affect the overall monitor calibration setup and only applies to the specific image you're working with. To set the overprint colors, follow these steps:

1. Choose Image➡Mode➡Duotone to display the Duotone Options dialog box. You can do this even if you're already in Duotone mode.

2. Click the Overprint Colors button to display the Overprint Colors dialog box (see Figure 2.25). The combinations that result when colors overprint are indicated here.

3. To display the Photoshop Color Picker, click the color swatch over the combination that you would like to adjust.

4. Select the color you want for this combination and then click OK.

Perform Steps 3 and 4 for all the color combinations you want to change before clicking OK in the Overprint Colors dialog box.

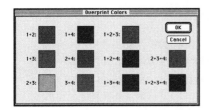

Figure 2.25

The possible color combinations are highlighted in the Overprint Colors dialog box.

Loading and Saving Duotone Curves

You can save the Duotone curve information in a file for later retrieval. Click the Save button in the Duotone Options dialog box and give the file a name that reflects the colors used. To load saved Duotone presets, click the Load button in the Duotone Options dialog box.

Creating a Monotone

Creating a monotone is a simple process. Monotone images are grayscale images that have a color specification assigned to them. If you specify a Custom Color (PANTONE 156, for example) and save the file in EPS format, you can import the file into a page layout application such as QuarkXPress or PageMaker and separate the file out to a color plate called Pantone 156. To create a monotone image, start out with a grayscale image and do the following:

1. Choose Image➡Mode➡Duotone to display the Duotone Options dialog box.

2. Select Monotone from the Type pull-down menu.

3. Select the color for your monotone by clicking the color box to the left of the color name. When the Photoshop Custom Color Picker appears, you can use any of the Custom Color models to select a color for your monotone or click the Picker button to specify a color mix in one of Photoshop's color spaces. If you choose a Custom spot color, be sure the color is named exactly as the color name in your page layout application (upper- and lowercase count as well). See "Selecting Custom Colors" later in this section for more information on specifying spot colors.

4. Click the Duotone Curve diagram to display the Monotone Curve dialog box. If you want to end up with a monotone image that represents the grayscale with a color, leave the Duotone curve linear (a straight line from the bottom left to the top right).

5. Click OK. If you want to readjust the color settings for your monotone, type (Command-Z)[Control-Z] to undo the conversion and try again.

6. Save the file in Photoshop EPS format if you want to import the monotone into a page layout application.

Creating a Tritone or Quadtone

Follow the preceding steps for creating a duotone, but specify three colors to create a tritone or four colors for a quadtone image. Custom presets for tritones and quadtones reside in the goodies directory (Windows) or the Goodies folder (Macintosh) in the Photoshop application's directory. The best way to get a feel for what settings to use for duotones, tritones, and quadtones is to experiment and examine some of the presets provided with Photoshop.

Setting Screen Angles for Duotones, Tritones, and Quadtones

A duotone, tritone, or quadtone creates overlapping areas of the grayscale image when it is created. In order for the halftone screens to print properly, the halftone screen angles for the color plates should be at least 30 degrees apart. For four-color process separations, black is usually set to a 45-degree angle with magenta and cyan 30 degrees away from that on either side (15 degrees and 75 degrees). Setting the angles 30 degrees apart ensures that an overlapping of the halftone dots does not create a moiré pattern. For CMYK printing the yellow plate is printed at 90 degrees (only 15 degrees away from the nearest color). Yellow is chosen as the color that must overlap because it is the least dominant of the four colors. Use this same setup for duotones, tritones, and quadtones. For quadtones, keep in mind that with four inks, one of them must overlap in the halftone dot area. Choose the lightest of the four colors to be set at the "yellow" angle.

Before you set the screen angles for your duotone, tritone, or quadtone images in Photoshop, consult your printer or service bureau. Many screening algorithms are in use today, such as Agfa's Balanced Screening and Linotype Hell's Diamond Screening, not to mention advanced screening technologies for stochastic screening, sometimes called FM (frequency modulation) screening. Setting the screen angles independently for the image in Photoshop may cause more harm than good because service bureaus and printers may use improved screening techniques that they can set up for your file during output. To set up the screen frequencies and angles yourself, follow these steps:

1. Open a duotone image and choose Page Setup from the File menu to display the Page Setup dialog box (see Figure 2.26).

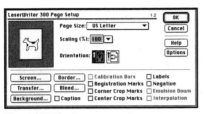

Figure 2.26

The Page Setup dialog box.

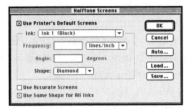

Figure 2.27

The Halftone Screens dialog box.

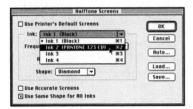

Figure 2.28

The colors used in your duotone, tritone, or quadtone are listed under the Ink drop-down menu.

Figure 2.29

The EPS Format dialog box.

2. Click the Screen button to display the Halftone Screens dialog box (see Figure 2.27).

3. Deselect the Use Printer's Default Screens checkbox and select the ink color from the drop-down menu (see Figure 2.28). Note that the ink color list is composed of the colors used in your duotone, tritone, or quadtone.

4. Enter a Screen Frequency and Angle for the color. Black should be at 45 degrees with other colors 30 degrees apart at either 15 degrees or 75 degrees. Talk to your printer for suggested angles.

5. Choose a dot shape from the drop-down list. For standard halftone screens, use a diamond dot. If you want all plates to have the same dot shape, click the Use Same Shape for All Inks checkbox.

6. Click the Use Accurate Screens checkbox if you plan to print your file to an output device using PostScript Level 2 or an Emerald controller or Emerald RIP (Raster Image Processor). If you check this box and do not print to one of these devices, the accurate screens setting has no effect.

7. Specify the screen information for each color in your image.

8. You can save your settings to reload for subsequent images by clicking the Save button in the Halftone Screens dialog box. Click the load button to reload the settings in the future. Click OK if you're done.

9. In order for the screens you just set up to be used for the image when it is saved as a Photoshop EPS file, you must click the Include Halftone Screens checkbox when saving the file in Photoshop EPS format (see Figure 2.29).

Indexed Color Mode

Indexed Color images are images that contain a specific color palette of up to 256 colors. An Indexed Color image can contain just the colors used in the image (if 256 or fewer), facilitating smaller file sizes and faster display in multimedia applications and Web pages. Indexed Color images are rarely used for printing purposes and are best suited for multimedia authoring applications such as Director and QuarkImmedia, presentation programs such as Persuasion and PowerPoint, and are ideal for creating graphics for Web pages. See Chapter 16, "Creating Web Graphics" for more information on using indexed color images on Web pages. When you convert a color image from one of the other color modes to indexed color, Photoshop creates a color lookup table (CLUT) to store the color values for the image. If the image contains more than 256 distinct colors, Photoshop finds the closest matches and builds an indexed color table with 256 colors. The color table generated for indexed color images can also be edited to reduce the number of colors used.

Converting to Indexed Color

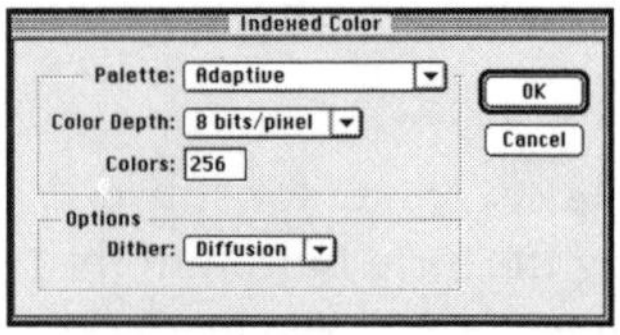

Choose Image➡Mode➡Indexed Color to display the Indexed Color dialog box (see Figure 2.30). These are the steps necessary to convert to indexed color:

1. Open a RGB image and choose Image➡Mode➡ Indexed Color.

2. Choose a palette. The Palette drop-down menu contains five palette choices to convert to Indexed Color. You can view the color table that is generated by choosing Image➡Mode➡Color Table or by displaying the Swatches palette. See "Choosing an Indexed Color Palette" later in this chapter for specific information on the choices in the Palette drop-down menu.

Figure 2.30

The Indexed Color dialog box.

3. Select a Color Depth. The Color Depth option is available only when you choose Uniform or Adaptive from the Palette drop-down list in the Indexed Color dialog box. Photoshop uses the Color Depth information to generate the Indexed Color file. The maximum setting is 8 bits per pixel here because 8 bits per pixel generates 256 colors. Choosing a number less than 8 bits per pixel results in fewer colors, although the Indexed Color image is still going to be an 8-bit-per-pixel image. When you choose Other as the Color Depth option, you can specify the exact number of colors desired.

4. Select a Dithering Option. When the color table generated by converting to Indexed Color mode does not contain the exact 256 colors used in the RGB image, the resulting image appears posterized to some extent, unless some form of dithering is applied to the image. When dithering is used, the missing colors in the image are simulated by the application of a pattern. If you use the Exact Palette, the Dithering options are grayed out (unavailable) because the image contains all the color values needed.

   ► When None is selected and the RGB image contains more than 256 colors, posterization (harsh color transitions) may become apparent because Photoshop fills in the blanks with the closest color in the palette.

   ► The Pattern method of dithering creates patterns of pixels to simulate the missing colors. You must be using one of the System Palette options to apply a Pattern dither.

   ► Diffusion offsets pixels to avoid an obvious pattern when dithering and is the most common choice for dithering, when dithering is necessary.

Choosing an Indexed Color Palette

The color palette you choose to generate an Indexed Color image is largely dependent on the colors in the image and the intended use of the image. Web graphics, for example, have a specific color palette that contains the 216 colors that display correctly on both Windows and MacOS platforms. When choosing a color palette for screen display, it's sometimes helpful to try a few of the following options to see which one yields the best results.

▶ The Exact Palette is created with the exact same colors used in the RGB file, assuming the RGB file contains 256 or fewer colors. If the RGB contains more than 256 distinct colors, the Exact option is grayed out.

▶ The System (Macintosh) palette uses the Macintosh default color palette. This palette contains an even sampling of the colors in the RGB color space. Note that the Macintosh color palette and Windows color palette may contain some of the same colors, but they are organized in a different order, so choose a System (Macintosh) color palette only when you're sure the image will be used on a Macintosh only.

▶ The System (Windows) palette uses the Windows default color palette. This palette contains an even sampling of the colors in the RGB color space. Note that the Windows color palette and Macintosh color palette may contain some of the same colors, but they are organized in a different order, so choose a System (Windows) color palette only when you're sure the image will be used on a Windows computer only.

▶ The Web Palette uses a palette of the 216 colors recognized by Web browser applications. If you have created graphics to be exported to GIF89a format, choose Web when converting to Indexed Color mode for the best results on both Macintosh and PC/Windows platforms.

▶ The Uniform Palette uses a uniform sampling of the colors in the RGB image's gamut of colors. The Uniform palette's colors are generated based on the Color Depth specified. Specify dithering for Uniform indexed colors with a color depth of less than 8 bits per pixel.

▶ The Adaptive Palette samples the colors used in the image and builds a color table based on the most common occurrences, which can be really helpful for images that are weighted in specific color areas because the indexed color image will contain fewer individual colors. You can also base the color table on a selected portion of the image. Select the portion of the image you want to base the indexed color table on before converting to Indexed mode. Photoshop uses the selected area of the image to weigh the color choices made for the color palette.

▶ The Custom Palette is used to build your own color table of up to 256 colors. When you choose this option the Color Table dialog box appears. See the section on "Editing the Indexed Color Table" later in this chapter for information on how to enter the colors for the color table.

► The Previous choice is available only if you chose the Custom or Adaptive options the last time you converted to Indexed Color. The Previous option uses the color palette from the previously generated "Custom" or "Adaptive" color palette, even if you didn't save the palette (see "Saving and Loading Color Tables" in this section).

Making Color Table Choices

The top of the Color Table dialog box contains six predefined color tables (see Figure 2.31). You can apply any of these color tables to the indexed color image.

► Custom represents any color table that is not a Photoshop built-in color table.

► Black Body is based on the colors a black body radiator radiates when heating up. The colors range from black to red, orange, yellow, then white.

► If you select Grayscale, the image is rebuilt using 256 levels of gray. Not to be confused with converting a color image to grayscale, selecting Grayscale as the color table remaps all of the color pixels to an ordered set of gray levels.

► The Macintosh System color table displays the Macintosh 256 color palette.

► The Spectrum palette contains transitions between the primary hues: violet, blue, green, yellow, orange, and red.

► The Windows System color table displays the Windows 256 color palette.

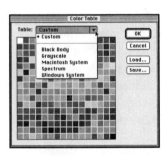

Figure 2.31

Display the Color Table dialog box by choosing Image➡Mode➡Color Table.

Saving and Loading Color Tables

You can save the displayed color table by clicking the Save button in the Color Table dialog box. To load a previously saved color table, click the Load button in the Color Table dialog box. You can also load the saved color tables into the Swatches Palette. To load a color table into the Swatches Palette, choose Load Swatches or Replace Swatches from the Swatches Palette menu. Locate a previously saved Swatch file or CLUT file and click the Open button.

Modifying the Color Table

The color table contains all of the colors (up to 256) that are contained in your indexed color image. You may want to modify the colors that make up your Indexed Color image to combine similar colors into one flat color or to change the values of individual colors for effect. To modify the colors contained in the color table of an Indexed Color image, follow these steps:

1. Choose Image➡Mode➡Color Table to display the Color Table dialog box.

2. Click a color to modify an individual color or click and drag through a range of colors.

3. The Photoshop Color Picker appears. If you clicked just one color swatch, choose a new color and click OK. If you selected a range of colors, choose the first new color for the range and click OK. The Color Picker reappears so you can select the last color in the range. The first color you pick also appears in the color picker the second time it is displayed, so simply clicking OK without entering a color changes the whole range of colors to the first color.

4. Click OK in the Color Table dialog box to apply the changes. If you click the Cancel button the color palette is restored.

Figure 2.32

The Multichannel mode creates numbered grayscale channels.

Multichannel Mode

When color images are converted to Multichannel mode, the color plates are recreated as 8-bit-per-pixel grayscale channels numbered from 1 (see Figure 2.32). Converting an RGB image to Multichannel mode, for example, would result in three channels numbered 1, 2, and 3 representing the Red, Green, and Blue channels of the RGB file. Converting a CMYK image to Multichannel mode would create four channels numbered 1, 2, 3, and 4 to represent the cyan, magenta, yellow, and black plates respectively. Multichannel mode is not an option for Grayscale, Bitmap, and Indexed Color images because these contain only one channel to begin with. After you have converted to Multichannel mode, you can convert back to the original color mode or Lab mode. Multichannel mode lends itself well to breaking out particular color channels to create specialized printing effects such as bump plates in which a fifth color is included to enhance a particular color value in the printed piece.

Calibrating Your Monitor

Monitor calibration is important because it helps to create a somewhat accurate viewing environment for Photoshop images. The following instructions tell you how to calibrate your monitor using Photoshop's calibration tools. Calibrating your monitor eliminates color casts, balances the grays and neutrals, and even helps you standardize how you view color images on different monitors. Calibrating your monitor in no way guarantees that the four color process printing you do is accurate and matches your screen. In fact, a computer monitor always displays RGB data and is not able to display exact CMYK colors. Because humans are highly dependent on visual input, however, having a calibrated monitor certainly helps you spot obvious color problems.

Functionally, the calibration process is the same for both the Macintosh and PC computers running Windows 3.x or Windows 95. The location of specific dialog boxes and places where you have to enter data, however, are different. The steps to calibrating your monitor are presented in the following sections individually in their entirety for both Macintosh and PC displays. Before you begin, make sure the monitor has been on for at least a half hour and set the room lighting conditions. The ambient lighting conditions in the room can greatly affect the color display on your monitor, so take steps to ensure that the lighting is consistent throughout the day. A darker room is preferable to a bright room because clothing and background colors may be reflected on the monitor in high lighting conditions.

Calibrating Windows 3.x or Windows 95 Monitors

Photoshop 4.0 for Windows incorporates the monitor calibration process directly in the application using the Monitor Setup dialog box. Unlike the MacOS where the calibration setings affect the entire system, Windows calibration only affects the display when working in Photoshop.

1. Adjust the Brightness and Contrast on your monitor using the controls on the monitor. When you're happy with the settings, tape down the controls or mark them in some way.

2. Turn off any background patterns or pictures, and change the color of your monitor's display to a light gray to avoid colors that affect your perception of color.

3. Choose File➡Color Settings➡Monitor Setup.

4. Type a value for Gamma in the Monitor Setup dialog box. A target gamma of 1.8 is best for

printing CMYK images. If you intend to print to an RGB device such as a color transparency film recorder or if you're creating images for display on a monitor, enter a gamma higher than 1.8. Television sets and very large display monitors (30 inches or larger) have a gamma of 2.2, so set this as your target gamma for images to be displayed in video. If you're not sure of the output device specifications, enter 1.8.

5. Click the Calibrate button in the Monitor Setup dialog box to display the Calibrate dialog box. You can preview your adjustments on an open Photoshop image by clicking the Preview button.

6. Hold up a piece of white paper that matches the whiteness of the paper you use for output. If you have a color proof handy, use the white of the proofing substrate. Click White Pt. and drag the three slider triangles until the whites on your monitor match the white of the paper in your hand. Monitors tend to have a blue tint when the whites are set too bright. You may also notice that your adjustments make the whites of the screen appear slightly yellow in tint; that's okay.

7. Adjust the gamma by dragging the Gamma Adjustment slider until the solid gray area matches the patterned gray area in the control strip above the Gamma Adjustment slider.

8. Adjust the color balance. Click Balance and drag the three slider triangles until the gray areas in the control strip become a neutral gray. Adjusting the color balance eliminates any color casts that are present.

9. Click Black Pt. and adjust the three triangle sliders until the shadow tones in the lower control strip contain no color cast. You should see an apparent gradation between each of the gray levels represented in the strip.

10. Check to make sure that these last adjustments did not affect previous adjustments. If so, you should go back and adjust the gamma and color balance settings. When you're happy with the setup, close the Calibrate dialog box.

You can save the calibration settings by clicking the Save Settings button in the Calibrate dialog box. You should save the settings just in case someone else changes the settings or you want to set up a profile for another output scenario in the future. Load the settings by clicking the Load Settings button in the Calibrate dialog box. You shouldn't have to recalibrate your monitor unless some of the original conditions have changed, such as room lighting or if you install a new monitor. Monitors also lose intensity with age, but unless there is something wrong with your monitor, this loss of intensity should not become apparent for years.

Calibrating Macintosh Monitors

1. Adjust the Brightness and Contrast on your monitor using the controls on the monitor. When you're happy with the settings, tape down the controls or mark them in some way.

2. Turn off any background patterns or pictures, and change the color of your monitor's display to a light gray to avoid colors that affect your perception of color.

3. Choose Control Panels from the Apple menu and double-click the Gamma control panel. When turned on, the Gamma control panel affects the entire monitor for all applications. Click the "on" radio button to activate the gamma correction in the Gamma control panel.

4. Select a target by clicking a target gamma radio button at the top of the Gamma control panel. A target gamma of 1.8 is best for printing CMYK images. If you intend to print to an RGB device such as a color transparency film recorder or if you're creating images for display on a monitor, choose a gamma higher than 1.8. Television sets and very large display monitors (30 inches or larger) have a gamma of 2.2, so set this as your target gamma for images to be displayed in video. If you're not sure of the output device specifications, choose 1.8.

Note

The Gamma control panel comes with Adobe Photoshop on the Macintosh. If it's not in your Photoshop folder or in the Control Panels folder in the System folder, look for it on the Photoshop install disks or CD.

5. Hold up a piece of white paper that matches the whiteness of the paper you use for output. If you have a color proof handy, use the white of the proofing substrate. Click White Pt. and drag the three slider triangles until the whites on your monitor match the white of the paper in your hand. Monitors tend to have a blue tint when the whites are set too hot. You may also notice that your adjustments make the whites of the screen appear slightly yellow in tint; that's okay.

6. Adjust the gamma by dragging the Gamma Adjustment slider until the solid gray area matches the patterned gray area in the control strip above the Gamma Adjustment slider.

7. Adjust the color balance. Click Balance and drag the three slider triangles until the gray areas in the control strip become a neutral gray. Adjusting the color balance eliminates any color casts that are present.

8. Click Black Pt. and adjust the three triangle sliders until the shadow tones in the lower control strip contain no color cast. You should see an apparent gradation between each of the gray levels represented in the strip.

9. Check to make sure that these last adjustments did not affect previous adjustments. If so, you should go back and adjust the gamma and color balance settings. When you're happy with the setup, close the Gamma control panel.

You can save the calibration settings by clicking the Save Settings button in the Gamma control panel. You should save the settings just in case someone else changes the settings or you want to set up a profile for another output scenario in the future. Load the settings by clicking the Load Settings button in the Gamma control panel. You shouldn't have to recalibrate your monitor unless some of the original conditions have changed, such as room lighting or if you install a new monitor. Monitors also lose intensity with age, but unless there is something wrong with your monitor, this loss of intensity should not become apparent for years.

Color Settings

Color Settings are available when you choose File➡Color Settings. Using the color settings options in Photoshop, you can specify precisely the printing conditions and conditions for viewing on the monitor in your office or room.

Before you adjust any of the color settings, it is suggested that you calibrate your monitor using the supplied software that comes with Photoshop (as detailed previously in "Calibrating Your Monitor"), or a third-party product that supports your color monitor. Most calibration tools enable you to adjust the gamma, color balance, and white and black points for your monitor. The Color Settings in Photoshop are used to specify how Photoshop converts from RGB to CMYK and to further control the way Photoshop images are displayed on your monitor.

Specifying Monitor Setup

After you have calibrated your monitor, the next step is to enter the monitor information in the Monitor Setup dialog box (see Figure 2.33). Photoshop uses this information to adjust the display of images in Photoshop. Aside from affecting the monitor display, the Monitor Setup information also determines the way colors convert between modes. On the Macintosh, the settings in the Monitor Setup dialog box affect the way RGB is converted to CMYK and how the CMYK colors display on the monitor. In Windows, the Monitor Setup information affects the way RGB is converted to CMYK but only affects the display of RGB images.

1. Choose File➡Color Settings➡Monitor Setup to display the Monitor Setup dialog box.

2. Select the type of monitor you are using from the Monitor drop-down menu (see Figure 2.34).

3. Type the gamma value you set in the Gamma control panel for Macintosh. In Windows, a value should already be entered here from when you calibrated your monitor. If you are using a third-party utility, enter the value determined by the calibration device.

4. If you are not using a third-party calibration device, choose 6500 degrees K for the white point. If you are using a third-party device, enter the white point value suggested by the calibration device. If the number you need is not listed in the drop-down menu, select Custom and enter it.

5. Select the type of monitor you are using from the Phosphors drop-down list. If you are not sure or if your monitor type is not listed here, choose Custom and enter the red, green, and blue values specified by the monitor manufacturer.

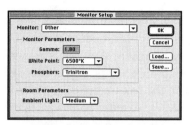

Figure 2.33

The Monitor Setup dialog box.

Figure 2.34

The choices in the drop-down menu.

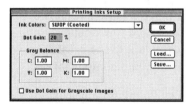

Figure 2.35

The Printing Inks Setup dialog box.

6. Compare the room lighting to the brightness of your monitor. If the room lighting is about the same as the monitor brightness, select Medium for Ambient Light. If the room light is brighter, select High, and if the room lighting is darker, select Low.

7. Click the OK button when you're happy with the settings. You can save and load the monitor settings by clicking the Load and Save buttons.

Specifying Printing Inks Setup

The Printing Inks Setup dialog box is where you set up the separation preferences to control ink, paper stock, and dot gain (see Figure 2.35). The information needed to make the choices for the Printing Inks Setup's dialog box are available from your printer, although there are some standard settings that return good results. Photoshop uses the information in the Printing Inks Setup dialog box to convert color values between modes. If you change the settings in the Printing Inks Setup dialog box after you have already converted an image from RGB to CMYK, the changes affect only the screen representation, leaving the data unchanged. Converting back and forth between RGB and CMYK is not a good idea because Photoshop has to recalculate the color values each time and may inadvertently cause a shift in color.

1. Choose File➡Color Settings➡Printing Inks Setup to display the Printing Inks Setup dialog box (see Figure 2.35).

2. Select the Ink Colors profile from the drop-down list. The default setting here is SWOP (Coated). SWOP stands for "Specifications for Web Offset Publications" and is the industry standard for color separation in the United States. The most common ink color specifications are available in this drop-down menu and you should choose the

Figure 2.36

Choose SWOP (Coated) for high quality printing if you are not sure.

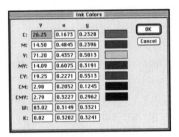

Figure 2.37

The Ink Colors dialog box.

one that best describes your printing needs (see Figure 2.36). This color profile adjusts the color display of your file to represent the type of paper and printing ink set specified here. If you choose Custom from this list, the Ink Colors dialog box appears (see Figure 2.37). To enter color values in the Ink Colors dialog box you need specific numbers acquired from a reflective densitometer's readings of a color proof or printed piece.

3. The Dot Gain field has a value in it if you chose a standard profile from the Ink Colors setting. Don't change this value unless you have already seen a proof and talked to the printer. The dot gain percentage indicated here represents compensation in the halftone dot size for press conditions that cause the halftone dot to grow during printing. A 20% setting in the Dot Gain field means that when the CMYK file is generated, a 50 percent dot is adjusted down to a 30 percent dot, so when the file is printed on press and the dot increases in size by 20 percent, it will be at the correct size (50 percent). Although dot gain can be identified on the proof (assuming the proofing system is calibrated to emulate dot gain), you should always talk to the printer before specifying any dot gain compensation.

4. You can check Use Dot Gain for Grayscale Images to have the screen reflect dot gain for grayscale and Duotone images, as well as individual channels of color files. You can then determine whether the image is too dark from the screen representation and make adjustments.

Specifying the Separation Setup

The Separation Setup dialog box contains settings used to generate the CMYK plates when converting from RGB mode (see Figure 2.38). The Separation Setup information controls the generation of CMYK for each pixel based on the RGB values for those same pixels. Where the Monitor Setup and Printing Inks Setup affect how the image is displayed onscreen, the Separation Setup modifies the pixel data to accommodate the settings in the Separation Setup dialog box. Once you have converted an image to CMYK, Photoshop reconverts the data back to RGB "internally" for display on the monitor. When you first use the settings in the Separation Setup and Printing Inks Setup dialog boxes to convert from RGB to CMYK, Photoshop stores a separation table with the specified values. This separation table is used for each successive conversion from RGB to CMYK until you change one or both of the Separation Setup and Printing Inks Setup values. The following options determine how the CMYK plates are separated in Photoshop:

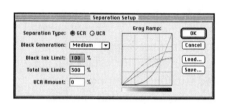

Figure 2.38

The Separation Setup dialog box.

▶ **UCR and GCR.** UCR (Undercolor Removal) and GCR (Gray Component Replacement) are settings used to determine how to generate the black plate when converting from RGB to CMYK mode. When GCR is selected, the black plate contains a wide range of grays and is usually used for images that contain dark saturated areas. Internally, the image data is evaluated to locate the areas of the image where combinations of all the colors contain a gray component that can be represented with black ink instead of a CMY combination. Undercolor Removal (UCR), on the other hand, leaves the gray components of the colors intact, generating a "skeleton" black plate that is concentrated in the shadows and detail areas of the image. Paper and press conditions are ultimately the deciding factors in choosing which method to use for black generation. Printers are quite familiar with these terms and can help you decide which method to use.

▶ **Black Generation.** There are six choices available for Black Generation: Light, Medium, Heavy,

Maximum, Custom, and None. Medium is the default setting in Photoshop and is the correct choice for most separation types. The Light setting creates a black plate that is only slightly lighter than the Medium setting. Use the Light setting if you think the overall darkness of the image is too high. The Heavy setting creates a black plate that is darker than that created with the Medium setting, but again, only to a small degree. Use Heavy if the image seems flat or too even in the darker areas. Maximum puts all of the gray areas on the black plate and is most useful for high contrast images that contain light backgrounds. Screen captures from a computer monitor or images that contain black text as part of the image are some examples. Custom is used to create a setting not represented in the Black Generation list. Selecting Custom displays a curve dialog box that contains a curve representative of the last setting for black generation before you selected Custom. A setting of None generates an empty black plate; all of the image detail is represented by CMY only.

▶ **Black Ink Limit.** The default setting for Black Ink Limit is 100 percent. This setting affects the generation of the black plate in concert with the black generation method you chose above. The black ink limit is also part of the Total Ink Limit.

▶ **Total Ink Limit.** The Total Ink Limit is the maximum ink density supported by the printing press on which the color separation is going to print. The default for Total Ink Limit is 300 percent, a value that works well for most high-quality print jobs. Note that when you change the Black Ink Limit or Total Ink Limit, the composite curve diagram in this dialog box reflects the change. Check with your printer before deciding on Total Ink Limit and Black Ink Limit.

▶ **UCA Amount.** The UCA (undercolor addition) Amount option is a choice only when you choose GCR as the separation type. UCA adds back some of the CMY color in the shadow areas where GCR removed the gray component to the black plate. UCA is a value between 1 percent and 100 percent; the default is 0 percent (no UCA). For the majority of printing conditions, leave this value at 0 percent. Your printer can tell you what value to plug in here.

Saving your settings can save you many future phone calls to your printer. If you use the same printer frequently for the same types of projects, ask the printer whether you can use these same settings for future projects as well. Saving your settings is a good habit to get into, and is especially important if you have created your own black generation by choosing Custom and adjusting the curve. Click the Save button in the Separation Setup dialog box, and give your file a name that will make sense in the future. Load saved settings by clicking the Load button in the Separation Setup dialog box.

Saving and Loading Separation Tables

The settings you selected in the Printing Inks Setup and Separation Setup dialog boxes generate a separation table when you convert from RGB to CMYK. You can save this table through the Separation Tables dialog box and reload the separation table at a later date. You may want to do this if you routinely generate separations with specific settings for different printers and printing conditions. It is important to note that the Monitor Setup information is not saved with the separation table. To display the Separation Tables dialog box choose File➡Color Settings➡ Separation Tables. Click the Save button and type a name for the separation table. This table contains the settings in the Printing Inks Setup and Separation Setup Dialog boxes. The Use Table radio buttons are grayed out until you load a separation table. Click the Load button and choose a separation table. Click the radio button next to Use Table to use the new separation table instead of the one generated by the Printing Inks Setup and Separation Setup (see Figure 2.39). After you load a separation table in the Separation Tables dialog box, it stays in effect for future conversions from RGB to CMYK. If you change the settings in Printing Inks Setup or Separation Setup, you must also change your selections in the Separation Tables dialog box.

You also can set up color separation tables with device profiles for color printers defined by the Apple ColorSync Manager (Macintosh) or the Kodak

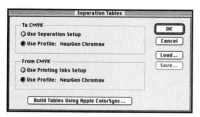

Figure 2.39

You have to load a previously saved separation table to select Use Table from the Separation Tables dialog box.

ICC Color Management System (Windows). Refer to the Photoshop documentation and the documentation of your particular color management system for specific details on how to use this function.

Summary

This chapter is packed with information about Photoshop's various color modes and color settings as well as some important information about calibrating your monitor. The key to good color reproduction in Photoshop is communication: communication with your printer and communication with your service bureau in particular. If you're creating images for print, ask questions to find out what settings you should enter or if you should change the settings at all. If you're creating graphics for the Web, see Chapter 16, "Creating Web Graphics," for information on which color modes to use and how to create indexed color images for Web graphics. In the following chapter you will learn how to paint and fill with color using the available color models in Photoshop.

Painting and Filling

Photoshop offers a variety of tools and methods for painting and filling the pixels in the image bitmap. The powerful options of the painting tools enable you to paint subtle changes to an existing image or create original artwork on a blank canvas. This chapter details the painting tools and fill commands as a reference for the exercises in this book.

Blending Modes

The Blending modes are available in many palettes in Photoshop, including all of the painting tool palettes. They affect the way the color you are painting with interacts with the underlying image. In the case of layers, the Blending modes affect the way the colors on one layer interact with the colors of underlying layers. The Blending modes are available whenever you add color to the Photoshop image, regardless of the technique used. The Blending modes available in Photoshop are:

► The Normal blending mode is the default mode in Photoshop. Normal mode replaces the values of the painted pixels with foreground color. The Normal mode is called Threshold when you are working in Bitmap mode.

► The Dissolve blending mode replaces the values of the pixels randomly, based on the Opacity setting in the Paintbrush Options palette. Choose a large brush size and set the opacity to something less than 100% to view the effect of this mode.

► The Behind blending mode works only on transparent layers. The transparent pixels are exclusively affected with this option.

► The Clear blending mode is available only when you are using the Line tool, Paint Bucket tool, or the Fill or Stroke command and only when you are working on a transparent layer. This option replaces the values of the pixels with the transparent value.

► The Multiply blending mode multiplies the color values of the image and the color you are painting with to arrive at a darker complementary color. Painting over the same area multiple times creates successively darker colors, whereas painting on either white or black yields no results.

► The Screen blending mode produces a bleaching effect making the painted area lighter depending on the color selected and the underlying color in the image. Painting with light colors has a stronger effect than painting with dark colors; therefore, darker colors create a subtler effect.

► The Overlay blending mode combines the color value of the foreground color with the colors of the image pixels while preserving the highlight and shadow values of the image. This mode is effective when colorizing a color image with the painting tools or compositing images on layers.

► The Soft Light blending mode darkens or lightens the image based on the color being used. A lighter color with a gray value less than 50% lightens the image creating a dodged effect with the foreground color. A darker color with a gray value greater than 50% darkens the image creating a burn effect.

▶ The Hard Light blending mode combines the effects of the Screen mode and the Multiply mode. When you paint with a color that has a gray value less than 50%, the effect is similar to the Screen mode described earlier. When you paint with a color that has a gray value greater than 50%, the effect is similar to the Multiply mode described earlier.

▶ The Color Dodge blending mode lightens the color of the image pixels to reflect the lightness value of the selected color. Painting with dark colors produces a subtler change than painting with light, bright colors. Painting with black yields no effect, whereas painting with white results in an overexposed blown-out effect.

▶ The Color Burn blending mode darkens the color of the image pixels based on the selected painting color. Painting with light, bright colors produces a more subtle effect than painting with dark colors. Painting with white yields no effect.

▶ The Darken blending mode changes the color of the pixels that contain values lighter than those of the foreground color. Pixels darker than the painting color are left unchanged.

▶ The Lighten blending mode changes the color of the pixels containing values darker than those of the foreground color. Pixels lighter than the painting color are left unchanged.

▶ The Difference blending mode evaluates the brightness values of the colors in each channel and compares these values with the comparable values in the selected color. The color with the lightest brightness value is subtracted from the color with the darkest brightness value resulting in the value for the image pixel. Painting with dark colors produces a subtler effect than painting with light, bright colors. Painting with white results in an inverse image, similar to a color negative.

▶ The Exclusion blending mode produces an effect similar to the Difference mode, but with a softer effect.

▶ The Hue blending mode replaces only the hue value of the image pixels, leaving the saturation and luminance values intact.

▶ The Saturation blending mode replaces the saturation value of the image pixels with the saturation value of the foreground color.

ADVANCED TIP

The Blending mode options are available under the context menu of the Paintbrush tool. Hold down the Control key and click anywhere in the canvas area to display the context menu on the Macintosh; click in the canvas area with the right mouse button in Windows.

► The Color blending mode replaces both the hue and saturation values of the image pixels with the hue and saturation values of the foreground color. Use this mode to paint in local color changes without affecting the grayscale portion of the image.

► The Luminosity blending mode maintains the hue and saturation of the image pixels, but it changes the luminance value to that of the foreground color or layer colors when compositing layers.

TIP

To paint in a straight line, click the canvas area with the paintbrush; Shift-click somewhere else in the canvas area to create a straight brush stroke from the first point. If you hold down the Shift key while painting with the Paintbrush tool, you can constrain painting to either a vertical or horizontal plane.

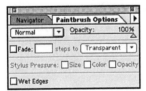

Figure 3.1

The Paintbrush Options palette.

Using the Paintbrush Tool

To use the Paintbrush tool, select the Paintbrush from the Toolbox or type the letter B and click and drag in the canvas area. Use the Paintbrush tool as you would an ordinary paint brush. The Paintbrush tool is used in Chapter 10, "Working in Layers," Chapter 11, "Using Adjustment Layers," Chapter 9, "Colorizing," and Chapter 13, "Adjusting Focus & Tone."

► Double-click the Paintbrush tool in the Toolbox to display the Paintbrush Options palette (see Figure 3.1).

► Select a Blending mode. The Blending modes for the Paintbrush tool are available under a drop-down menu in the upper-left corner of the Paintbrush Options palette (see Figure 3.2). See "Blending Modes" at the beginning of this chapter for more information on the available Blending modes.

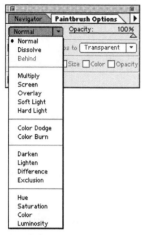

Figure 3.2

The Blending modes available for the Paintbrush tool.

TIP

When using the Paintbrush tool, hold down (Option)[Alt] and click the image to sample a color from the image and load it as the foreground color.

TIP

To paint in a straight line, click the canvas area with the Airbrush; Shift-click somewhere else in the canvas area to create a straight brush stroke from the first point. If you hold down the Shift key while painting with the Airbrush tool, you can constrain painting to either a vertical or horizontal plane.

▶ To set the opacity level of the Paintbrush tool to a value from 1% to 100%, drag the triangle slider in the upper-right corner of the Paintbrush Options palette or type a number on the keyboard. Simply type a single digit number from 0 through 9 to specify the opacity in 10% increments. Typing 6, for example, changes the opacity setting to 60%; typing a 0 changes the opacity to 100%. If you type the numbers quickly, you can type an exact percentage, such as 31%.

▶ To specify the fade-out rate for the Paintbrush tool, check the Fade checkbox in the Paintbrush Options palette and type the number of steps in the fade. You can type a value from 1 to 9999 for the fade steps; each step represents a single brush mark. Keep in mind that this value is affected by the brushes spacing value explained in the Brushes palette section in this chapter. Choose whether the brush stroke is to fade to transparency or the background color from the drop-down menu.

▶ Click the Wet Edges checkbox in the Paintbrush Options palette to create watercolor effects. The painting color is lighter in the middle with the solid color built up on the edges.

Using the Airbrush Tool

To use the Airbrush tool, select the Airbrush from the Toolbox or type the letter A for airbrush and click and drag in the canvas area. Think of the Airbrush as spraying droplets of paint onto the canvas. If you stay on one spot, the paint accumulates in a spray pattern that matches the selected brush type.

If you have a digitizing tablet, you can adjust the pressure of the stylus for the painting tools. The three checkbox items in the Paintbrush Options palette offer three methods to describe how applying pressure with the stylus affects the Paintbrush tool.

▶ Click the **Size** checkbox if you want the size of the Paintbrush to increase when pressure is increased.

▶ When the **Color** checkbox is selected, applying light pressure to the stylus paints with the background color, whereas applying heavy pressure paints with the foreground color. Painting with medium pressure on the stylus results in a color between the foreground and background color.

▶ Click the **Opacity** checkbox if you want the stylus pressure to affect the opacity of the color you are painting with. Light pressure results in a lower opacity and high pressure results in a more opaque color.

TIP

When using the Airbrush tool, hold down (Option)[Alt] and click the image to sample a color from the image and load it as the foreground color.

▶ Double-click the Airbrush tool in the Toolbox to display the Airbrush Options palette (see Figure 3.3).

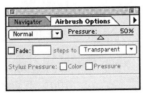

Figure 3.3

The Airbrush Options palette.

▶ The Blending mode options for the Airbrush tool are available under a drop-down menu in the upper-left corner of the Airbrush palette. The available Blending modes are detailed in the "Blending Modes" section at the beginning of this chapter.

▶ The pressure setting for the Airbrush tool controls how fast the paint builds up on the canvas and can be set to a value from 1% to 100% by dragging the triangle slider in the upper-right corner of the Airbrush Options palette or by typing a number on the keyboard.

▶ To specify the fade-out rate for the Airbrush tool, click the Fade checkbox in the Airbrush Options palette and type the number of steps in the fade. You can type a value from 1 to 9999 for the fade steps; each step represents a single brush mark. Keep in mind that this value is affected by the brushes spacing value explained in the section on the Brushes palette in this chapter. Choose whether the brush stroke is to fade to transparency or the background color from the drop-down menu.

Using the Line Tool

To use the Line tool, select the Line tool from the Toolbox or type the letter N and click and drag in the canvas area. Select where you want to end the line and let go of the mouse button.

► Double-click the Line tool in the Toolbox to display the Line Tool Options palette (see Figure 3.4). The Line tool is not affected by the brush size selected.

Figure 3.4

The Line Tool Options palette.

► Select a Blending mode. The Blending modes for the Line tool are available under a drop-down menu in the upper-left corner of the Line Tool palette. The Blending options affect the way the color of the line you are drawing interacts with the underlying image. The section on the Paintbrush tool earlier in this chapter discusses the available choices in detail.

► The opacity level of the Line tool can be set to a value from 1% to 100% by dragging the triangle slider in the upper-right corner of the Line Tool Options palette or by typing a number on the keyboard or numeric keypad.

► To specify the line width for the Line tool in pixels, type a number between 0 and 1000. Because the Line tool can be set to a width as high as 1000 pixels, you may want to consider using the line tool to draw filled rectangles in some cases.

TIP

When using the Line tool, hold down the (Option)[Alt] key and click the image to sample a color from the image with the eyedropper.

TIP

If you need to determine the angle of a part of an image, display the Info palette by choosing Show Info from the Window menu. Set the Line width for the Line tool to 0 (zero) and draw a line along the path you want to measure, viewing the "A" value for angle and the "D" value for distance in the Info palette.

▶ Click the Anti-aliased checkbox in the Line Tool Options palette to blend lines with the background image. Keep in mind, however, that a thin line may look fuzzy or out of focus with an anti-aliased edge.

▶ The Line tool can draw lines with arrowheads on one or both ends of a line. Click the Start checkbox to put the arrowhead where you start drawing. Click the End checkbox to put an arrowhead where you stop drawing. To edit the shape of the arrowhead, click the Shape button in the lower-right corner of the Line Tool palette. The following settings control the shape and size of the arrowheads:

The **width** value can range from 10 to 1000 and represents a percentage of the line width. If you specify an arrowhead width of 500%, for example, the arrowhead will be five times larger than the width of the line.

The **length** value can range from 10 to 5000 and represents a percentage of the line width. If, for example, you specify an arrowhead length of 1000%, the arrowhead will be equal to ten times the width of the line.

The **concavity** value can range from –50% to +50% and determines where the line and the arrowhead meet. Think of the line as pushing or pulling the wall of the arrowhead to which it connects. When you set a positive value such as 50%, the wall of the arrowhead is pushed toward the center of the arrowhead. When you set a negative value such as –50%, the wall of the arrow is pulled out from the center and looks more like a diamond shape.

TIP

To paint in a vertical or horizontal line with the Pencil tool, hold down the Shift key while dragging.

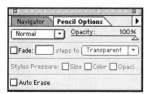

Figure 3.5

The Pencil Options palette.

TIP

When using the Pencil tool, hold down (Option)[Alt] and click the image to sample a color from the image and load it as the foreground color.

Using the Pencil Tool

To use the Pencil tool, select the Pencil tool from the Toolbox or type the letter Y and click and drag in the canvas area. The Pencil tool is a freehand drawing tool that draws hard-edged lines. The brushes palette contains only hard-edged brushes when using the Pencil tool.

▶ Double-click the Pencil tool in the Toolbox to display the Pencil Options palette (see Figure 3.5).

▶ The Blending modes for the Pencil tool are available under a drop-down menu in the upper-left corner of the Pencil Options palette. See the section on "Blending Modes" at the beginning of this chapter for more information about the available blending modes.

▶ The opacity level of the Pencil tool can be set to a value from 1% to 100% by dragging the triangle slider in the upper-right corner of the Pencil Options palette or by typing a number on the keyboard.

▶ To specify the fade-out rate for the Pencil tool, click the Fade checkbox in the Pencil Options palette and type the number of steps in the fade. You can type a value from 1 to 9999 for the fade steps; each step representing a single brush mark. Choose whether the line is to fade to transparency or the background color from the drop-down menu.

ADVANCED TIP

If you have a digitizing tablet, you can set three options to control drawing with the stylus.

▶ Click the **Size** checkbox if you want the size of the Pencil to increase when pressure is increased.

▶ When the **Color** checkbox is selected, applying light pressure to the stylus paints with the background color, whereas applying heavy pressure paints with the foreground color. Painting with medium pressure on the stylus results in a color between the foreground and background color.

▶ Click the **Opacity** checkbox if you want the stylus pressure to affect the opacity of the color you are painting with. Light pressure results in a lower opacity and high pressure results in a more opaque color.

TIP

You can cycle through the available Eraser tools in the drop-down list by (Option-clicking)[Alt-clicking] the Eraser tool in the Toolbox or by typing the letter E on the keyboard.

6. Click the Auto Erase checkbox in the Pencil Options palette to turn on Auto Erase. When you paint over a part of your image painted with the foreground color, the Pencil paints with the background color. This option makes a lot more sense when you work on a bitmapped image in which the foreground color is black and the background color white. When working on transparent layers, the Auto Erase function makes the pixels transparent instead of the background color.

Using the Eraser Tool

To use the Eraser tool, select the Eraser tool from the Toolbox or type the letter E. Click and drag in the canvas area. The Eraser tool paints with the background color or erases to transparency in the case of transparent layers.

▶ Double-click the Eraser tool in the Toolbox to display the Eraser Options palette (see Figure 3.6).

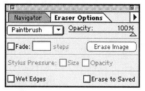

Figure 3.6

The Eraser Options palette.

▶ Four tools can be used as Eraser tools and are available under a drop-down menu in the upper-left corner of the Eraser Options palette.

▶ The Blending modes affect the way the color of the area you are painting interacts with the underlying image. See the "Blending Modes" section at the beginning of this chapter for further information on the available blending modes.

ADVANCED TIP

The Stylus Pressure Options for the Eraser tool depend on the tool used as the Eraser tool. Size and Opacity are available for the Paintbrush, Pencil, and Block tool; Size and Pressure are available for the Airbrush tool.

► Click the **Size** checkbox if you want the size of the Eraser to increase when pressure is increased.

► Click the **Opacity** checkbox if you want the stylus pressure to affect the opacity of the color you are painting with. Light pressure results in a lower opacity and high pressure results in a more opaque color.

► Click the **Pressure** checkbox if you want to control the pressure setting with the stylus. Set the low pressure setting in the Eraser Options palette by dragging the triangle sliders for Pressure. Applying pressure with the stylus increases the pressure from this starting point up to 100 percent.

► The opacity settings are available when you are using the Paintbrush or Pencil tool as an eraser in the Eraser Options palette. The pressure setting is available when you use the Airbrush as an eraser. The opacity and pressure settings can be set to a value from 1 percent to 100 percent by dragging the triangle slider in the upper right corner of the Eraser Options palette or by typing a number on the keyboard or numeric keypad.

► To specify the fade-out rate for the Eraser tool, select either the Paintbrush, Pencil, or Airbrush from the drop down menu in the Eraser Options palette and click the Fade checkbox in the Eraser Options palette. Type the number of steps in the fade. You can type a value from 1 to 9999 for the fade steps; each step represents a single brush mark. The Eraser tool always fades from the background color to transparency on the Background layer and from transparency to 100 percent opacity on transparent layers.

► Click the Erase Image button in the Eraser Options palette to erase the entire image and replace it with the background color. If you have layers in your image, this button changes to Erase Layer and erases the entire layer to transparency.

► Click the Erase to Saved checkbox in the Eraser Options palette to turn on the Magic Eraser. This option is only available after you have made changes to a saved file. Painting with the Eraser tool with the Magic Eraser turned on restores the image from the most recently saved version.

► Wet Edges is available only when you are using the Paintbrush as the Eraser tool. In this case the erased effect builds up on the edges.

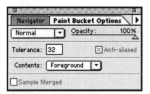

Figure 3.7

The Paint Bucket Options palette.

Using the Paint Bucket Tool

The Paint Bucket tool combines the effects of the Magic Wand tool (see Chapter 4, "Making Selections") and the Fill command. The Paint Bucket fills the pixel you click and adjacent pixels based on a tolerance setting with either the foreground color or a defined pattern. To use the Paint Bucket tool, select the Paint Bucket tool from the Toolbox or type the letter K.

▶ Double-click the Paint Bucket tool in the Toolbox to display the Paint Bucket Options palette (see Figure 3.7). The Blending modes available in the drop-down menu in the upper-left corner of the Paint Bucket Options palette and the Opacity settings in the upper-right corner are the same as all of the other painting tools described in this chapter. Refer to the section on the Paintbrush tool earlier in this chapter for details on the Blending modes and Opacity setting.

▶ The Tolerance setting requires a number from 0 to 255 and determines how close in gray level or color the adjacent pixels must be to the pixel you click. See Chapter 2, "Color and Resolution in Photoshop," for specific information about the 256 gray levels in Photoshop channels. A setting of 0 (zero) selects only the adjacent pixels that have the exact same color value as the one you click when Anti-aliased is not turned on. When Anti-aliased is turned on, extra edge pixels are selected to smooth the edges of the selection. If you set the tolerance to 255, every pixel in the image is affected regardless of the pixel you click.

▶ The Foreground and Pattern options are for contents. Choose Foreground to fill with the foreground color and Pattern to fill with a pre-defined pattern. To define a pattern, drag a rectangular marquee around a portion of an image to use as a pattern and choose Define Pattern from the Edit menu.

Using the Gradient Tool

The Gradient tool enables you to create a smooth blend between two or more colors. You can create either a linear blend, which blends in a straight line from one point to another, or the radial blend, which blends from the center of a circle out to a point you specify in all directions. Note that the Gradient tool is not available for bitmapped or indexed-color images because a full range of gray levels (256) are necessary to create a smooth gradient.

Creating a Blend

1. Select the part of your image you want to fill with a gradient. If you do not create a selection, the gradient fills the entire image area.

2. Double-click the Gradient tool in the Toolbox to display the Gradient Tool Options (see Figure 3.8).

3. Choose the type of Gradient you want to use from the drop-down menu in the Gradient Tool Options palette (see Figure 3.9).

4. Select Linear or Radial from the Type drop-down menu in the Gradient Tool Options palette.

5. Click the Mask checkbox to turn on the transparency mask for the gradient fill. This setting enables the transparency mask specified for the blend. See "Editing the Gradient Transparency Mask" later in this section for an explanation of the transparency mask. If you uncheck the Mask checkbox, the opacity settings are ignored for the blend.

6. Click the Dither checkbox to create a smoother blend with less chance of banding.

7. Click the image where you want to begin the blend, drag to the point you want it to end, and

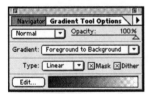

Figure 3.8

The Gradient Tool Options palette.

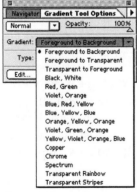

Figure 3.9

The default gradient choices in the Gradient drop-down menu.

release the mouse button. If you hold down the Shift key while dragging, you can constrain the blend to a straight line or 45° increments. Radial blends are created from the center out, so click where you want the center of the radial blend to be as the first point.

Creating and Editing Gradients

You can edit a gradient fill type or create one of your own by clicking the Edit button in the lower-left corner of the Gradient Tool Options palette. To create or edit a gradient fill:

1. Click the Edit button in the Gradient Tool Options palette to display the Gradient Editor dialog box (see Figure 3.10)

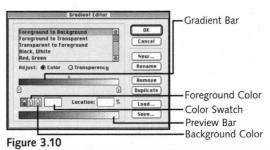

Figure 3.10

The Gradient Editor dialog box.

2. Select the Color radio button next to the word Adjust in the Gradient Editor dialog box.

3. To create a new gradient fill click the New button and give your gradient a name, or to edit an existing gradient, select it in the scroll list. If you want to create a duplicate of an existing gradient and edit it, select it in the list and click Duplicate to give it a new name.

4. Click the far left box under the gradient bar. Notice that the triangle above the box turns black to indicate that this is the part of the gradient you are modifying.

5. Select the starting color by doing one of the following:

   ► Click the Color Swatch in the Gradient Editor dialog box and select a color using the Photoshop Color Picker.

   ► Position the cursor over the gradient bar and click with the eyedropper cursor to select a color in the gradient.

   ► Click the foreground (F) or background (B) color selection box in the Gradient Editor dialog box.

6. Define the ending color by clicking the far right square below the gradient bar and choose from the options described in Step 5.

7. Define the midpoint color by clicking the diamond centered above the gradient bar and choose from the options described in Step 5.

8. Adjust the starting point, midpoint, and ending point by dragging the boxes under the gradient bar or type a location in the Location box that defines at what percent of the gradient length the color begins to blend. Note that when you change the starting and ending points the midpoint stays constant relative to the start and end positions.

9. To add intermediate colors between the starting and ending points, click the space under the gradient bar and define the colors. Note that midpoint diamonds appear above the gradient bar between each set of defined points.

10. To remove any of the intermediate color points, click the box and drag it away from the gradient bar.

11. When you're satisfied with your new blend, click the OK button.

Editing the Gradient Transparency Mask

Gradient fills contain a transparency mask that determines the transparency of the fill at given points. The default transparency mask is set to 100 percent opacity, but you can change that by clicking the Transparency radio button in the Gradient Editor dialog box (see Figure 3.11). The transparency mask can be turned off in the Gradient Tool Options palette by unchecking the Mask checkbox. When the transparency mask is turned off in the Gradient Tool Options palette, all levels of opacity become 100% opaque. Perform the following steps to adjust the transparency mask:

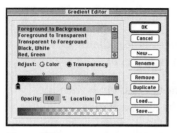

Figure 3.11

The Transparency options in the Gradient Editor dialog box.

TIP

Save the gradient fills you define by clicking the Save button in the Gradient Editor dialog box. This is particularly important if you must delete the preferences file for Photoshop at some point because that's where the gradient fills are stored. Click the Load button to load saved gradient fills.

1. Click the Transparency radio button for Adjust in the Gradient Editor dialog box.

2. Click the far left box under the gradient bar to adjust the starting opacity.

3. Type an opacity value and the starting location percentage.

4. Click the far right box under the gradient bar to adjust the ending opacity.

5. Type an opacity value and the ending location percentage.

6. To adjust the midpoint value, click the diamond above the gradient bar and set the Opacity and midpoint Location.

7. Create intermediate transparency points by clicking under the gradient bar and setting the appropriate values.

8. You can preview the effect of the mask on the gradient bar at the bottom of the Gradient Editor dialog box. Click OK if you're done or select the Color radio button to perform further adjustments to the color values.

Filling with Color

The Fill command enables you to fill selected areas or the entire image area with colors, patterns, or selections from the saved image.

1. Choose Fill from the Edit menu to display the Fill dialog box (see Figure 3.12).

2. Select the type of fill to use from the Use drop-down menu in the Fill dialog box.

3. Choose a Blending mode from the pull-down menu and select the opacity for the fill. The

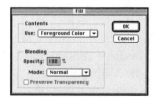

Figure 3.12

The Fill dialog box.

Keyboard Shortcuts to Fill

► To fill with the background color when on the Background layer, press (Delete) [Backspace]. This keystroke deletes to transparency on a transparent layer.

► To fill with the background color when on a transparent layer, press (Command-Delete)[Control-Backspace].

► To fill with the foreground color, press (Option-Delete) [Alt-Backspace].

► When on a transparent layer, to preserve the transparency and fill only the non-transparent pixels with the foreground color, press (Option-Shift-Delete) [Alt-Shift-Backspace].

► When on a transparent layer, to preserve the transparency and fill only the non-transparent pixels with the background color, press (Command-Option-Delete)[Control-Alt-Backspace].

► To display the Fill dialog box, press (Shift-Delete) [Shift-Backspace].

TIP

Hold down (Option)[Alt] as you drag with the Smudge tool to temporarily activate the Finger Painting option.

Preserve Transparency option is available when you are applying a fill to a transparent layer.

Using the Smudge Tool

The Smudge tool (represented by the finger icon in the Toolbox) simulates dragging your finger through wet paint. The color of the pixels where you start dragging is blended in the direction of the point at which you end.

► Double-click the Smudge tool in the Toolbox to display the Smudge Tool Options palette (see Figure 3.13). The Blending modes available in the pull-down menu in the Smudge Tool Options palette and the Pressure settings in the upper-right corner are the same as those used for the Airbrush tool described earlier in this chapter.

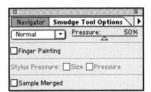

Figure 3.13

The Smudge Tool Options palette.

► When you click the Finger Painting checkbox in the Smudge Tool Options palette, the point at which you begin dragging smudges with the foreground color.

Summary

In this chapter you learned about the various tools and commands to change the color and opacity values of pixels in a Photoshop image. The information presented here is put to use in many of the chapters to come and is elementary to working in all aspects of Photoshop. In the next chapter you will

TIP

The Blending modes for the Smudge tool are available under the context menu when using the Smudge tool. Hold down the Control key and click anywhere in the canvas area to display the context menu on the Macintosh; click in the canvas area with the right mouse button in Windows.

examine the methods to select pixels in the Photoshop image using selection tools such as the Marquee tool, Lasso tool and Magic Wand tool. After you have mastered selecting pixels and changing the color values of pixels, you're more than half way to working effectively in this program.

ADVANCED TIP

There are two options for Stylus Pressure in the Smudge Tool Options palette: Size and Pressure.

▶ Click the **Size** checkbox if you want the size of the Smudge tool's brush to increase when pressure is increased.

▶ Click the **Pressure** checkbox if you want to control the pressure setting with the stylus. Set the low pressure setting in the Smudge Tool Options palette by dragging the triangle sliders for Pressure. Applying pressure with the stylus increases the pressure from this starting point up to 100 percent.

▶ When you click the Sample Merged checkbox in the Smudge Tool Options palette, the Smudge tool affects the current layer and all layers (including the background layer) beneath it.

Making Selections

In this chapter you are going to use the selection tools to make selections in an image. The ability to make accurate selections is an integral part of working in Photoshop, at any level. Using the selection tools, you will isolate parts of images, enabling you to cut, copy, and move the selected areas as well as modify the pixel values in the selected area. The Channels palette enables you to save selections into mask channels so that you can load the selections again at a later time. In the following exercises you will learn how to make selections using the selection tools in the Toolbox, how to make selections using Quick Mask mode, how to make selections using the Color Range command, and how to load mask channels and apply the effects of mask channels to your image.

Using the Selection Tools

The selection tools are the four tools located at the top of the Toolbox: the Marquee tool, the

Move tool, the Lasso tool, and the Magic Wand tool. In this exercise you will use the selection tools to select shapes and move, copy, cut, and paste the shapes into a cutout of the same shape (see Figure 4.1).

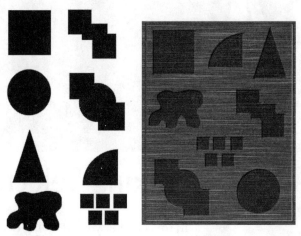

Figure 4.1

The object of this exercise is to move the shapes from the left into the box on the right.

Selecting with the Marquee Tools

To select a particular Marquee tool, click and hold the Marquee tool in the Toolbox or type the letter M to toggle between the rectangular Marquee and the elliptical Marquee.There is no shortcut key available to select the Single Row or Single Column Marquee tools. Type the letter C to select the Crop tool, also included with the Marquee tools in the Toolbox. (Option-Click)[Alt-Click] the Marquee tool in the Toolbox to cycle through all of the Marquee tools and the Crop tool.

In the following exercise we are going to use the selection tools to select areas of an image, reposition the marquee, cut and move or copy and move the selected image area, learn shortcuts to constrain selections to exact squares or circles, and discover methods to add to or subtract from selections.

1. Open lessons/chap4/select.psd from the CD-ROM that accompanies this book.

2. Select the rectangular Marquee tool in the Toolbox or type the letter M to toggle between the rectangular and elliptical Marquee tools.

3. Hold down (Command-Spacebar)[Control-Spacebar] to access the Zoom tool and zoom in close to the blue box in the upper-left corner by dragging a marquee around the box with the Zoom tool.

4. Position the cursor in the upper-left corner of the blue box; click and drag to the lower-right corner and release the mouse button (see Figure 4.2). Hold down the Shift key while you drag to constrain the selection marquee to an exact square.

> **TIP**
>
> Hold down the Spacebar to reposition the selection you are dragging while you're creating it. Remember to hold down the other keys when you let go of the Spacebar to continue dragging the selection. This function is especially helpful when selecting circles because the center point is often difficult to locate precisely.

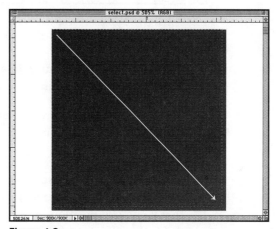

Figure 4.2

Click and drag with the Marquee tool to make a selection.

5. To deselect, click with the Marquee tool anywhere outside the selection area or press (Command-D)[Control-D].

> **TIP**
>
> You can press (Command-Z) [Control-Z] to undo the last thing you did or choose Edit➡Undo from the menu bar.

6. To reposition the marquee selection without moving the underlying pixels, click inside the selection area and drag (see Figure 4.3). Note that when you position the cursor inside the selection, the cursor display changes to indicate that clicking and dragging will move only the selection marquee.

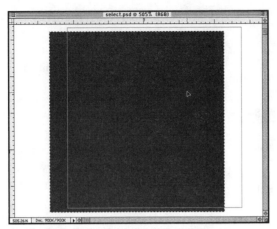

Figure 4.3

Click inside the selection and drag to move the marquee only.

7. Zoom out so that the entire image fits the window by double-clicking the Hand tool in the Toolbox.

8. Press D to set the foreground and background colors to the default setting of black foreground, white background.

9. Cut and move the blue box. With the (Command)[Control] key held down, position the cursor inside the selected blue box and drag the blue box into the square template on the right (see Figure 4.4). Note that when you position the cursor inside the selection and hold down the (Command)[Control] key, the cursor changes, indicating that dragging will cut the pixels from the image and move them. When you cut the pixels out of the image, the background color (white in this case) is left behind unless you are working on a layer, in which case the pixels are made transparent.

10. Press (Command-D)[Control-D] to deselect.

Circular and oval shaped selections are created using the eliptical Marquee tool. When you select an area with the elliptical Marquee, the edges are anti-aliased to help the image blend with the background you move it onto as well as to preserve the smooth edges. Anti-aliased edges have pixels with varying opacity to create smooth arcs.

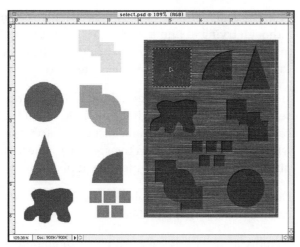

Figure 4.4

(Command)[Control] drag to cut and move the selected pixels.

1. Choose the elliptical Marquee tool from the Toolbox or press M to switch from the rectangular Marquee tool to the elliptical Marquee tool.

2. Hold down (Command-Spacebar)[Control-Spacebar] to access the Zoom tool and drag a marquee around the red circle with the Zoom tool to enlarge it to fit the window (see Figure 4.5). The circle appears blurry because the edge of the circle is anti-aliased.

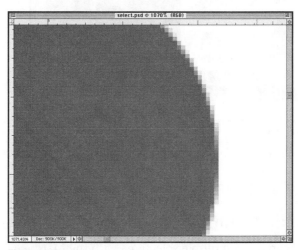

Figure 4.5

The edge of the circle is anti-aliased to create a smooth curve.

3. The elliptical Marquee works much like the rectangular Marquee, although trying to find a corner to start at is a problem. In this instance, you'll drag the circular selection from the center. Position the cursor where you think the center of the circle is located.

4. Hold down (Option)[Alt] and drag from the center to make the selection. After you start dragging, hold down the Shift key to constrain the selection to an exact circle. To reposition the selection while dragging, hold down the spacebar. Select only the solid red pixels and leave off the lighter-edged pixels.

5. Double-click the Hand tool or type (Command-0)[Control-0] to change the view to Fit on Screen.

6. To move a copy of the selected pixels, hold down (Command-Option)[Control-Alt] and drag the red circle onto the circular template to the right (see Figure 4.6). Note that the cursor changes to indicate that dragging will create a duplicate (clone).

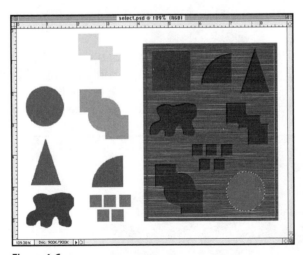

Figure 4.6

(Command-Option)[Control-Alt] dragging leaves a copy behind.

7. Press (Command-D)[Control-D] to deselect.

Making Multiple Selections

You can make multiple selections with the Marquee tools by holding down the Shift key, the same key used to constrain selections to exact squares and circles. The trick is using the Shift key to make multiple selections as exact squares or circles. When you overlap selections created using any of the selection tools, the result is a selection that combines one selection with the other.

1. Select the rectangular Marquee tool in the Toolbox or press M to toggle between the elliptical and rectangular Marquee tools.

2. You are going to select the yellow shape by combining three rectangular selections. Hold down (Command-Spacebar)[Control-Spacebar] to access the Zoom tool and zoom in closer to the yellow shape.

3. Drag a marquee in the shape of a square to select the upper-left box.

4. Hold down the Shift key and drag a rectangular-shaped selection that overlaps the first selection where necessary. It's easier to make the second selection if you start at one of the outside corners. Note that the cursor icon changes, indicating that the new selection will be added to the previous selection(s).

5. Hold down the Shift key and drag another square-shaped selection to complete the selection of the yellow shape.

6. Zoom out to the Fit on Screen view by double-clicking the Hand tool or choose View➥Fit on Screen.

7. Select the rectangular Marquee tool again. Hold down the (Command)[Control] key and drag the selected pixels onto the template on the right or hold down (Command-Option)[Control-Alt] and drag to move a copy of the pixels.

8. Press (Command-D)[Control-D] to deselect.

Note

To deselect a portion of an existing selection, hold down the (Option)[Alt] key and drag a new selection in the shape that you want to deselect.

9. To select the orange shape made up of two squares and a circle, select the elliptical Marquee from the Toolbox or press M.

10. Hold down the (Option)[Alt] key and start dragging the selection from the center of the circle. Once you start dragging, hold down the Shift key to constrain the selection to an exact circle.

11. Switch to the rectangular Marquee by pressing M. Hold down the Shift key and begin dragging a square selection from an outside corner. Once you start dragging, lift the Shift key while keeping the mouse button down and press the Shift key again to constrain the shape to an exact square. Add the other square shape to the selection.

12. Reduce the view to fit onscreen and select the rectangular Marquee tool again. Hold down the (Command)[Control] key and drag the selected pixels onto the template on the right or hold down (Command-Option)[Control-Alt] and drag to move a copy of the pixels.

13. Press (Command-D)[Control-D] to deselect.

14. To select the five brown boxes, use the rectangular Marquee tool and drag the first square selection, and then hold down the Shift key and drag the other four selections. Remember that you can hold down the Shift key while drawing to make a square selection. Move the selected pixels onto the template at right.

Selecting an Intersection

It is sometimes necessary to select the intersection of two distinct selections. The intersection of two selections is the pixels included in both selections.

1. To select the pink object, you will have to select the intersection of a square and circular selection. Select the elliptical Marquee to make the circular selection.

2. The lower-right corner of the pink shape is approximately the middle of the circle. (Option)[Alt] drag from this point to create an elliptical selection that follows the curved edge.

3. Switch to the rectangular Marquee by pressing M.

4. Hold down (Option-Shift)[Alt-Shift] and drag a rectangular selection that intersects the ellipse selection. Release the mouse button to select the intersection of the two selections (see Figure 4.7).

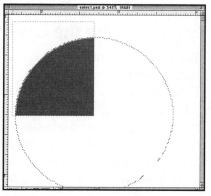 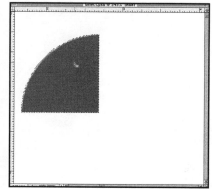

Figure 4.7

The intersection of two selections.

5. With the Marquee tool selected, hold down the (Command) [Control] key and drag the selected pixels onto the template on the right or hold down (Command-Option)[Control-Alt] and drag to move a copy of the pixels.

6. Press (Command-D)[Control-D] to deselect.

Stroking a Selection

You can specify a stroke in the foreground color to paint the border of a selection. To specify a stroke, perform the following steps:

1. Create a selection in your image to stroke.

2. Choose Edit➡Stroke to display the Stroke dialog box.

3. Type a width value from 1 to 16 pixels.

4. Select the location of the stroke. Choose Inside to stroke inside the selection area, Center to center the stroke on the selection marquee, or Outside to stroke outside the selection area.

5. Enter an opacity value in the Opacity box.

6. Choose a Blending mode from the Mode drop-down menu in the Stroke dialog box. Preserve Transparency is available when you are on a transparent layer.

Selecting with the Lasso Tools

The Toolbox has two available Lasso tools: the Free-hand Lasso tool and the Polygon Lasso tool. The Freehand Lasso tool enables you to create an irregular selection by "drawing" it freehand. The Polygon Lasso enables you to create a selection by clicking to define anchor points that join straight segments. When creating a selection with the Lasso tools, you must end at the point you started to close the selection.

1. Open lessons/chap4/select.psd from the CD-ROM that accompanies this book.

2. Select the Freehand Lasso tool in the Toolbox or press L to toggle between the Freehand and Polygon Lasso tools.

3. Zoom in close to the purple shape by dragging a marquee around the shape with the Zoom tool.

4. Click and drag with the Freehand Lasso tool, following the edge of the shape you want to select. If you let go of the mouse button before returning to the point you started dragging, the selection will be closed by a straight line seg-ment. The easiest way to make a complex selec-tion using the Freehand Lasso tool is to make a bunch of smaller selections that overlap. Hold down the Shift key and drag multiple closed selections that overlap each other to build a larger and larger selection (see Figure 4.8).

5. If you make a mistake and go outside the desired selection area, hold down the (Option)[Alt] key and drag a new selection around the area that's sticking out to deselect that portion of the selection (see Figure 4.9).

> **TIP**
>
> You can access the Zoom tool when any other tool is selected in the Toolbox by holding down (Command-Spacebar)[Control-Spacebar].

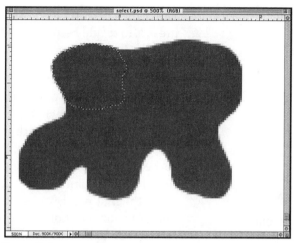

Figure 4.8

Hold down the Shift key and overlap small selection areas to create a complex selection.

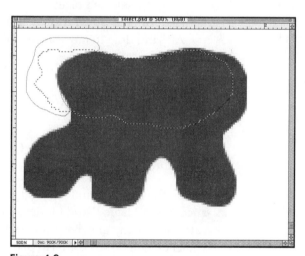

Figure 4.9

Hold down (Option)[Alt] to deselect a portion of an existing selection.

6. With the Lasso or Marquee tool selected, hold down the (Command)[Control] key and drag the selected pixels onto the template on the right or hold down (Command-Option)[Control-Alt] and drag to move a copy of the pixels.

7. Press (Command-D)[Control-D] to deselect.

8. Select the Polygon Lasso from the Toolbox or press L to toggle between the Freehand and Polygon Lasso tools.

9. To select the green triangle shape, position the cursor over a corner of the triangle and click once. The cursor now has a "rubber band" attached to display the path the selection will take the next time you click. Point at another corner and click once. Make your way around this shape by pointing and clicking until you reach the first point. When you reach the starting point of your selection the cursor will display a closed loop to indicate that clicking here will close the selection.

10. Hold down the (Command)[Control] key and drag the selected pixels onto the template on the right or hold down (Command-Option)[Control-Alt] and drag to move a copy of the pixels.

11. Press (Command-D)[Control-D] to deselect.

Using the Magic Wand Tool

The Magic Wand tool enables you to select a range of pixels based on gray levels (see Chapter 2, "Color and Resolution in Photoshop").

To use the Magic Wand tool you simply set a tolerance in the Magic Wand Options palette that indicates how many gray levels on each side of the pixel you click will be selected. All pixels that are within the range specified are selected, as long as they are contiguous (touching each other). For example, if you set the tolerance level to 10 and click a pixel with a gray value of 150, the selection will include all contiguous pixels in the range 140 to 160—10 above the selected pixel and 10 below (see Figure 4.10).

For RGB images, the Red, Green, and Blue values must meet the criteria on all color channels. If, for

TIP

If you hold down the (Option) [Alt] key while using the Polygon Lasso Tool, you can drag freehand. If you hold down the (Option)[Alt] key while using the Freehand Lasso Tool, you can select using straight segments like the Polygon Lasso tool.

example, you set the tolerance to 10 and click a pixel that is 100 Red, 100 Green, and 100 Blue and the pixel right next to it is 100 Red, 100 Green, 111 Blue, the latter pixel will not be selected because the Blue value is outside the range of 90 to 110. A tolerance value of 0 selects only the contiguous pixels that exactly match the value of the pixel you click on.

It works out that colors close in hue are also close in their luminosity values. Don't worry; you will not have to examine each pixel in your image to use the Magic Wand tool. As a rule of thumb, when I'm trying to make a selection with the Magic Wand, I start with a relatively low tolerance of 32 (Photoshop's default). If a tolerance of 32 does not select enough pixels, I double it to 64. If this selects too many pixels, I pick a number in between or if it doesn't select enough pixels, I double it again, and so forth.

139	145	102	169	177	210	161	158	160	158
9	140	7	102	140	155	250	200	162	162
155	152	132	139	153	160	255	255	150	162
150	150	132	161	150	144	144	142	163	162
150	102	211	139	156	157	40	47	210	250
91	150	105	161	158	158	33	33	217	221
91	90	100	147	139	160	142	142	200	202
142	150	151	15	17	148	148	160	161	129
151	158	160	18	153	126	203	202	162	162
3	74	91	161	165	139	202	202	139	136

Figure 4.10

The result of clicking a pixel with a gray value of 150 with a tolerance setting of 10.

1. Open lessons/chap4/grays.psd on the CD-ROM that accompanies this book (see Figure 4.11).

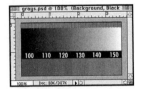

Figure 4.11

The grays.psd file.

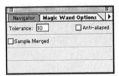

Figure 4.12

The Magic Wand Options palette.

2. Display the Info palette by choosing Window➡Show Info.

3. Select the Magic Wand tool in the Toolbox or press W.

4. Double-click the Magic Wand tool in the Toolbox to display the Magic Wand Options palette (see Figure 4.12).

5. This 72 ppi image contains the entire gray scale from 0 to 255. Each column of pixels in the middle section of the image is one of the gray levels. Because this image displays too smoothly to distinguish the pixels from each other when zoomed in, a comb of black and white pixels is provided at the top of the image representing a single pixel width. Zoom in as close as possible (1600%) to an area that includes the comb at the top of the image and the gray pixel ramp underneath (see Figure 4.13).

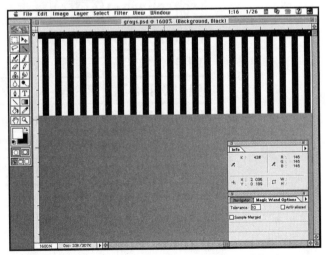

Figure 4.13

Each black and white bar represents a single pixel width.

6. Click the tiny eyedropper icon in the upper-left section of the Info palette and choose Grayscale

Figure 4.14

The Info palette.

Note

When Anti-aliased is checked, an additional pixel is selected on each end of the selection. The Anti-aliased option selects additional edge pixels so that the selected area does not have harsh edges when copied or cut and pasted. I recommend having the Anti-aliased option on when using the Magic Wand tool for most selections.

to display the ink percentage. Click the tiny eyedropper icon in the upper-right section of the Info palette and choose RGB Color to display the gray level information. See Figure 4.14.

7. Position the cursor over the gray pixels directly under the black-and-white pixel markers and note that each pixel from left to right has a different gray value displayed in the RGB section of the Info palette. The gray values range from 0 (zero) on the left to 255 on the right.

8. Set the Tolerance value to 10 in the Magic Wand Options palette.

9. Make sure Anti-aliased is not checked in the Magic Wand Options palette.

10. Position the cursor over a gray pixel and note its gray value in the RGB section of the Info palette, and then click that pixel with the Magic Wand tool.

11. The selected area includes all the pixels whose value is in the range of 10 less than the pixel you clicked and 10 more than the pixel you clicked. If, for example, you clicked a pixel with a value of 140, 10 pixels to the left and 10 pixels to right are selected (a range of 130 to 150). See Figure 4.15.

12. Press (Command-D)[Control-D] to deselect or choose Select➡None from the menu bar.

13. This time, check Anti-aliased in the Magic Wand Options palette and click the same pixel.

14. The large gray boxes at the bottom of this image represent gray levels incremented by 10, starting at 100 and ending at 150. Experiment with different Tolerance settings in increments of 10 for a bigger picture of how the Magic Wand tool selects pixels.

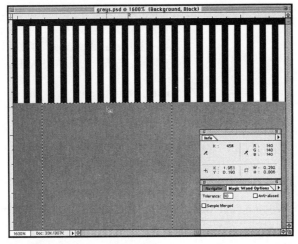

Figure 4.15

A Tolerance value of 10 selects 21 total columns of pixels: the pixel you click and 10 pixels above and below the selected pixel's gray level.

Using the Magic Wand to Select Color Ranges

The preceding exercise explained how the Magic Wand tool works to select pixels arranged in order. This exercise illustrates how to use the Magic Wand tool to select areas of photographic image where the luminosity values are not obvious. For the most part, when you select pixels with the Magic Wand tool, it's best to experiment with Tolerance settings. You will use the Magic Wand tool to make a selection of some yellow feathers and change their color to orange.

1. Open lessons/chap4/parrots.psd on the CD-ROM that accompanies this book.

2. Select the Magic Wand tool in the Toolbox or press W.

3. Double-click the Magic Wand tool to display the Magic Wand Options palette.

4. Set the Tolerance value to 32 to start with and check the Anti-aliased box. The Sample Merged checkbox applies only to files with layers, enabling you to select a color range that includes pixels from the current layer and any underlying layers. This image does not contain layers, so you can leave the Sample Merged box unchecked.

5. Position the cursor over the yellow feathers in the parrot and click once to create a selection (see Figure 4.16).

Figure 4.16

Try to find a tolerance value that will select most of the color you want.

6. If the selection does not include all the color, double the tolerance setting to 64 and try again. A tolerance of 64 selects most (but not all) of the yellow pixels.

7. To expand the selection choose Select➡Modify➡Expand and type a value of 1 or 2 in the dialog box that appears. This expands the selection created by the Magic Wand 1 or 2 pixels in all directions.

8. If your selection contains some unselected pixels within the overall selected area, choose Select➡Modify➡Smooth and type a number in the dialog box to expand the selection only within the selected area's borders. In other words, the selection will not grow, but the unselected pixels inside the selection border will be absorbed.

9. You can Shift-click areas to add them to the selection area using the Magic Wand's tolerance setting. Shift-click the unselected areas with the Magic Wand tool. This is one way to include non-contiguous pixels in your selection as well.

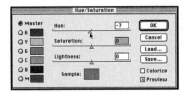

Figure 4.17

The Hue/Saturation dialog box.

10. After you have selected the yellow area of the parrot, you can perform any of Photoshop's effects and adjustments to the selected area. For this example, you're going to change the color of the feathers using Hue/Saturation. Colorizing using Hue/Saturation is covered in Chapter 9, "Colorizing." Type (Command-U)[Control-U] or choose Image➡Adjust➡Hue/Saturation to display the Hue/Saturation dialog box (see Figure 4.17).

11. Change the Hue value to –7 to slightly adjust the color of the feathers toward orange. Click OK. Leave this file open if you are proceeding to the next section on Quick Mask mode.

Using the Quick Mask

Quick Mask is another way to make or modify selections. Using Quick Mask, you can utilize the painting tools to create a selection. Quick Mask is simply another representation of a selection using a painted mask to represent the selected area or non-selected area depending on which preference you choose for the mask. For this reason, it is best to think of Quick Mask as a mode—one that you will toggle in and out of when making selections.

1. Open lessons/chap4/parrots.psd on the CD-ROM that accompanies this book (if it isn't still open from the previous exercise).

2. Make a selection of the yellow feathers on the left parrot using the Magic Wand or any of the previously described selection tools (see Figure 4.18). Don't worry if the selection is not exact because you will use Quick Mask to adjust the selection.

Figure 4.18

The yellow feathers selection.

3. Turn on Quick Mask mode by clicking the Quick Mask icon in the Toolbox or by pressing Q to toggle on and off Quick Mask.

4. Choose Window➭Show Channels to display the Channels palette (see Figure 4.19). The Quick Mask is represented in the Channels palette as a temporary channel at the bottom of the list where the masked areas are black and the unmasked areas white in the thumbnail preview.

Figure 4.19

The Quick Mask is added to the Channels palette as a temporary (indicated by italic type) mask channel.

5. The "marching ants" disappear and are now represented by a mask that covers the entire image with the exception of the selected area. To modify the mask, you will paint with black as the foreground color to add to the mask or white as the foreground color to remove the mask. You can also paint the mask with levels of gray to represent levels of opacity because the Quick Mask is an 8-bit-per-pixel (256 gray levels) mask. The mask color is red to emulate a rubylith mask, a familiar paradigm to many graphic artists. Think of the mask as a transparent sheet of red acetate on top of your image. When you remove the red, you reveal (unmask) the image (see Figure 4.20).

Setting the Quick Mask Display Options

To change the properties of the Quick Mask, double-click the Quick Mask icon in the Toolbox or double-click the Quick Mask channel in the Channels palette. This displays the Quick Mask Options dialog box (see Figure 4.21). Click a radio button to choose whether the Quick Mask represents the selected areas or the unselected areas (Masked Areas). Click the color swatch to change the mask color and set an opacity value for the color mask. I find that the default red mask color with a 50% opacity on the Masked Areas makes the most sense if, like me, you liken the Quick Mask to the traditional rubylith mask.

Figure 4.20

The unmasked areas represent the selection area.

6. Select the Paintbrush tool from the Toolbox or press B.

7. Choose Window➡Show Brushes to display the Brushes palette and choose a medium sized brush with hard edges to start with (see Figure 4.22).

8. Double-click the Paintbrush tool in the Toolbox to display the Paintbrush Options palette and make sure the Opacity is set to 100% and the Blending mode is Normal (see Figure 4.23).

9. To add to the selection area, you will paint with white. Set the default colors by pressing D. Set the foreground color to white by pressing X to swap the foreground and background colors.

10. With white as the foreground color, paint the image to remove the mask and expand the selection area. If you make a mistake, press X to make black the foreground color and paint the mask back in.

Figure 4.21

The Quick Mask Options dialog box.

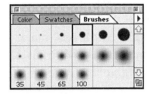

Figure 4.22

Select a medium sized brush from the Brushes palette.

Figure 4.23

The Paintbrush Options palette.

11. Switch out of Quick Mask mode by pressing Q or clicking the selection icon to the left of the Quick Mask icon in the Toolbox. Note that the selection area has changed to reflect the changes you made while in Quick Mask mode.

12. Toggle in and out of Quick Mask mode to adjust the selection. You can use the soft-edged brushes to create a selection that has soft edges. See the section "Saving and Loading Selections" to learn how to make use of your selections.

Selecting with Color Range

A selection made with the Color Range command will select all pixels in the image that meet a selection criteria based on color that you determine. The Color Range command is great to make selections when an image contains isolated and well defined colors. In this exercise you will make selections in the image based on a range of colors.

1. Open lessons/chap4/parrots.psd on the CD-ROM that accompanies this book.

2. Choose Select➡Color Range to display the Color Range dialog box. Position the Color Range dialog box so that you can see the parrot with the yellow feathers.

3. Set the Select option in the Color Range dialog box to Sampled Colors, the Fuzziness to 40, and click the Selection radio button to display a selection mask in the preview window of the Color Range dialog box. Set the Selection Preview option to None for now and be sure the Invert checkbox is not checked.

4. Select the left eyedropper in the Color Range dialog box, then position the eyedropper cursor over the blue feathers in the image and click once. The preview window displays the selected area in white (see Figure 4.24).

Figure 4.24

The selected area is indicated in the preview window of the Color Range dialog box.

5. To add to the selection, choose the middle eyedropper with the plus sign (+) and drag around in the blue areas of the image to expand the selection (see Figure 4.25). To remove unwanted areas from the selection, choose the right eyedropper with the minus (-) sign and drag in the image area.

Figure 4.25

The eyedropper with the plus sign expands the selection throughout the image.

6. Drag the Fuzziness slider to adjust the range of colors selected. The fuzziness is similar to the tolerance setting for the Magic Wand. Decrease the fuzziness to make the color selection more exact or increase the fuzziness setting to add more similar colors.

7. Click the Image radio button in the Color Range dialog box to display the image in the preview window. Choose one of the Selection Preview options to view your selection on the image itself:

> ► If you choose Grayscale, the image window will display a black-and-white representation of the selection.

- ▶ Choose Black Matte to display the selected areas in color with the unselected areas masked in black.

- ▶ Choose White Matte to display the selected areas with the unselected areas masked in white.

- ▶ Choose Quick Mask to display the selected areas with the unselected areas displayed in the Quick Mask color.

- ▶ Check the Invert checkbox to invert the way the selection is represented in both the preview window of the Color Range dialog box when the Selection radio button is chosen and the image area when a Selection Preview is selected.

8. You can save the settings in the Color Range dialog box for later use by clicking the Save button. Load any previously saved settings by clicking the Load button in the Color Range dialog box.

9. When you are satisfied with the selection area, click OK to make the selection (see Figure 4.26).

Figure 4.26

The result of the Color Range selection.

Saving and Loading Selections

After you have created a selection, you can save it to a mask channel called an alpha channel. The mask channels store the selection as a

Note

Alpha channels are grayscale channels added to the channels already contained in your image to facilitate saving and loading a selection. You can create an alpha channel based on a selection you make in the image or by painting directly on the alpha channel. Alpha channels are 8-bit grayscale channels that can contain up to 256 gray levels that represent levels of opacity when you use the alpha channel to make a selection. To apply the opacity levels of the alpha channel you must cut, copy, and paste, or fill the selection loaded from the alpha channel. Each image can contain a total of 24 channels, which includes the channels used to create the image, like the Red, Green and Blue channels or the Cyan, Magenta, Yellow, and Black channels.

grayscale mask so that you can load the selection again later. In the following exercises you will make selections, save them in alpha channels as masks, load the channels to reselect parts of the image, and explore some special effects that can be achieved with mask channels. You are going to quickly create a composite image and import some stylized text created in Adobe Illustrator to make a promotional ad for a travel magazine (see Figure 4.27). If you want to see two variations of the completed ad in color, open lessons/chap4/hawaii.tif and lessons/chap4/hawaii2.tif.

Figure 4.27

An advertisement for a travel magazine.

You can save a selection to an alpha channel and then use the selection as a mask for the image. You can also add your selection to an existing alpha channel, subtract it from an existing alpha channel, or replace an existing channel. After you create the alpha channel, you can load it as a selection at any time and save it with the file in a limited number of file formats.

1. Open lessons/chap4/parrots.psd on the CD-ROM that accompanies this book.

2. Use the Lasso tool to select the larger red parrot on the right side (see Figure 4.28).

Figure 4.28

The red parrot is selected.

3. Choose Window➡Show Channels to display the Channels palette.

4. To save the selection to an alpha channel choose Select➡Save Selection to display the Save Selection dialog box (see Figure 4.29).

5. The destination of the new alpha channel you are creating is the present file, so choose parrots.psd for the Document choice. Because you have created no other channels for this document, the choice for Channel is New and the Operation radio button for New Channel is selected. Click OK to create the alpha channel. The new alpha channel resides in the Channels palette under the RGB color channels and is automatically named "#4" because it is the fourth channel; the Red, Green, and Blue channels are the first three (see Figure 4.30).

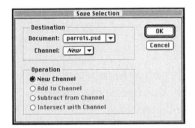

Figure 4.29

The Save Selection dialog box.

Figure 4.30

The alpha (mask) channel is added to bottom of the Channels palette.

Figure 4.31

Drag the alpha channel onto the selection icon to load the alpha channel as a selection.

6. Press (Command-D)[Control-D] to deselect and save your file in Photoshop format.

7. To load the alpha channel as a selection choose Select➡Load Selection to display the Load Selection dialog box or drag the alpha channel (#4) onto the selection icon at the bottom of the Channels palette (see Figure 4.31) or (Command) [Control] click the alpha channel in the Channels palette.

8. Choose Select➡Inverse or type (Command-Shift-I)[Control-Shift-I] to invert the selection so that everything but the parrot is selected.

9. Click the mask icon at the bottom of Channels palette to save the selection as an alpha channel without displaying the Save Selection dialog box.

10. Save your changes and press (Command-D) [Control-D] to deselect.

Now that you have saved selections for the parrots and the background as alpha channels, you can load the selections from the alpha channels to isolate the parts of the image you want to change.

1. Leave the parrots.psd file open and open lessons/chap4/islands.psd on the CD-ROM that accompanies this book.

2. Press (Command-A)[Control-A] to select the entire image and copy this image to the clipboard. Close the islands.psd file.

3. In the parrots.psd file load the background selection by (Command)[Control] clicking the alpha channel (#5).

4. Choose Edit➡Paste Into to paste the clipboard contents into the selection area or press (Shift-Command-V)[Shift-Control-V] (see Figure 4.32).

Figure 4.32

Paste the clipboard contents into the selected area.

5. Choose Window➡Show Layers to display the Layers palette. Notice that the image you just pasted into the selection is now on a separate layer with a layer mask that is identical to the alpha channel you pasted into. You can do more with the layer a little later; for now keep the Layers palette and the Channels palette on the screen so that you can monitor any additional layers that you create. See Chapter 10, "Working in Layers," for more information on creating layers and layer masks.

6. Add the stylized text created in Illustrator. Choose File➡Place and navigate to the CD-ROM that accompanies this book and choose lessons/chap4/hawaii.eps. Click the Place button.

7. Move the placed text to the lower-right corner of the image and enlarge it by dragging one of the corner points of the placed Illustrator file. Hold down the Shift key while dragging to maintain the aspect ratio of the text while enlarging (see Figure 4.33).

8. Double-click inside the placed Illustrator text transformation box to apply the enlargement. The placed image is converted to a bitmapped image at the resolution of the image and is placed on its own layer in the Layers palette named hawaii.eps.

Figure 4.33

Position and enlarge the placed Illustrator text.

9. Press (Command-S)[Control-S] to save what you have done so far. Saving the file in Photoshop format enables you to keep a version of the file that includes the layers and alpha channels so that you can come back at a later time and modify this promotional ad.

10. To save the file without having to merge the layers or flatten the image, choose File➡Save a Copy to display the Save a Copy dialog box (see Figure 4.34). Check the Flatten Image and Don't Include Alpha Channels checkboxes or choose a file format first from the drop-down menu and the checkboxes will be selected for you. If you choose TIFF, for example, you can still include the alpha channels, but if you choose Photoshop EPS, both checkboxes are checked.

Figure 4.34

The Save a Copy dialog box enables you to save a flattened version of your file without alpha channels.

Now that you have saved a completed version of the promotional ad for Hawaii, you may want to create alternative versions to present to the client. Because all the pieces to this ad are on separate layers, you can create an unlimited number of alternatives.

Display the Layers palette if it is not already onscreen.

1. Select the layer that contains the background image of the island by clicking the thumbnail in the Layers palette. Be sure to click the thumbnail that displays the island image and not the layer mask thumbnail (see Figure 4.35).

2. Drag the Opacity slider at the top of the Layers palette to 62% or type 62 on the numeric keypad to set the opacity of the islands image, which overlays the parrots on the Background layer (see Figure 4.36).

Layer mask thumbnail

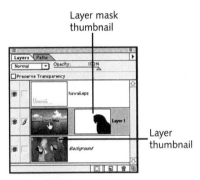

Layer thumbnail

Figure 4.35

The paintbrush icon to the left of the layer thumbnail indicates that the image—not the layer mask—is selected.

Figure 4.36

Changing the opacity of Layer 1 to 62% enables 38% of the underlying image to show through.

3. Choose File➡ Save a Copy to save this version as an alternative to present to the client.

Summary

I could fill the next 50 pages with variations of this particular image using the Layers palette and alpha channels. Experiment with the layer settings and use the alpha channels to adjust parts of the image to see what kind of variations you can create. Chapter 5, "Vignettes and Edge Effects," contains more information on how to use alpha channels and Chapter 10, "Working in Layers," provides detailed information on working with the Layers palette.

Vignettes and Edge Effects

You can use a variety of methods to create vignettes and edge effects in Photoshop. In this chapter you look at methods for creating vignettes in any shape, as well as how to apply filter effects to the edges of pictures. Because layers are such an integral part of creating special effects and compositing images in Photoshop, you examine methods to create vignettes and edge effects using layers. In this chapter, you create three vignettes (see Figure 5.1) and four edge effects (see Figure 5.2).

Original Image   Rectangle Vignette   Oval Vignette   Brush Stroke Vignette

Figure 5.1

The three types of vignettes covered in this chapter.

Original Image   Reticulated Edge   Charcoal Edge

Embossed Edge   Layered Composite

Figure 5.2

The four edge effects covered in this chapter.

Creating Vignettes

Vignettes are images with softly blended edges, usually in some geometric shape, such as a circle, oval, or square. In this section, you examine the vignette action in the Actions palette and then perform the same effect using fewer steps. If you are familiar with recording actions, you may want to record the steps you perform in this chapter. See Chapter 15, "Using Actions," for information on how to record actions.

Creating a Rectangle Vignette

In this section you look at the action Photoshop supplies in the Actions palette, and then you learn to create the same effect with more control and fewer steps.

1. Open lessons/chap5/portrait.psd on the CD-ROM that accompanies this book.

2. Choose Window➡Show Actions to display the Actions palette (see Figure 5.3).

3. Set the Actions palette to Button mode by clicking the arrow in the upper-right corner of the Actions palette to choose Button mode from the drop-down menu (see Figure 5.4). Now that you are in Button Mode, click the Vignette (full image) button in the Actions palette to create a vignette of portrait.psd.

The resulting image is a decent vignette, although you didn't really have much control over the process. If you want to see how the vignette was created, switch out of Button Mode by choosing Button Mode again in the Actions palette menu.

Click the triangle to the left of Vignette (full image) to display the parts of the action. Click the triangle next to the parts to display the steps for each part

> **Note**
>
> If you use Photoshop 4, the Actions palette contains an action to perform a rudimentary vignette that uses the Feather command on the outside edge of your image to create the effect.

Figure 5.3

The Actions palette.

Figure 5.4

Choose Button Mode from the drop-down menu.

(see Figure 5.5). You will notice that this action selects the entire image, makes an alpha channel of the selection, enlarges the canvas area, creates a new layer, loads the selection from the alpha channel, paints the new layer white using the inverse of the selection with a feathered edge, and then deletes the alpha channel. You can achieve the same results without creating alpha channels or layers.

1. Choose File➡Revert to load the original image again. If you have already saved the image under a new name, open lessons/chap5/portrait.psd again.

2. Set the background color to white by typing D for default colors.

3. Choose Image➡Canvas Size to display the Canvas Size dialog box and set the width and height to 110% (see Figure 5.6). Be sure the gray box is in the middle of the Anchor grid because you are adding white space around the image. Click OK. You added the white space around the image so that you can create the vignette without reducing the size of the image area too much (see Figure 5.7).

> **Note**
>
> Photoshop comes with the six actions shown in Figure 5.3. If you have removed the pre-installed actions, you can load them again by choosing Reset Actions from the Actions palette menu.

Figure 5.5

Evaluate an action by clicking the triangles next to the actions.

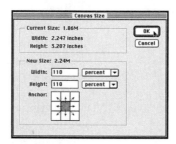

Figure 5.6

The Canvas Size dialog box.

Figure 5.7

The white space around the image gives you room to create a vignette.

Figure 5.8

The Marquee Options palette.

4. Double-click the Rectangle Marquee tool in the Toolbox to display the Marquee Options palette and set the Feather value to 20 pixels (see Figure 5.8).

5. Drag a selection around the portrait area with the Rectangle Marquee tool (see Figure 5.9).

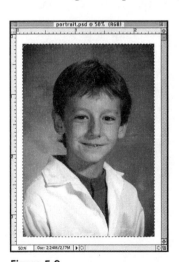

Figure 5.9

Select the picture area with the Marquee tool.

6. Choose Select➥Modify➥Contract to display the Contract dialog box and type 10 to reduce the selection area by ten pixels. The maximum number you can type in the Contract dialog box is 16. You want to contract the selection a total of 20 pixels, so perform the Contract function two times (10 pixels each time). See Figure 5.10.

Figure 5.10

Contract the selection 20 pixels.

7. Choose Select➥Inverse from the menu bar or type (Command-Shift-I) [Control-Shift-I] to select the outside area of the image (see Figure 5.11).

Figure 5.11

Inverse the selection.

Figure 5.12

The feathered edge creates the vignette.

Figure 5.13

The Marquee Options palette.

Figure 5.14

Select an oval area of the image.

8. Type the (delete)[backspace] key to fill the selected area with the background color (white). If you want the edges to be softer, type the (delete)[backspace] key a second or third time. The feathered edge on the original selection creates the vignette effect (see Figure 5.12).

9. Experiment with a larger feather radius and try filling with black instead of white. If you don't mind reducing the image area of your picture, perform the indicated steps without enlarging the canvas area.

Creating an Oval Vignette

The steps to creating an oval vignette are similar to those used to create the rectangle vignette. In this exercise you create the oval vignette without adding any extra canvas area around the image.

1. Open lessons/chap5/portrait.psd on the CD-ROM that accompanies this book.

2. Double-click the Ellipse Marquee tool in the Toolbox to display the Marquee Options palette and set the feather radius to 15 pixels (see Figure 5.13).

3. Drag an oval selection on the image to include most of the subject's face, but do not go out to the edges of the image (see Figure 5.14).

TIP

Once you draw a selection with the Marquee tools, you can click inside the selection area and drag the marquee to reposition it.

4. Type the letter D to set the foreground and background colors to the default black foreground/white background.

5. Choose Select➥Inverse to select the outside area of the image (see Figure 5.15).

Figure 5.15

Inverse the selection area.

6. Type the (delete)[backspace] key to fill the selected area with white (see Figure 5.16).

Creating Vignettes on Layers

You use layers in this exercise to illustrate how you can overlay a vignette on another image. To learn more about working in layers, refer to Chapter 10, "Working in Layers."

1. Open lessons/chap5/bkgrnd.psd and lessons/chap5/portrait.psd on the CD-ROM that accompanies this book.

2. Use the Move tool to drag the image in portrait.psd onto the bkgrnd.psd image area (see Figure 5.17).

Figure 5.16

Fill the selected area with white to create the vignette.

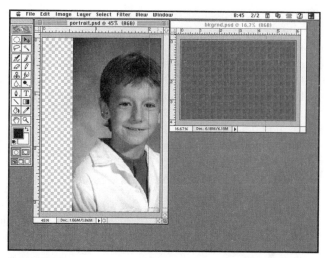

Figure 5.17

Drag the portrait image to the background image with the Move tool.

3. Choose Window➡Show Layers to display the Layers palette if it is not already onscreen. Note that dragging the portrait file onto the background file creates a new layer (Layer 1).

4. With the Move tool still selected, drag the portrait image you just moved to the background file to position it on the left side (see Figure 5.18). Close the portrait.psd file.

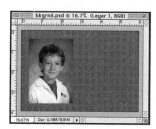

Figure 5.18

Use the Move tool to adjust the position of the new layer.

5. Select Layer 1 in the Layers palette if it is not already selected and choose Duplicate Layer from the Layers palette menu. Name the new layer "Layer 2."

6. The duplicate layer is placed directly on top of the original layer. Use the Move tool to position the image on Layer 2 on the right side (see Figure 5.19).

TIP

You can duplicate a layer by dragging the layer in the Layers palette onto the New Layer icon at the bottom of the Layers palette. This method does not display the Duplicate Layer dialog box. Duplicate Layer is also available under the Layer menu in the menu bar.

TIP

If you hold down the Shift key while dragging the image from left to right, the image will be constrained to a horizontal move.

TIP

(Option-Click)[Alt-Click] the Eye icon to the left of the layer thumbnail to hide all but the selected layer. (Option-Click)[Alt-Click] the Eye icon again to make all layers visible.

Figure 5.21

Drag an oval shaped selection.

Figure 5.19

Move the image on Layer 2 to the right side.

7. Select Layer 1 in the Layers palette. Selected layers are highlighted in the Layers palette and a paintbrush icon is displayed to the left of the layer thumbnail picture.

8. Double-click the Ellipse Marquee tool in the Toolbox to display the Marquee Options palette and set the Feather to 20 pixels. Anti-aliased should remain checked because you want the edge pixels to blend with the background (see Figure 5.20).

Figure 5.20

The Marquee Options palette.

9. Drag an oval-shaped selection over the picture on the left (see Figure 5.21) and Choose Select➡Inverse or type (Command-Shift-I) [Control-Shift-I] to select the inverse area of the selection.

10. Type the (delete)[backspace] key to delete the selected area, replacing it with transparent pixels. The 20-pixel feather radius you defined for the Ellipse Marquee tool blends the image to transparency (see Figure 5.22).

Figure 5.22

The feather radius of 20 pixels blends the vignette to transparency.

Figure 5.23

The Layer Mask thumbnail is displayed to the right of the layer thumbnail.

Add a layer mask to a layer to precisely control the vignette effect without destroying the present image. Once you have created a layer mask you're happy with you can apply the mask to the image and make the changes permanent.

1. Select Layer 2 in the Layers palette so that you can work on the image on the right.

2. Click the Mask icon the bottom of the Layers palette to add a layer mask to "Layer 2." You also can choose Layer➡Add Layer Mask➡Reveal All from the menu bar. The layer mask thumbnail is displayed to the right of the layer thumbnail for Layer 2 and is automatically selected (see Figure 5.23).

3. The Layer Mask works very much like an alpha channel. Unlike with alpha channels, however, the changes you make to the layer mask are dynamic, displaying the results immediately. Using the layer mask you can mask parts of the image on a layer in a non-destructive way by painting with black, white, or levels of gray. Painting with black masks out parts of the image, making them transparent. Painting with white restores the image, removing the mask. Painting with levels of gray paints with corresponding levels of opacity. To switch between the layer mask and the actual layer, click their respective thumbnail pictures in the Layers palette.

4. Click the thumbnail of the layer mask for Layer 2.

5. Use the Ellipse Marquee tool in the Toolbox to drag an oval selection around the image on the right.

6. Choose Select➡Inverse or type (Command-Shift-I) [Control-Shift-I] to select the inverse area of the selection. Remember, you're working on the layer mask of Layer 2 right now.

Figure 5.24

The masked areas become transparent, blending with opacity to create the vignette.

7. Be sure the foreground color is set to black. Type (Option-delete)[Alt-backspace] to fill the selected area with the foreground color (black) and note the change to the layer mask thumbnail picture (see Figure 5.24).

8. (Option-click)[Alt-click] the Layer Mask thumbnail to display only the layer mask (see Figure 5.25). (Option-click)[Alt-click] the Layer Mask thumbnail again to display the image. Note that you are still working on the layer mask.

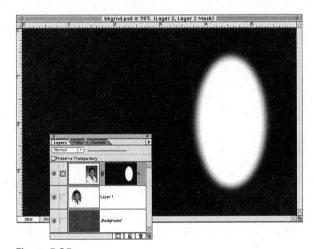

Figure 5.25

The Layer Mask.

9. Shift-click the Layer Mask thumbnail to hide the effects of the mask (see Figure 5.26). Shift-click again to turn the mask on.

Figure 5.26

Shift-click the Layer Mask thumbnail to turn off the mask effect.

10. Select the Paintbrush tool in the Toolbox and select a medium sized, soft brush from the brushes palette. Paint the Layer Mask with black, using the Paintbrush tool to remove portions of the image. If you make a mistake, change the foreground color to white and paint to restore the image.

To permanently apply the layer mask to the layer, drag the layer mask thumbnail onto the Trash Can icon at the bottom of the Layers palette or choose Layer➡Remove Layer Mask and click the Apply button when the dialog box appears. Save this file in Photoshop format to preserve the layers. Choose File➡Save a Copy to save a flattened copy of the file in another format besides Photoshop format. To flatten the image, choose Layer➡Flatten Image or choose Flatten Image from the Layers palette menu.

Creating Edge Effects

You can create an infinite number of edge effects on your images by following a few simple steps to select the area to change, then applying filters or color adjustments to the selected area. You create three examples of edge effects in the following exercise. After you've done a few of these, you can create any edge effect desired. This section introduces you to some special effects filters available under the Filter menu. For the most part, filters are selected and applied based on their visual effect, which will vary from image to image. Experimenting with the variety of available filters will give you an idea of how they work and when they are applicable to the job at hand. Many of the special effects filters are only available in RGB mode, something to keep in mind if you want to use these edge effects on your own images.

1. Open lessons/chap5/harbor.psd on the CD-ROM that accompanies this book.

2. Choose Select➡All or type (Command-A)[Control-A] to select the entire image.

3. Choose Select➡Modify➡Border to display the Border dialog box and type 64 for pixel width. 64 is the maximum pixel width allowed here (see Figure 5.27). Click OK. The selection marquee changes to display a selected area that is 32 pixels wide around the edges of the image (see Figure 5.28). The Border command creates a selection border that is built by adding 32 pixels to the outside of the marquee and 32 pixels to the inside of the marquee (64 pixels) in our example. Because the selection marquee was right out to the edge of the image, only 32 pixels were added to the inside of the marquee to create the border.

Figure 5.27

The Border dialog box.

Figure 5.28

The border pixels are selected.

4. A 32-pixel border isn't really large enough for the effects you want to create, so the next task is to enlarge this selection. Choose Select➥Modify➥ Expand to display the Expand Selection dialog box.

5. The maximum value for this dialog box is 16 pixels. Type 16 pixels to add 16 pixels to the width of the selection.

6. Choose Filter➥Artistic➥Fresco to display the Fresco dialog box (see Figure 5.29).

7. Click inside the preview picture in the Fresco dialog box and drag with the Hand icon to position the edge of the image in the window. The fresco effect is previewed in the picture window along the edges of the image.

Figure 5.29

The Fresco filter dialog box.

8. Choose the settings you want from the Options in the Fresco dialog box. For example, I selected a Brush Size of 8, Brush Detail of 5 and Texture of 3 to create a somewhat exaggerated effect. You can use these settings or try some of your own. Click OK when you're satisfied with the preview picture to apply the effect to the image (see Figure 5.30).

Figure 5.30

The Fresco effect applied to the border selection.

Type (Command-H)[Control-H] to hide the selection marquee without deselecting. Type (Command-H)[Control-H] again to make the marching ants visible again.

Figure 5.31

The Fade dialog box.

9. To blend the Fresco effect more precisely with the image, choose Filter→Fade Fresco to display the Fade dialog box (see Figure 5.31).

10. The Fade option is available for many of the filters in Photoshop and must be applied immediately after applying the filter effect. Set the Opacity value to something less than 100% to blend the Fresco effect with the image. You may also want to experiment with some of the Blending Modes available. See Chapter 3, "Painting and Filling," for information on the available blending modes. Click OK to apply the change to the image.

11. If you want to save this image choose File→Save a Copy and save the file to your hard disk. Saving a copy of the file leaves the filename intact so that you can revert to the saved image instead of opening it again from the CD-ROM. Open lessons/chap5/harbor2.psd on the CD-ROM that accompanies this book to see the completed image.

In the following example, we will use the Texturizer filter to add a texture to the border of an image and then adjust the texture using the Fade option. The steps to select a border area of the image are the same as the previous example. Refer to the preceding example for instructions on selecting a border area.

1. Open lessons/chap5/thinker.psd on the CD-ROM that accompanies this book.

2. Select a border area of 48 pixels as described in the previous exercise.

3. Choose Filter➧Texture➧Texturizer to display the Texturizer dialog box (see Figure 5.32).

4. You can choose from four textures: Brick, Burlap, Canvas and Sandstone, or load a grayscale file as a texture. For this exercise, set the Texture to Sandstone, the Scaling to 200%, Relief to 25, and Light direction to Top (see Figure 5.33).

Figure 5.32

The Texturizer dialog box.

Figure 5.33

An enlarged view showing the Sandstone texture effect.

5. Choose Filter➧Fade Texturizer and set the opacity to 70 percent in the Fade dialog box to blend the filter effect with the image.

In the following example we will create an edge effect in much the same way we did for the two previous examples, though this time we'll use the Add Noise filter to create the edge effect. Refer to the first example in this section for instructions on selecting the border pixels of the image.

1. Open lessons/chap5/mariner.psd on the CD-ROM that accompanies this book.

2. Perform steps detailed in the first example in this section to select a 48 pixel border of the image.

3. Choose Filter➤Noise➤Add Noise to display the Add Noise dialog box (see Figure 5.34).

4. Click and drag inside the preview picture window in the Add Noise dialog box to position the edge of the image in the window. Set the Amount to 999, choose Gaussian and check the Monochromatic check box. The Gaussian choice will disperse the noise in a less apparent pattern. Checking the Monochromatic check box creates noise in black and white instead of multiple colors. Click OK to apply the filter effect to the image (see Figure 5.35).

Figure 5.34

The Add Noise dialog box.

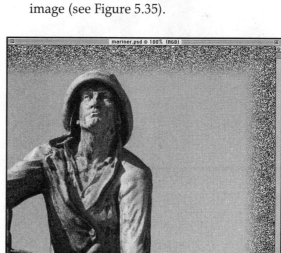

Figure 5.35

An enlarged view showing the Add Noise filter effect.

5. Choose Filter➡Fade Add Noise to display the Fade dialog box. Set the opacity to 100% and choose Multiply from the Blending Mode drop-down menu in the Fade dialog box. The Screen blending mode creates a recessed box effect on the image.

Creating Edge Effects with Layers

In the previous examples, you created edge effects by modifying the pixels in an existing image. In this exercise you use layers to composite two images together to apply the burnt paper edges effect to a photograph taken of East Berlin through the Berlin wall.

1. Open lessons/chap5/berlin.psd and lessons/chap5/paper.psd on the CD-ROM that accompanies this book.

2. Select the Move tool in the Toolbox. Click the image window of berlin.psd and drag the image into the paper.psd window (see Figure 5.37).

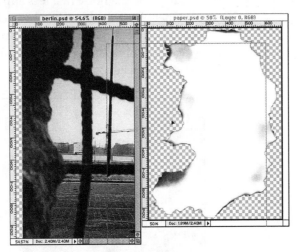

Figure 5.36

Drag the image from berlin.psd onto paper.psd with the Move tool.

3. Adjust the position of the image you just dragged into paper.psd by dragging with the Move tool.

4. Choose Window➡Show Layers to display the Layers palette if it isn't already onscreen.

Figure 5.37

The Berlin image clipped to the shape of the paper image.

5. Be sure Layer 1 is selected in the Layers palette. Choose Layer➡Group with Previous or type (Command-G)[Control-G] to create a clipping group of the Berlin picture and the burnt paper. The paper image on Layer 0 is used to clip the image on Layer 1 (see Figure 5.37).

6. With Layer 1 still selected in the Layers palette, choose Multiply from the Blending Mode drop-down menu in the Layers palette (see Figure 5.38). Refer to Chapter 3, "Painting and Filling," for information on the available blending modes. The burnt paper effect becomes visible after applying the Multiply blending mode (see Figure 5.39).

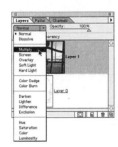

Figure 5.38

Choose Multiply for a Blending Mode.

7. Save this composite image in Photoshop format if you want to preserve the layers or choose Layer➡Flatten Image to the reduce the image to a background layer and save in any format you want.

Summary

This chapter has introduced you to some simple methods to create vignettes and edge effects, as well as some of the special effects filters available in Photoshop. You can apply the techniques covered in this chapter to layers, layer masks and alpha channels, or combine multiple filter effects to the same

Figure 5.39

The burnt paper effect is multiplied with the image pixels of the Berlin image.

image to create stunning graphic imagery. In the next chapter you will learn how to create paths using Photoshop's Bézier pen tool, and save these paths as clipping paths with the exported file to create silhouetted images for use in page layout applications.

Creating Paths

The Path tools in Photoshop enable you to create clipping paths for your images. Clipping paths can be saved with the file and applied to the images in page layout applications such as QuarkXPress and PageMaker.

Clipping paths are necessary when you want to place a masked image onto a background in a page layout program. The path tools create PostScript paths around a portion of the image that you define and take up very little space in the Photoshop file. For this reason, paths are a good way to save multiple selection paths for later use.

Finally, paths can be filled and stroked using a variety of painting and toning tools. In this chapter, you explore the techniques necessary to create effective paths for use in Photoshop and as clipping paths for placement into page layout programs.

Practicing with the Path Tools

If you are familiar with illustration programs such as Illustrator and FreeHand, the path tools in Photoshop work in much the same way as the pen tools in these programs. When we create paths in Photoshop, we are creating separate elements used to outline portions of an image. We create these elements by drawing with a pen tool that connects line segments using anchor points. We can create straight line segments and curved line segments to help us outline a shape in our image. After we have created some paths, we can use them as selections to fill or stroke areas of the image. The paths we create reside in the Paths palette and can be turned on or off at any time. The most common use of paths is to create a clipping path for an image. When a path is defined as a clipping path and saved with the Photoshop image in EPS format, the image will be clipped to the shape of the path when placed in a page layout application such as QuarkXPress or PageMaker. The following exercise covers the basics of how to use the Pen tool to create paths and introduces some techniques to help you work productively. Like any tool, the path tools take some practice, so let's practice (see Figure 6.1).

Figure 6.1

A file to practice using paths.

1. Open lessons/chap6/paths.psd on the CD-ROM that accompanies this book.

2. Choose Window➡Show Paths to display the Paths palette (see Figure 6.2).

Note

For detailed information on the Paths palette see Chapter 1, "Photoshop Basics."

Figure 6.2

The Paths palette.

3. The Path tools are located in the Toolbox. You can access the Path tools by typing the letter P. Press P to toggle through the Path tools, (Option-Click)[Alt-Click] the Path tools, or select the desired tool by clicking and holding the Path tool to display the tool menu.

4. Zoom in close to the blue box in the upper-left corner of paths.psd.

5. Select the Pen tool in the Toolbox.

6. Position the cursor over one of the red dots in the corners of the blue square and click. This first point is the anchor point and the place where you end the path to close it.

7. Hold down the Shift key and position the cursor over another red dot. Holding down the Shift key creates a straight vertical or horizontal path or a path at increments of 45 degrees. Click to create a straight path from the first anchor point.

8. Keep the Shift key held down and click the other red dots. When you get back to the first anchor point, the pen cursor contains a tiny loop that indicates you are about to close a path. Click when you see the loop to close the square path (see Figure 6.3).

Figure 6.3

Close the path by clicking the first anchor point again.

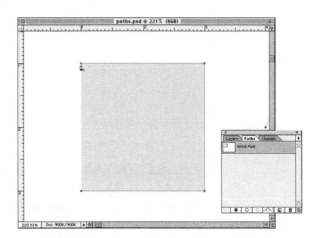

The path you just created is now listed in the Paths palette as Work Path. The work path is a temporary path and is not saved with the file. The first thing you should do after creating a work path is make the work path into a named path in the Paths palette.

1. Double-click Work Path in the Paths palette to display the Save Path dialog box. You can name this path anything you want because the path names exist only to help you keep track of your paths. Leave this one named Path 1.

2. Click the empty space under Path 1 in the Paths palette to hide the path.

3. Zoom in to the wave shape in the upper-right corner of the paths.psd file.

4. Click the leftmost red dot with the Pen tool to insert an anchor point.

5. Position the cursor over the red dot in the center of the wave. Click and drag down and to the right to create an arced path (see Figure 6.4). Clicking and dragging at the same time creates a curve point. Curve points have two handles that are used to adjust the arc of the curve. Don't worry if your curve isn't exactly right—you'll come back and fix it later.

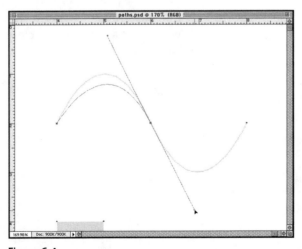

Figure 6.4

Click and drag to insert a curve point.

6. Position the cursor over the rightmost red dot. Click and drag up and to the right to create the arc (see Figure 6.5). Curve points have two sides to them, each curve arcing in a different direction.

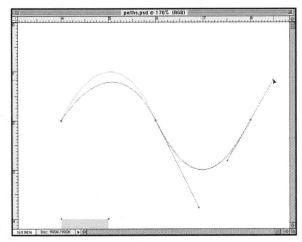

Figure 6.5

Click and drag up to create an arc in the opposite direction.

7. Use the Direct Selection tool to adjust the anchor points on your path, as well as the handles of the curve points. You can select the Direct Selection tool in the Toolbox by clicking the Pen tool to display the tool menu or by typing the letter P until the Direct Selection tool appears.

8. Click and drag the anchor points on your path with the Direct Selection tool to reposition them. Click and drag the handles of curve points to adjust the arc of the curved path (see Figure 6.6). Click and drag path segments to move the walls of the path.

TIP

To quickly access the Direct Selection tool while using the Pen tool, hold down the (Command)[Control] key.

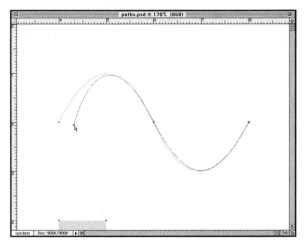

Figure 6.6

Use the Direct Selection tool to adjust anchor points and curve handles.

9. When you draw an open path such as the one you just drew for the wave shape, it is necessary to deselect the path before creating a new path. If you don't deselect the path, the next anchor point you click connects to the last anchor point of the open path. To deselect the path, click anywhere off the path with the Direct Selection tool. The path remains visible, but the anchor points and handles disappear.

Now that you know how to create straight paths and curve paths, the next steps instruct you in how to combine straight line segments with curve segments. Once you master these techniques, creating a path will be a breeze.

1. Position the shape at the bottom of paths.psd in the window and select the Pen tool in the Toolbox.

2. Start in the lower-left corner and click an anchor point. Click the upper-left corner to create a straight path. Continue adding points until you come to the first arc.

3. Click and drag the red dot in the center of the two humps to create the arc from the straight path segment (see Figure 6.7).

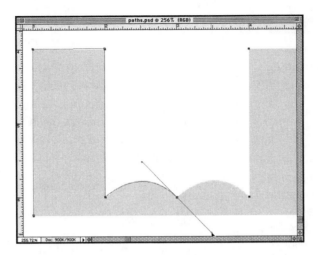

Figure 6.7

Click and drag to connect a curved arc to a straight segment of the path.

4. Before you can continue you must remove the right handle of the corner point because if you don't, the next curve point you add creates an arc in the opposite direction. (Option-Click)[Alt-Click] the active anchor point (not the curve handles) to retract the right handle into the curve point (see Figure 6.8).

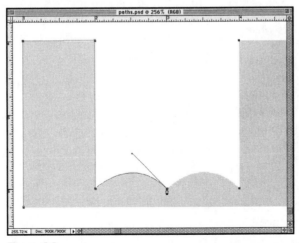

Figure 6.8

(Option-Click)[Alt-Click] the current anchor point to retract the curve handle that applies to the next curve.

If you make a mistake when creating a path, do not use the (Delete)[Backspace] key to remove the anchor point. You can press (Command-Z) [Control-Z] to undo the last point or hold down the (Command)[Control] key and use the Direct Selection tool to adjust the position of the point. When you use the (Delete)[Backspace] key, the most recent anchor point is deleted, but the rest of the anchor points in your path are activated. Pressing (Delete) [Backspace] a second time deletes the entire path.

TIP

To add or remove points while using the standard Pen tool, Macintosh users can hold down the Control key and point along the path to add a point or point at an existing point to remove it. Windows users can click with the right mouse button. To add or remove points when the Pointer tool is selected, hold down (Command-Option)[Control-Alt] and click the path or anchor point.

5. Click and drag the next red dot to create the curved path in the same direction as the previous arc.

6. To connect the curve point you just made to a straight line segment, you must again retract the handle of the curve point. (Option-Click) [Alt-Click] the current point before clicking to create the straight segment.

7. Use these techniques to make your way around this shape. Be sure to close the path by clicking the first point.

8. Because you deselected Path 1 in the Paths palette, the new paths you created for the wave shape and the shape at the bottom of the file are on a new Work Path. Double-click the work path and name the new path Path 2.

9. Select Path 1 in the Paths palette and click the path around the box with the Direct Selection tool.

10. Choose the Pen tool with the plus sign (+) to add points along an existing path. Use the Pen tool with the minus sign (–) to remove points on an existing path.

After you have created a closed path you can fill the path with any of the fill options or stroke the path using a variety of tools from the Toolbox. When you have more than one path created the individual paths are referred to as subpaths by Photoshop.

1. Choose Fill Subpath from the Paths palette menu to display the Fill Path dialog box.

2. Choose Stroke to display the Stroke Subpath dialog box. Choose a tool from the Stroke Subpath dialog box. You paint the path using the settings for the tool you choose and the brush size currently selected for that tool.

3. To fill the path with the foreground color click the solid circle icon at the bottom of the Paths palette. To stroke the path with the foreground color click the open circle icon at the bottom of the Paths palette.

4. To load the path as a selection, choose Make Selection from the Paths palette menu or click the selection icon at the bottom of the Paths palette.

5. To create a work path from a selection, choose Make Work Path from the Paths palette menu or click the path icon at the bottom of the Paths palette.

Saving a Clipping Path

Clipping paths are necessary to create silhouetted images for placement in page layout applications, such as QuarkXPress and PageMaker. The clipping path crops the image area inside the path so that the image can be placed on another background. In other words, even though the entire image is saved as an EPS file, when a clipping path is included only the image area inside the path is used in the page layout application for both display and printing.

In this exercise you create a clipping path for two images to be used as an automobile dealership marketing piece (see Figure 6.9).

Figure 6.9

A typical example of the use of clipping paths in a page layout application.

1. Open lessons/chap6/car.psd on the CD-ROM that accompanies this book.

2. Choose Window➡Show Paths to display the Paths palette.

3. Select the Pen tool in the Toolbox and create a path around the shape of the car (including the tires). Use as few anchor points as possible to create an efficient path that prints without a problem to a PostScript printer (see Figure 6.10).

Figure 6.10

The car path.

4. After the path is created, double-click the Work Path in the Paths palette and name the path "car path."

Now that you have created a path, the next step before saving the file is to define one of your paths as the clipping path. You must do this even if you have only one path defined.

1. Choose Clipping Path from the Paths palette menu and select car path from the Path drop-down menu (see Figure 6.11). Leave the flatness setting blank because entering a flatness value affects the way the file is output. A flatness value of 3 or 4 is good if you have a particularly complex path that does not print to your laser printer, but a value higher than 3 or 4 usually causes the curved paths to appear jagged. High resolution output devices have built-in flatness settings, so leaving the flatness value blank applies the flatness setting of the output device.

2. Note that the name of the path (car path) appears in outline text in the Paths palette. Only one path can be exported with the file for use in other applications. If you have more than one path

Note

Clipping paths will only print on a PostScript Level 2 or higher printer. If you have a laser printer purchased before PostScript Level 2 was implemented, you will not be able to print files that contain clipping paths.

Figure 6.11

Select a path from the Path drop-down menu to be used as the clipping path for the saved file.

defined, the one with outline text is the clipping path that should be saved with the file.

3. Choose File➡Save As to display the Save dialog box and choose Photoshop EPS from the Format drop-down menu. Click the Save button to display the EPS Format dialog box (see Figure 6.12).

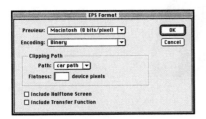

Figure 6.12

The EPS Format dialog box.

4. Choose Preview and Encoding options. Make sure car path is selected in the Path drop-down menu. You can select another path to save with your file at this point, even though you defined the clipping path in the Paths palette. Click OK to save the EPS file.

Creating Paths in Paths

Photoshop uses a method called even-odd fill to handle paths within paths. The outermost path clips the image from the background. If you add another closed path inside this path, the contents of the inside path clip changes to transparent. Adding successive paths inside this path continue along the same lines (see Figure 6.13). You must create subpaths within paths to punch out areas of the image that are inside the overall clipping path. In this section you create a clipping path that includes subpaths inside the silhouette path (see Figure 6.14).

Figure 6.13

The clipping paths on the left image result in cycling transparent and solid image areas in the placed EPS file.

Figure 6.14

The hollow areas of this monument must be created as paths to knock out on the placed image.

1. Open lessons/chap6/mariner.psd on the CD-ROM that accompanies this book.

2. Choose Window➥Show Paths to display the Paths palette.

3. Use the Pen tool to first create a path around the perimeter of the statue. Be sure to close this path by clicking the first anchor point.

4. Double-click the work path in the Paths palette to name the path. Name this path anything you want.

5. Leave the new path selected in the Paths palette and create new closed paths for all hollow areas on the statue.

6. After you have created all the inside paths, choose Clipping Path from the Paths palette menu to define the path as a clipping path.

7. Save the file as a Photoshop EPS file.

8. Place the saved EPS file in your page layout application. If you are using QuarkXPress, set the background color to none to make the clipped parts of the image transparent. Text run-arounds follow the clipping path with an outset you define in the layout program.

Exporting Paths to Illustrator

After you have created a path in Photoshop, you can export the path to an Illustrator format file. When the path is in the Illustrator application you can use the path to create text on a path or to fill and stroke the path to create flash and varnish plates.

► Flash plates are typically used in screen printing to print a solid white area before applying color to dark materials, such as a black T-shirt.

► Varnish plates are used in offset printing to create a gloss or matte finish on parts of a printed page.

In a page layout program, you can place the varnish plate or flash plate over the silhouetted image and overprint the plate to generate an extra printing plate.

1. Choose File➡Export➡Paths to Illustrator to display the Export paths dialog box.

2. Select a path to export from the Write drop-down menu. If you choose Document Bounds here, a rectangle path at the dimensions of the Photoshop image is exported.

3. Use the .ai extension when exporting the path. Click Save.

4. Open the exported path in Illustrator. The paths are not stroked, so you must turn off Preview to see the paths in Illustrator.

Summary

In this chapter you learned how to create paths in Photoshop to facilitate filling and stroking areas of the image and most importantly to enable you to create a silhouette path to be used in a page layout application. In the next chapter you will learn how to specify color in Photoshop using a variety of tools and palettes.

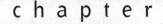
Specifying Color

Photoshop offers many ways to specify color. Regardless of the method you use to choose a color, all of the colors you define in Photoshop are either a foreground or background color. You will specify foreground and background colors to use the painting tools, Fill and Stroke commands, and in the case of the Gradient tool, to specify blend colors. Aside from defining colors using the Color Picker, you can also sample colors from existing images and load them into the foreground and background colors. You can define colors using any of Photoshop's available color models.

Understanding Photoshop's Color Models

The choices you have for specifying color in Photoshop are HSB, Lab, RGB, and CMYK. Three of the four-color models have corresponding color modes in Photoshop (RGB, Lab, and CMYK). The HSB color model is the color model that is used by the available color pickers to display color and is the model used by many of the commands that change the color of pixels. You can specify color in any one of the four-color models; the corresponding values for the other three are automatically inserted by Photoshop.

RGB Color

The RGB (red, green, blue) color model is representative of colors created using light. Televisions, scanners, and color monitors are examples of devices that must use RGB light to create color. The red, green, and blue levels are specified by integers between 0 and 255, indicating the amount of light used to create a pixel's color. The RGB colors are referred to as the additive or light primaries because when red, green, and blue light are generated at full and equal intensity on the same spot, they create white light. Necessity dictates the use of the RGB color model for color monitors, although colors can vary significantly between different monitors and even between two monitors of the same make and model. RGB color is also the color model used by all scanners, even if the scanner is capable of generating color in other color spaces. To specify RGB color in the Photoshop Color Picker, enter a value from 0 (zero) to 255 for each of the RGB colors.

CMYK Color

Four-color process printing is achieved by combining cyan, magenta, yellow, and black (the process colors) to produce a full range of colors. Black is indicated by the letter "K" to avoid confusion with the color blue (B). Process color guides are available from a variety of vendors such as Trumatch, Pantone, and Agfa to aide in the specification of CMYK color mixes. In the Photoshop color picker, specify percentages of ink from 0% to 100% for each of the process colors.

Lab Color

The Lab color model encompasses all the colors within the RGB and CMYK color models, and it is used internally by Photoshop to convert between RGB and CMYK. Based on the CIE XYZ color model, developed in 1931 by the Commission Internationale de l'Eclairage (the International Committee on Illumination), the Lab color model has recently gained wide acceptance because it is a device-independent color model. Color management systems developed by companies such as Kodak, Apple, and Agfa are built around the Lab color model. A telling indicator of the widespread support of this color model is its support in Adobe's PostScript Level 2, the current version of PostScript in use today. The three components used in the Lab color model are Luminance (lightness) and two color components—component "a" ranges from green to red and component "b" ranges from blue to yellow.

HSB Color

The HSB color model describes colors by the three attributes used to describe color: hue, saturation, and brightness. Hues are usually described with a common color name (brown, purple, or pink, to name a few). The HSB color model is graphically depicted as a cylinder. Hue is specified by degrees, indicating a position around the circumference of the cylinder. Hues follow a progression of red, orange, yellow, green, blue, indigo, violet, and back to red again (see Figure 7.1). The saturation values are depicted from the center out. A saturation value at the center or core of the cylinder is at 0% saturation, a neutral gray. The cylinder's horizontally sliced sections represent the brightness value, with the darkest values at the bottom (100%) and the brightest at the top (0%). Each slice of this cylinder represents a color wheel at a particular brightness percentage. Figure 7.2 depicts the Apple color picker to illustrate the HSB color wheel. In the Apple color picker, degrees around the wheel represent the hue, saturation is the value from the center of the wheel out, and the horizontal slider under the color wheel controls brightness. The Photoshop Color Picker uses the HSB color model to graphically depict color selections, although not with the usual color wheel (see Figure 7.3).

The Photoshop Color Picker graphically depicts specified colors in the HSB color space. The large square (Figure 7.3) contains brightness and saturation values for a particular hue, represented by the "rainbow" color slider to its right. Saturation percentage runs from 0% (left) to 100% (right) of the selected hue. Brightness percentage runs from 100% (top) to 0% (bottom) in the color square. Click inside the large square horizontally to change the saturation and vertically to affect the brightness.

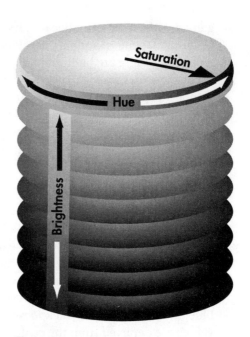

Figure 7.1

The HSB color model.

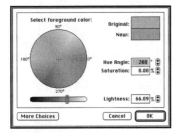

Figure 7.2

The Apple color picker.

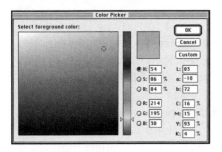

Figure 7.3

The Photoshop Color Picker.

Custom Colors

Aside from specifying color in all the available Photoshop color spaces, you can also specify color using a variety of Custom Color choices (see Figure 7.4). Photoshop does not provide a method to save spot colors in addition to the four process color plates. If you are in RGB mode and choose a custom spot color, the color is converted into its RGB equivalent based on its CMYK breakdown. Conversely, when you are in CMYK mode, the spot color you choose is converted to the process color match based on built-in tables that conform with the color system's standard formulas. Photoshop supports the PANTONE Matching System, the TRUMATCH Swatching System, the FOCOLTONE Colour System,

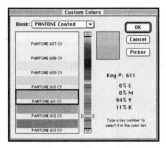

Figure 7.4

Custom colors in the Photoshop Color Picker.

Spot Color Choices in Photoshop

Pantone Matching System— Pantone is the most popular system for selecting spot color inks in the United States. Pantone color guides come in a variety of formats, each geared to a particular use. Some of the Pantone color guides display CMYK equivalents to facilitate choosing matches for Pantone colors with confidence. The Pantone color gamut is signifi- cantly larger than that of CMYK, so many Pantone colors cannot be simulated accurately using CMYK inks. In other words, some colors can be matched closely using CMYK inks, while others will be quite far off or not achievable at all. In Photoshop, you can choose from PANTONE Coated, PAN- TONE Uncoated, PANTONE Process, and PANTONE ProSim, which represent particular color guides or books you can acquire from Pantone.

the Toyo 88 ColorFinder 1050 System, the ANPA- Color System and the DIC Color Guide. Each of these custom color systems has a corresponding printed color guide, available at most art stores or directly from the vendor (see sidebar).

Understanding Color Gamut

The range of colors available in a specific color model is that model's color gamut. The visible spectrum (the range of colors you can see with your eyes) is significantly larger than any of the available color model's color gamut. In Photoshop, Lab mode encompasses the largest color gamut including all the colors in the RGB and CMYK gamut. The RGB gamut contains all the colors that computer monitors and television screens can generate. The CMYK gamut, the smallest of all the color gamuts in Photoshop, contains all the colors that can be printed using the cyan, magenta, yellow, and black process color inks. Because the RGB gamut is quite different than the CMYK gamut, it stands to reason that some colors that can be displayed on the monitor cannot be represented by process color inks and vice versa. When colors displayed on the monitor are outside the range (gamut) of colors that can be produced using process color inks, these colors are considered to be "out of gamut." Photoshop displays an exclama- tion point (!) inside a triangle to indicate out-of- gamut colors in the Photoshop Color Picker (see Figure 7.5), as well as the in Color palette (see Figure 7.6). The gamut warning symbol appears next to a color swatch that shows the closest color within the CMYK gamut. Click the gamut warning symbol in either the Color Picker or Color palette to adjust the out-of-gamut color to the closest color within the CMYK gamut.

Trumatch Swatching System— The Trumatch system covers the colors in the visible spectrum that reproduce well in CMYK. There are approximately 2,000 color choices created as 40 variations of each hue, including four-color grays.

Focoltone Colour System—The Focoltone system contains 763 CMYK colors selected for their ability to blend well with other CMYK colors, hence avoiding trapping problems with process color plates.

Toyo 88 ColorFinder 1050—The Toyo 88 system contains more than 1,000 colors based the standard printing inks used in Japan. The *Toyo Color Finder 1050 Book* is available in the United States at many art supply stores.

ANPA-Color—The *ANPA-Color ROP Newspaper Color Ink Book* contains the colors that print well on newsprint.

DIC Color—The *DIC Color Guide* is used primarily for printing projects in Japan.

Out of Gamut Warning

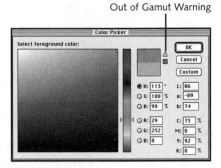

Figure 7.5

The Photoshop Color Picker displays the out-of-gamut warning under a color swatch representing the closest match within the CMYK gamut.

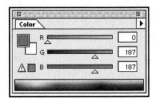

Figure 7.6

The out-of-gamut warning symbol is displayed in the lower-left corner of the Color palette, next to a swatch to indicate the closest CMYK color.

Setting Foreground and Background Color

When you launch Photoshop for the first time (or if you delete the preferences file from your hard disk), Photoshop's default colors of black foreground and white background are set. You can set the foreground and background colors back to the default colors anytime by typing the letter D or by clicking the default colors icon in the Toolbox (see Figure 7.7). The foreground and background colors can also be swapped by typing the letter X or by clicking the icon in the Toolbox.

To change the foreground or background color:

1. Click the foreground or background swatch in the Toolbox pictured in Figure 7.7.

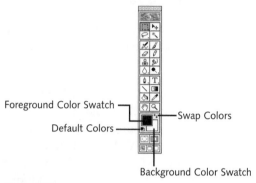

Foreground Color Swatch

Default Colors

Swap Colors

Background Color Swatch

Figure 7.7

The Foreground and Background colors.

2. The color picker that is displayed is determined by which color picker you have selected in the Display & Cursors preference—Photoshop, Apple, or Windows. If you have not changed the preference since you installed Photoshop, the default color picker is the Photoshop Color Picker (see Figure 7.3). See the section on Setting Preferences in Chapter 1, "Photoshop Basics," for instructions on selecting the color picker.

3. Create a color using one of the available color spaces and click OK.

4. The color swatch in the Toolbox displays the selected color. When the Color Picker dialog box appears, you can also click the Custom button to select a color from the available color books.

Specifying Custom Colors

You can specify custom colors from the Color Picker as well as from the Color palette's menu. To select a custom color from the Color Picker:

1. Open the Photoshop Color Picker by clicking either the foreground or background color swatch in the Toolbox or Color palette.

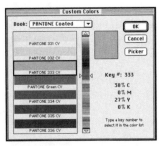

Figure 7.8

The Custom Colors dialog box.

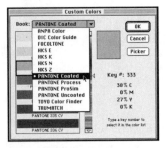

Figure 7.9

The color book choices in the Custom Colors dialog box.

2. Click the Custom button to display the Custom Colors dialog box (see Figure 7.8). The color shown is the closest match for the color currently selected. The color system displayed is the last one used.

3. Choose the color system from the drop-down menu to the right of the word "Book" (see Figure 7.9).

4. Locate the color by typing the color number, clicking the color bar or scrolling through the list by dragging the triangles in the color bar. Click the top and bottom arrows of the color bar to move forward and backward one color at a time. Note that there is no field for typing in the code number for the color you want and you only have to type the number part of the color description.

5. The CMYK breakdown of the custom color you select is displayed in the Custom Colors dialog box. Click the Picker button to see what the color equivalents are in other color models. Remember that Photoshop converts all spot colors to CMYK, except in the case of Duotone mode. See Chapter 2, "Color and Resolution in Photoshop," for more information on Duotone mode.

Specifying Colors with the Color Palette

To change the foreground and background colors using the Color palette:

1. Choose Window➡ Show Color to display the Color palette (Figure 7.10).

2. The Color palette is another way to set the foreground and background colors and it contains foreground and background swatches. If you click the active color swatch (outlined in

Foreground Color

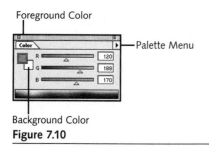

Palette Menu

Background Color

Figure 7.10

The Color palette.

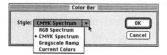

Figure 7.11

Choose a color slider from the palette menu of the Color palette.

Figure 7.12

The Color Bar choices.

black), the Color Picker dialog box appears. Click the inactive color swatch (not outlined in black) to make it active.

3. Select the color model for the Color palette by clicking the triangle in the upper-right corner of the Color palette and making a selection from the palette menu (see Figure 7.11).

4. The color bar at the bottom of the Color palette enables you to select a color from a selected color model's spectrum. Click the triangle in the upper-right corner of the Color palette to display the palette menu choices and select Color Bar to choose which color ramp appears at the bottom of the Color palette (Figure 7.12). If you choose Current Colors as the color ramp to display at the bottom of the Color palette, a blend between the foreground color and background color will be available.

5. Drag the triangle sliders in the Color palette to mix a color.

Specifying Colors with the Swatches Palette

The Swatches palette enables you to save the foreground or background color into a palette of colors for use later on. The colors in the Swatches palette can be selected as the foreground or background color. You can create a color palette from scratch, add to the palette displayed, save the color palette, and load previously saved color palettes. The default swatches contain the current palette. To use the Swatches palette:

1. Choose Window➡Show Swatches to display the Swatches palette (see Figure 7.13).

Figure 7.13

The Swatches palette.

2. Position your cursor over one of the color swatches in the Swatches palette. The cursor changes to an eyedropper cursor.

3. Click a swatch to load that color as the foreground color.

4. (Option-click)[Alt-click] a color swatch to load that color as the background Color.

5. To add a color, position your cursor over an empty space in the Swatches palette. If no empty spaces are available, click and drag in the lower-right corner of the Swatches palette to change the height and reveal empty spaces. The cursor changes to a paint bucket. Click the empty space to add the foreground color to the palette.

6. To replace a color in the Swatches palette, Shift-click the swatch (the cursor changes to a paint bucket) to change the swatch color to the foreground color.

7. To insert a color swatch, position the cursor over a color swatch in the palette. Hold down (Shift-Option)[Shift-Alt] (the cursor changes to a paint bucket) and click the swatch to insert a new swatch in front of it in the foreground color.

8. To delete a color swatch in the Swatches palette, hold down (Command)[Control]. When the cursor changes to a pair of scissors, click a swatch to delete it.

9. To reset the swatches palette to the default swatch colors, click the triangle in the upper-right corner of the Swatches palette to display the palette menu and choose Reset Swatches. A dialog box appears so that you can choose whether to replace all the current swatches with the default color swatches or append the default color swatches to the current swatches.

10. To save a custom set of color swatches, click the triangle in the upper-right corner of the Swatches palette and choose Save Swatches from the palette menu. Navigate to the folder or directory you want to save the swatches in and click the Save button. Save your swatches if you want to use them on another image at a later date. Opening an indexed color image or converting an image to indexed color replaces the custom color palette with the indexed colors. See Chapter 2, "Color and Resolution in Photoshop" for more information on Indexed color mode.

11. To replace the current swatches with swatches previously saved, click the triangle in the upper-right corner of the Swatches palette and select Replace Swatches from the palette menu. Navigate to the folder or directory containing the saved swatches and click the Open button. The previously saved swatches replace the current swatches.

12. To append swatches previously saved, click the triangle in the upper-right corner of the Swatches palette and select Load Swatches from the palette menu. Navigate to the folder or directory containing the saved swatches and click the Open button. The loaded swatches are appended to the current set.

13. To sample colors from your image to add to the swatches palette, use the Eyedropper tool and click the image to load the image colors as the foreground color. Click an empty space in the Swatches palette to add the colors. See the following section, "Sampling Colors," for more details.

Sampling Colors

The Eyedropper tool enables you to sample colors from an image and load them as the foreground or background color. You can sample the color of a specific pixel in the image or the average color of a square-pixel area. To sample colors from an image:

1. Double-click the Eyedropper tool in the toolbox to display the Eyedropper Options palette and select a Sample Size from the drop-down menu in the Eyedropper Options palette (Figure 7.14).

   ► Choose Point Sample to set the Eyedropper tool to select the color of a single pixel.

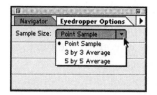

Figure 7.14

The Eyedropper Options palette.

TIP

Type the letter I to select the Eyedropper tool in the toolbox. If you are zoomed in close to sample a color, hold down the Spacebar to display the Hand tool. Click and drag with the hand tool to move the canvas area around in the window.

▶ Choose 3 by 3 Average to set the Eyedropper tool to load a color that is the average of the color values in each color channel of a 3-pixel-by-3-pixel area.

▶ Choose 5 by 5 Average to set the Eyedropper tool to load a color that is the average of the color values in each color channel of a 5-pixel-by-5-pixel area.

2. To define a foreground color, select the Eyedropper tool from the toolbox and position the cursor over the part of the image that contains the color you want to sample, and then click. If you hold down the mouse button and drag around the image with the Eyedropper tool selected, you can view the sampled colors in the color swatch in the toolbox.

3. To define a background color, select the Eyedropper tool from the toolbox and position the Eyedropper cursor over the part of the image that contains the color you want to sample. (Option-click)[Alt-click] to load the color as the background color. If you hold down the mouse button and drag around the image with the Eyedropper tool selected, you can view the sampled colors in the color swatch in the toolbox.

Summary

You will use what you learned in this chapter throughout this book. It may take some time to familiarize yourself with all the possibilities of specifying color, although each project you undertake will help you become comfortable with the techniques that are most useful to you. In the next chapter we will delve into the techniques used to adjust the colors of existing Photoshop files using a variety of commands and tools.

Adjusting Color and Grayscale

The capability to make color adjustments to scanned imagery is an important part of the pre-layout process. A color cast can be introduced when an image is scanned, especially on flatbed scanners. Local color changes are often necessary to correct for color shifts that take place when an RGB image is converted to CMYK. Color adjustment techniques are also used for special effects or to pump up color in parts of an image. Good tonal balance is the key to producing accurate color, balancing the shadows, midtones, and highlights to best represent the scanned image.

In this chapter, you perform some color adjustments and adjust the gray balance of images. To become an expert at color correction and adjustment, you should learn as much as possible about the color theory behind RGB and CMYK. Because scanners and computer monitors deal in RGB only, understanding the relationship between the RGB colors and CMYK printing ink colors will help you get the color adjustment right the first time and remove some of the guess work. The finer points of color theory and the CMYK printing process are outside the scope of this book, though there are a plethora of books on these subjects from this publisher and others at your local book outlets.

Adjusting Grayscale

When adjusting a grayscale image, there are three particular areas of importance in regards to gray balance:

► **Black point.** The *black point* is the darkest area on your image, theoretically; the part of the image that will print solid black.

► **White point.** The *white point* is the brightest point in the image; the part of the image that will print white.

► **Midtones.** The *midtones* are the middle grays of the image and often constitute the largest area on normal key images.

In the following exercise, the final product for the image we will adjust is an offset printed piece. To make judgements about tonal balance and adjustment for offset printing, you must know the following:

► **Screen frequency.** To scan the grayscale image at the correct resolution, you must know the screen frequency (line screen) the piece will be printed with. The only people who can tell you what line screen to use are the folks at the printing company. After you know the screen frequency, multiply the screen frequency by 1.5 to arrive at the proper resolution.

► **Dot gain.** Dot gain is specified in percentage and is the amount of growth a 50% halftone dot experiences when printed. Dot gain varies greatly from printing press to printing press and is affected by such things as ink properties, plating procedures, paper type, and the type of printing press used. Always ask your printer about dot gain when discussing a print job.

► **Textured or colored paper.** Textured and colored paper do not reflect as much light as white coated paper. Therefore, it might be necessary to compensate on the image by increasing contrast and brightness.

Figure 8.1

The original image on top is too dark in the shadows, too bright in the highlights, and somewhat dark and flat in the midtones. The corrected image directly above displays more detail and an even balance of brightness and contrast.

In this exercise, the photograph is going to be placed in a business magazine that prints on white coated paper. The magazine prints on a Web printing press that gets 15% dot gain and is printed at a screen frequency of 150 lpi (lines per inch). Now that we know the parameters of our target image, we can make the proper adjustments to the gray balance of the photograph (see Figure 8.1).

1. Open lessons/chap8/ann.psd on the CD-ROM that accompanies this book.

2. Choose Window➥Show Info to display the Info palette (see Figure 8.2). Make sure the "K" values are displayed in one of the upper sections of the Info palette. Click the tiny triangle next to one of the eyedropper icons in the Info palette to change the color to Actual Color if the "K" value is not displayed.

Figure 8.2

The Info palette.

3. Choose Image➥Histogram to display the histogram for this image (see Figure 8.3). The values in the Histogram dialog box represent the following data about the image:

   ▶ **Mean.** The mean represents the average brightness level of the entire image. This value is a good indicator of whether the image may be too bright or too dark. The mean value of this image is 101.25, which means that most of image resides in the midtone range (around 128 gray level).

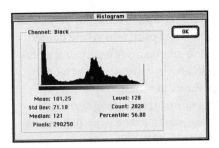

Figure 8.3

The Histogram dialog box.

Note

The *histogram* is a graphical depiction of the distribution of the pixels in the image. The darkest pixels (shadow) are on the left, and the brightest pixels (highlights) on the right. The pixels are represented in gray levels from 0 on the left to 255 on the right. You can see this value in the Info palette by choosing RGB from one of the Eyedropper menus in the Info palette. Position the cursor in the histogram to get information about the distribution of the pixels or click and drag to select a range of pixels. Notice the large peak on the left side of the histogram, indicating that there are a significant number of dark pixels.

▶ **Standard Deviation.** Standard deviation (Std Dev) indicates how widely the pixel values vary from the mean.

▶ **Median.** The median value is the middle value within the total range of values for the image or selected area. A good median value for this image is around 128 (halfway between 0 and 255). The median value of 121 indicates that the image is well balanced in the midtones.

▶ **Pixels.** The pixels field displays the total number of pixels in the entire image or selected area. The mean, standard deviation, and median statistics are derived from this value. There are 290,250 total pixels in the image.

▶ **Level.** The level field displays the gray level of a specific point or range of values (0–255) in the histogram. To view the information for a specific point, position the cursor over a point in the histogram or click and drag to display a range of values.

▶ **Count.** When selecting a specific point or range of values in the histogram, the count field displays the total number of pixels with these values.

▶ **Percentile.** The percentile field displays the percentage of pixels below (darker than) the value displayed in the level field.

4. Click OK after you have evaluated the histogram for this image. The histogram is simply a tool to view the distribution of the pixels and does not change the image in any way.

The histogram indicated that the image may be too heavily weighted in the shadow areas. Looking at the image onscreen, there is likely some detail that will be revealed if we adjust the shadow areas. Move the cursor over the image and observe the values in the

Info palette to get a feel for where the gray levels are distributed in the image. Note that the highlight areas in the hair are entirely blown out to 255 (0% K) and the shadow areas are pretty flat, showing little detail.

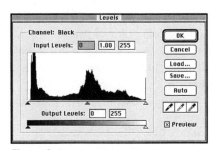

Figure 8.4

The Levels dialog box.

1. Choose Image➡Adjust➡Levels, or type (Command-L)[Control-L], to display the Levels dialog box (see Figure 8.4). The Levels dialog box contains the same histogram we saw when viewing the histogram of the image.

2. The first thing we need to do is define the black point (darkest shadow) and white point (brightest highlight) of our image. Double-click the white eyedropper in the Levels dialog box to display the Color Picker.

3. Enter 96% in the Brightness (B) value box and set the Hue (H) and Saturation (S) to 0. This means that the brightest pixels in our image will be a 4% printable dot. Keep in mind that some dot gain will occur, though not as much as indicated for the 50% dot. Basically, we are telling Photoshop that when we specify the white point, the value will be 245 gray (4% K) instead of 255 gray (0% K). Click OK in the Color Picker after you enter the value for the highlight pixels.

4. With the Levels dialog box still open, click the highlight area in your image with the white eyedropper tool. Look for the brightest highlight (hair) in the image. The value of the highlight pixels you clicked are set to 245 gray level (4% ink) and the values of the pixels in the entire image are proportionately adjusted to accommodate this new highlight level. Any pixels with values greater than the pixels you clicked with the white eyedropper tool become specular whites (no gray value).

5. Without closing the Levels dialog box, drag around in the image to find the shadow pixels.

TIP

The RGB values in the Info palette display the before and after values if you position your cursor over pixels in the image while the Levels dialog box is open.

Note

If you make a mistake in selecting the pixels for the highlight value, you can reset the Levels dialog box by (Option-clicking)[Alt-clicking] the Reset button. This resetting method applies to most of Photoshop's dialog boxes.

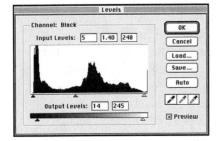

Figure 8.5

The Levels dialog with changes to the Input and Output levels.

Take care not to click in the image area yet. View the values of the pixels in the Info palette.

6. Double-click the black eyedropper tool in the Levels dialog box and enter 10% in the Brightness (B) value box and set the Hue and Saturation to 0. A 10% brightness value results in a 91% printable dot, the desired shadow value. Again, keep in mind that some dot gain will occur, making the 91% dot print closer to 100%. Click OK in the Color Picker after you enter a value for the shadows.

7. With the Levels dialog box still open, locate the darkest area in the image and click the image with the black eyedropper tool. The darkest area on the image now prints a 91% dot. The values of the pixels in the entire image are proportionately adjusted to accommodate this new shadow level. Any pixels with values lower than the pixels you clicked with the black eyedropper tool now have a gray level of 0 (100% black). The Info palette displays the before and after values for the pixels in the image while the Levels dialog box is open.

8. Now that we have set the black and white points of the image, let's adjust the gamma (midtones) of the image. Click and drag the middle triangle slider under the histogram to the left until the Input Level in the middle box reads 1.40. We can now see detail in the jacket and sweater.

9. Finally, drag the left triangle slider under the histogram to the right until it is under where the histogram begins (an input level of 5). Drag the right triangle slider to the left until the Input Level is 248. The input levels adjust the distribution of the pixels in the image, whereas the output levels adjust the white point and black point (see Figure 8.5). Click OK to save the changes to the image.

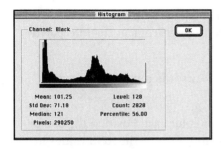

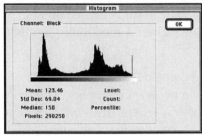

Figure 8.6

Note the difference in the shadow areas of the top histogram compared to the original histogram directly above.

10. Choose Image➡Histogram to display the histogram for the image and compare this histogram to the original values (see Figure 8.6).

Adjusting RGB

When working in RGB, think of the RGB values as intensities of colored light. Colors are darker when the level of light is lower and brighter when the levels are higher. A dim red light, for example, appears darker than a bright red light. RGB values are indicated on a scale of 0–255 that represents the 256 gray levels (levels of light). A value of 0 represents the absence of color, whereas a value of 255 is the maximum amount of color.

Neutral gray colors have red, green, and blue values that are the same or close. If two of the colors are relatively the same and the third is different by more than 10 levels in a neutral colored area, the image probably has a color cast. Color casts are evidenced by a dominant color tint to a photograph when it is proofed or printed. Color cast is easier to correct when the image is scanned using a gray wedge that is scanned with the image. A gray wedge is a photographic strip that contains percentages of gray in ten percent increments usually and can be purchased at many graphic arts and camera stores. When you do not have the benefit of a gray wedge, you will have to evaluate the colors in the image to determine if a color cast is present. Color casts are introduced into an image during scanning and may not be apparent at first glance when you do not have the original photograph to compare to the screen representation. See "Calibrating Your Monitor" in Chapter 2, "Color and Resolution in Photoshop" to calibrate the monitor for gray level and color balance if you want the benefit of spotting a color cast on the monitor.

1. Open lessons/chap8/cablecar.psd on the CD-ROM that accompanies this book.

2. Choose Window➡Show Info to display the Info palette. Click the tiny triangle next to one of the eyedropper icons in the Info palette, and choose RGB Color.

3. Select the Marquee tool so that the cursor is represented by a crosshair icon.

4. Shadows are good places to look for color cast. Position the cursor over the shadow behind the truck and observe the RGB values in the Info palette. Do the same for the shadow of the trolley car. The Green and Blue values are relatively close in value to each other, whereas the Red value is significantly higher—a good indication that this image has a red cast to it.

5. The white areas in the image should contain RGB values that are close in value and close to 255. We do not want any areas that are 255 Red, 255 Green, and 255 Blue because these areas will be blown out, lacking a printed halftone dot. The white areas, however, should have RGB values between 245 and 250. Position the cursor over the white shirt of the man standing on the corner and the white stripes in the road to evaluate the balance for the whites in the image. In this case, the Red and Green values are relatively close, whereas the Blue value is somewhat lower. Blue helps to make whites whiter, so we will probably have to add some blue to the highlight areas to get better whites. You can also observe the imbalance of blue in the sky, which appears somewhat yellow without the blue highlight.

Now that we've evaluated the values in the image, we use the Curves dialog box to make adjustments to the images. We start off by adjusting the white (highlight) and black (shadow) points because defining the shadows and highlights will help us make accurate adjustments to the midtones of the image.

1. The shadow areas of this image are pretty dark and could probably stand some adjustment. Before we make any color changes, let's fix the shadow areas. Choose Image➡Adjust➡Curves, or type (Command-M)[Control-M], to display the Curves dialog box (see Figure 8.7).

2. The grayscale of the image is represented in the Curves dialog box. The blend bar under the grid depicts the values of the grayscale. All of the gray values in the image are plotted along the linear curve displayed in the grid. These are the input values—the values currently

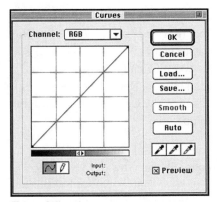

Figure 8.7

The Curves dialog box.

in the image. Notice that the Curves dialog box also has eyedropper tools to specify the black point and white point, as well as an eyedropper to specify the 50% gray value. For now, we are going to define only the black and white points.

3. You can adjust the curve for the composite RGB image or for each individual RGB channel. Make sure RGB is selected in the Channel drop-down menu at the top of the Curves dialog box.

4. Double-click the white eyedropper in the Curves dialog box to display the Color Picker.

5. Enter 245 for the Red, Green, and Blue values in the color picker, and then click OK.

6. With the Curves dialog box still open, click the highlight area in the image with the white eyedropper tool. Look for the brightest highlight (sky) in the image. The value of the highlight pixels you clicked are set to 245 gray level, and the values of the pixels in the entire image are proportionately adjusted to accommodate this new highlight level. Any pixels with values greater than the pixels you clicked with the white eyedropper tool become specular whites (no gray value). Observe that the RGB values in the Info palette display the before and after values if you position your cursor over pixels in the image while the Curves dialog box is open.

7. Double-click the black eyedropper tool in the Curves dialog box and enter 10 for the Red, Green, and Blue values. Click OK.

8. With the Curves dialog box still open, locate the darkest area in the image and click the image with the black eyedropper tool. The darkest area on the image should have RGB values of 0 or close to 0. The values of the pixels in the entire image are proportionately adjusted to accommodate this

new shadow level. Any pixels with values lower than the pixels you clicked with the black eyedropper tool now have a gray level of 0. The Info palette displays the before and after values for the pixels in the image while the Curves dialog box is open. Click OK when you are happy with the black and white point settings. Remember, you can hold down the (Option)[Alt] key to change the Cancel button into the Reset button and reset the Curves dialog box.

Now that we have set the black and white points of the image, let's adjust the gamma (midtones) of the image. By the way, did you notice that the red color cast is not as prominent now that we've set the black and white points? Setting the white and black points to equivalent values adjusts the overall color balance of the image.

1. Choose Image➡Adjust➡Curves or type (Command-M)[Control-M] to display the Curves dialog box again. Make sure that none of the eyedroppers in the Curves dialog box are selected. If one is selected, click it again to deselect it. To identify the midtone values in your image, position the cursor over the image and click. Hold down the mouse button and note the floating circle in the Curves dialog box. The circle shows you where the values you are clicking are located on the curve (see Figure 8.8).

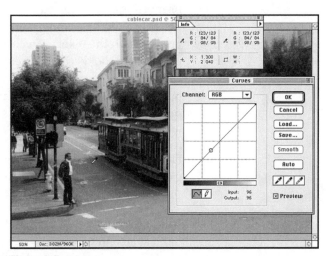

Figure 8.8

With the Curves dialog box open, click and drag the image to find the place on the curve for the area you are clicking.

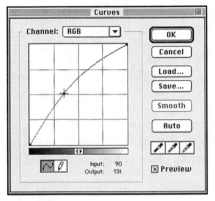

Figure 8.9

Click and drag the curve to adjust the midtone values.

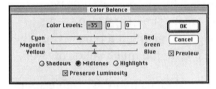

Figure 8.10

The Color Balance dialog box.

Figure 8.11

The input and output values are indicated in the Info palette separated by a slash.

2. To adjust the midtones of the image, click the center of the grid in the Curves dialog box and drag towards the lower-right corner to darken the midtones or toward the upper-right corner to brighten the midtones. Note the input and output values under the grid when you are dragging the midpoint of the curve. Drag the center point of the curve until the input value is 90 and the output value is 131 (see Figure 8.9). Click OK.

3. To adjust the red color cast, choose Image➡Adjust➡Color Balance to display the Color Balance dialog box (see Figure 8.10).

4. Click the Midtones radio button to adjust the color balance of the midtones, because that is where most of our color cast is. Check the Preserve Luminosity check box to preserve the gray balance of the image.

5. Drag the top triangle slider toward Cyan and away from Red until the Color Level reads -35. Before you click OK, move the cursor around on the image and observe the values in the Info palette. The values to the left of the slash are the original color values, and the values on the right of the slash are the new values (see Figure 8.11).

6. Save this image to your hard disk under a new name and open the original file to compare the two images. The corrected image is also on the CD-ROM that accompanies this book; open lessons/chap8/colrcst.psd to see the corrected image.

Adjusting CMYK

The CMYK values are percentages of printing inks. After an image has been converted to CMYK mode, it is best to work on the image in CMYK rather than converting it back to RGB because the colors will shift with each conversion. In this exercise, we are going to use the Curves dialog box to adjust the color of the image. The method for adjusting the image is the same as previously explained for RGB images, although with CMYK images we are dealing with color inks.

1. Open lessons/chap8/mktplace.psd on the CD-ROM that accompanies this book.

2. Choose Window➡Show Info to display the Info palette. Click the tiny triangle next to one of the eyedropper icons in the Info palette, and then choose CMYK Color or Actual Color to display the CMYK values in a section of the palette.

3. Select the Marquee in the toolbox so that the cursor is represented by a crosshair icon.

4. Move the cursor around the image and observe the CMYK values in the Info palette. Notice that there are a lot of areas with heavy ink coverage, especially in the shadow areas. The image also seems to have a little too much cyan and magenta, giving it a purple tint. The white areas in the image (highlights) have too much yellow as well.

Now that you have evaluated the image and identified the trouble spots to keep an eye on when making color adjustments, use the Curves dialog box to make adjustments to the color balance of the image.

1. Choose Image➡Adjust➡Curves, or type (Command-M)[Control-M], to display the Curves dialog box.

2. The grayscale of the image is represented in the CMYK channel of the Curves dialog box. The blend bar under the grid depicts the values of the grayscale. All of the gray values in the image are plotted along the linear curve displayed in the grid. These are the input values—the values currently in the image.

3. Make sure CMYK is selected in the Channel drop-down menu at the top of the Curves dialog box.

4. Double-click the white eyedropper in the Curves dialog box to display the Color Picker.

5. Enter 5, 3, 3, 0 for the CMYK values in the Color Picker to define the ink percentages that will be used for the whitest points in the image, and then click OK.

6. With the Curves dialog box still open, click the highlight area in the image with the white eyedropper tool. Look for the brightest highlight (top of tent in middle of image) in the image. The value of the highlight pixels you clicked are set to those you specified for the white point color. Any pixels with values greater than the pixels you clicked with the white eyedropper tool become specular whites (no color value). Observe that the CMYK values in the Info palette display the before and after values if you position your cursor over pixels in the image while the Curves dialog box is open.

7. Double-click the black eyedropper tool in the Curves dialog box and enter 65, 50, 50, 95 for the CMYK values respectively. These values give a black that has total ink density of 260%, which is safe for most printing projects. Total ink density is the maximum amount of ink that can safely be printed in one spot on the printing press. Ask your printer about total ink density for your printing projects. Click OK.

8. With the Curves dialog box still open, locate the darkest area in the image and click the image with the black eyedropper tool. The values of the pixels in the entire image are proportionately adjusted to accommodate this new shadow level. Any pixels with values lower than the pixels you clicked with the black eyedropper tool now have the value specified for the black eyedropper tool.

After you have defined the highlight and shadow values in the image you can adjust the midtone values between these two settings. When you adjust the midtone values in the Curves dialog box, all of the values in the image are adjusted to some degree along the arc of the curve. Color adjustments are made to the individual color channels using the Curves dialog box.

TIP

The Info palette displays the before and after values for the pixels in the image while the Curves dialog box is open. Drag the cursor around on your image to read the color values in the Info palette.

TIP

You can hold down the (Option)[Alt] key to change the Cancel button into the Reset button in the Curves dialog box to reset the original values.

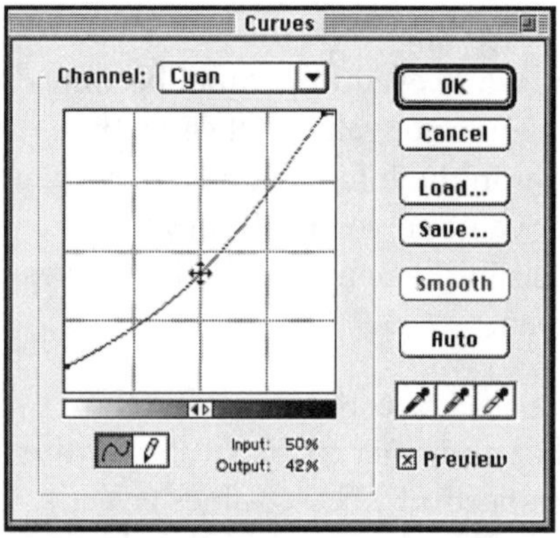

Figure 8.12

Adjust the color balance by adjust-
ing the curve for the individual
colors.

1. Click the center of the line in the grid of the Curves dialog box to adjust the midtone brightness of the image. Drag the center of the curve until the Input value under the grid reads 58% and the Output value reads 50%.

2. Select Cyan from the Channel drop-down menu to display the curve for Cyan. Click in the center of the curve and drag down and to the right until the Input value reads 50% and the Output value reads 42%. Basically, we are reducing the amount of cyan ink by 8% in the midtones and in lesser degrees along the rest of the curve (see Figure 8.12).

3. Select Magenta from the Channel drop-down menu. Make sure the eyedropper tools in the Curves dialog box are not selected. If one is selected, click it again to deselect it. Click the image with the Eyedropper tool in the areas that have a purple tinge to locate the spot on the curve to adjust.

4. Click the curve in the grid and drag the curve until the Input value reads 40% and the output value 35%. Click OK.

5. Open lessons/chap8/colrcst2.psd on the CD-ROM that accompanies this book to see the corrected image. You can also save your corrected image to your hard disk under a different name and compare it to the original image.

Using Replace Color

The Replace Color command enables us to select parts of the image based on color and adjust the hue, saturation, and brightness of the selected areas. In the following exercise, we are going change a summer scene into a fall scene using the Replace Color dialog box.

1. Open lessons/chap8/summer.psd on the CD-ROM that accompanies this book.

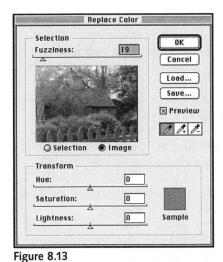

Figure 8.13

The Replace Color dialog box.

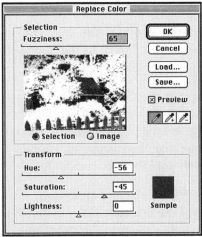

Figure 8.14

The selected areas are indicated in white in the preview window of the Replace Color dialog box.

2. Choose Image➡ Adjust➡ Replace Color to display the Replace Color dialog box (see Figure 8.13).

3. Check the Preview checkbox if it is not already checked.

4. Click the Selection radio button to display a selection mask in the image preview window.

5. Click a green area on the image with the Eyedropper tool. The mask reflects the selected colors.

6. Hold down the Shift key and drag in the green areas only of the image to enlarge the selection area.

7. Drag the Fuzziness triangle slider to the right to increase the selection or to the left to decrease the selection.

8. You do not have to select all of the green areas, but be sure the silhouette of the house and chimney are apparent in the preview window (see Figure 8.14).

9. Change the Hue value to -56 by dragging the triangle slider under Hue to the left.

10. Change the Saturation value to +45 by dragging the triangle slider under Saturation to the right.

11. Drag the Fuzziness slider until you are happy with the Fall foliage, and then click OK.

12. Open lessons/chap8/fall.psd to see the adjusted image.

Using Selective Color

The Selective Color dialog box enables us to make color adjustments in CMYK based on the primary colors in our image. In the following exercise, for example, we will make the grass greener by selecting the yellows and adding cyan. Cyan will be added only to the yellows of the image and nowhere else. The Selective Color dialog box also offers a way to make color adjustments to the black, white, and neutral values in the image.

1. Open lessons/chap8/rook.psd on the CD-ROM that accompanies this book.

2. Choose Image➡Adjust➡Selective Color to display the Selective Color dialog box (see Figure 8.15).

3. Check the Preview checkbox to see the changes to your image as you make them.

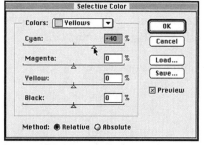

Figure 8.15

The Selective Color dialog box.

4. Select Relative as the Method at the bottom of the Selective Color dialog box. Relative makes changes to the ink percentages based on the value of the color. If we increase Cyan 20% in the Selective Color dialog box, for example, a 50% Cyan value in our image will increase by 10% (20% of 50%) resulting in 60% Cyan. When the Absolute method is used, the 20% Cyan is added to the 50% Cyan, resulting in 70% Cyan.

5. Choose Neutrals from the Colors drop-down menu at the top of the Selective Color dialog box. To decrease the amount of magenta in the neutral areas of the image, drag the triangle slider under Magenta to the left until the value reads -20%.

6. Choose Yellows from the Colors drop-down menu at the top of the Selective Color dialog box. Drag the Cyan triangle slider to the right until the value box reads +50% to increase the amount of cyan in the yellow areas of the image, making the grass greener.

7. Click OK to apply the changes. Save this file with a different name to your hard disk and open the original image to compare the before and after side by side. Open lessons/chap8/selectv.psd on the CD-ROM that accompanies this book to see the adjusted image.

Summary

In this chapter we examined the tools and techniques used to adjust color in Photoshop images. Using these techniques you can confidently color-correct your own scanned images. Like all of the functions of Photoshop, practice makes perfect, so don't be overwhelmed at what at first glance seems complicated and confusing. As stated in the introduction to this chapter, you should learn as much as you can about color theory, especially when it pertains to color prepress. Your printer can be an excellent resource to help you decide what settings to specify in dialog boxes for color settings and color conversion options. In the next chapter we will examine techniques to colorize both color and grayscale imagery using tools and menu commands specifically for this purpose.

Colorizing

Colorizing in Photoshop is relatively simple once the basic rules are understood. When colorizing an image in Photoshop, it is important to preserve the luminosity (gray scale) of the image, whether colorizing a grayscale, full-color RGB, or CMYK image. Each pixel in a Photoshop image has a hue, saturation, and brightness value that corresponds to the gray, RGB, LAB, and CMYK color values. The hue value determines what color the pixel is while the saturation value determines how saturated the color is. The brightness value is the value that determines the pixels gray level and is the value that creates the detail in the image. Therefore, we apply the hue and saturation component of the colors we use to colorize to the image, leaving the brightness value (luminosity) intact. In the following exercises, we are going to paint our changes on layers so that we can adjust them and correct overpainting with a layer mask. We will be working in the 100% view most of the time, and the Navigator palette will help us move around the image.

Colorizing a Grayscale Image

When colorizing a grayscale image, the object is to achieve a tinted effect, much like the color-tinted black and white photographs before color photography was available. In this section, we will use the Paintbrush and Airbrush tools at a low opacity setting to add hue and saturation values to a grayscale image.

1. Open lessons/chap9/sleeping.psd on the CD-ROM that accompanies this book.

2. Choose Window➥Show Layers to display the Layers palette.

3. Choose Image➥Mode➥RGB Color to convert the grayscale image to RGB color.

4. Choose Window➥Show Color to display the Color palette.

5. Choose Window➥Show Brushes to display the Brushes palette.

6. Choose Window➥Show Navigator to display the Navigator palette.

7. Double-click the Paintbrush tool in the toolbox to display the Paintbrush Options palette (see Figure 9.1). The Paintbrush Options are grouped with the Navigator palette. If you plan on using the Navigator palette, drag the tab out of the group to separate it from the Options palette.

Figure 9.1

The Paintbrush Options palette.

Let's start off by tinting the leopard spots on the pillows. We will leave the black areas alone and tint the light and medium gray areas orange.

1. Mix an orange color in the Color palette. I used a color that was 234 Red, 170 Green, and 46 Blue (5% Cyan, 38% Magenta, 89% Yellow).

TIP

To change the Opacity in the Paintbrush palette, type single-digit numbers on the numeric keypad to set the opacity in increments of 10. Type 2 for 20%, for example, and 0 for 100%. Type two digits on the numeric keypad to set a specific opacity, such as 23%. For an opacity less than 10%, precede the number by a zero; 04 to get 4% for example.

TIP

To switch to the next or previous brush in the Brushes palette, (Control-click)[Click with the right mouse button] the image to display the context menu.

Figure 9.2

Change the blending mode in the Layers palette to further adjust the color overlay.

2. Choose Color as the blending mode in the Paintbrush Options palette, and then set the Opacity for the Paintbrush to 20%.

3. Zoom in to the 100% view and position the image in the window so that you can see the pillows.

4. Choose a medium-sized brush with a soft edge from the Brushes palette.

5. Choose Layer➥New➥Layer and create a new layer called "leopard spots."

6. Paint over the medium gray areas with the Paintbrush set to a 20% opacity. Paint the lighter gray areas using a 10% opacity. Try not to stop and paint over the same area again because this will add another application of the foreground color to the existing color.

7. Slightly darken the orange color and paint the stuffed animal's light areas with a 15% Opacity setting in the Paintbrush Options palette.

8. Choose Multiply for a blending mode in the Layers palette to create a realistic colorization (see Figure 9.2).

9. Create a new layer named "shirt."

10. Mix a medium blue color in the Color palette for the foreground color. I used 0 Red, 101 Green, and 162 Blue (93% Cyan, 44% Magenta, 5% Yellow and 4% Black).

11. Paint the gray stripes, sleeve, and cuff of the boy's shirt with the Color blending mode set for the Paintbrush. Use a 20% opacity paintbrush.

12. After painting the shirt, set the blending mode for this layer to Overlay to preserve the highlight areas (see Figure 9.3).

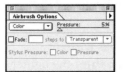

Figure 9.3

Use the Overlay blending mode to preserve the highlights in the image.

Figure 9.4

The Airbrush Options palette.

13. Create a new layer and name it "face."

14. Mix a light skin tone color in the Color palette (I used 7% Magenta, 7% Yellow, and 13% Black).

15. Double-click the Airbrush tool in the toolbox to display the Airbrush Options palette (see Figure 9.4). Choose Color as the blending mode for the airbrush and set the Pressure to 5%.

16. Select a relatively large brush in the Brushes palette, and then paint over the entire face area.

17. Set the blending mode for the face layer to Multiply, and then adjust the opacity slightly if the color is too dark.

18. Add a little magenta or red to the foreground color and paint the lips with a small soft brush. Do this on the face layer to view the multiply effect while painting.

19. Use the techniques outlined in the preceding steps to complete the image. Choose complimentary colors for the afghan and couch.

Open lessons/chap9/complete.psd on the CD-ROM that accompanies this book to see the completed colorized image.

Colorizing Selections

To colorize an image that is already in color, we can paint with the hue of a color, the saturation of a color, or a combination of both. In this exercise, we will take a rather dark monotone-looking color image and add some color to it using a combination of layers and adjustment layers.

1. Open lessons/chap9/whale.psd on the CD-ROM that accompanies this book.

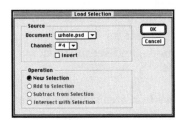

Figure 9.5

The Load Selection dialog box.

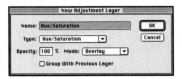

Figure 9.6

The New Adjustment Layer dialog box.

Figure 9.7

The Hue/Saturation Layer dialog box.

2. Choose Window➡Show Layers to display the Layers palette. We will put our adjustments on layers so that we can remove them and start again, if necessary.

3. Choose Select➡Load Selection to display the Load Selection dialog box (see Figure 9.5).

4. Select #4 from the Channel drop-down menu, and then click OK.

5. Choose Layer➡New➡Adjustment Layer to display the New Adjustment Layer dialog box (see Figure 9.6).

6. Select Hue/Saturation from the Type drop-down menu.

7. Choose Overlay from the Mode drop-down menu, and then click OK to display the Hue/Saturation Layer dialog box (see Figure 9.7).

8. Check the Colorize check box in the Hue/Saturation Layer dialog box. Set the Hue to –157, the Saturation to 13, and the Lightness to 0. Click OK to create the adjustment layer. The adjustment layer automatically has a mask that protects the whale and the sky from changes because a selection was active when we created the adjustment layer.

9. Drag the Opacity slider in the Layers palette to the left to set the Opacity for the Hue/Saturation layer to 75%.

10. Choose Layer➡New➡Layer to create a new layer and name it "sky."

11. Set the foreground color to 100% Cyan and the background color to 78% Magenta, 76% Yellow.

12. Choose Select➡Load Selection to display the Load Selection dialog box, and then choose #5 from the Channel drop-down menu.

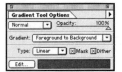

Figure 9.8

The Gradient Tool Options palette.

13. Double-click the Gradient tool in the toolbox to display the Gradient Tool Options palette (see Figure 9.8).

14. Choose Foreground to Background from the Gradient drop-down menu in the Gradient Tool Options palette. Select Linear for Type, select Normal for blending mode, and set the Opacity to 100%.

15. Drag a blend in the selection area starting at the top of the selection area and ending at the bottom to create a blend from blue to red (see Figure 9.9).

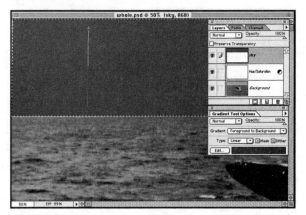

Figure 9.9

Drag with the Gradient tool to create a linear blend.

16. Choose Overlay from the blending mode drop-down menu in the Layers palette for the sky layer. Set the Opacity for the sky layer to 60%.

17. Save this image to the hard disk and compare it to the original image.

 Open lessons/chap9/whale2.psd on the CD-ROM that accompanies this book to see the completed image.

Colorizing with Hue

To make subtle color changes to an image we can adjust the hue component of the color, which is the color component. When we paint with the hue blending mode, the saturation and brightness levels of the pixels do not change.

1. Open lessons/chap9/sunset.psd on the CD-ROM that accompanies this book.

2. Choose Window➡Show Brushes to display the Brushes palette.

3. Choose Window➡Show Color to display the Color palette. Set the Color palette slider to CMYK by choosing CMYK Sliders from the palette menu.

4. Double-click the Paintbrush tool in the toolbox to display the Paintbrush Options palette (see Figure 9.10).

5. Set the blending mode for the Paintbrush tool to Hue, and the Opacity to 50%.

6. Select the 65 pixel brush from the Brushes palette (see Figure 9.11).

7. Set the foreground color to 100% Magenta.

8. Paint over the water starting at the horizon where the sun is and ending where the water starts to get darker in the foreground of the image. The reflection on the water will have a pink hue.

9. Set the foreground color to 100% Cyan, 50% Magenta, a medium Blue.

10. Set the Opacity for the Paintbrush tool to 70% in the Paintbrush Options palette.

Figure 9.10

The Paintbrush Options palette.

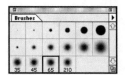

Figure 9.11

The 65 pixel brush selected in the Brushes palette.

11. Paint the sky and the tops of the trees with the Paintbrush tool. Paint the water in the foreground of the image with the blue color as well.

12. Save the file to your hard disk and compare it to the original file.

 Open lessons/chap9/sunset2.psd on the CD-ROM that accompanies this book to see the completed image.

Colorizing a Posterized Image

In this section, we are going to take a grayscale image and posterize it, reducing the number of grays used to create the image from 256 to just 6 (see Figure 9.12). We will create separate layers for each of the six gray levels, and then colorize the parts to create a special effect. The techniques you will learn in this section are useful to create an illustrated graphic from a photograph. We can also apply this same technique to color images to break a color image down into a limited number of colors. Screen printers often use this method to create an image with 10 or more spot colors, because printing CMYK separations is not often an option in screen printing.

Figure 9.12

The grayscale image is first posterized and then colorized.

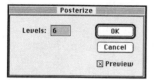

Figure 9.13

The Posterize dialog box.

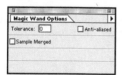

Figure 9.14

The Magic Wand Options palette.

Figure 9.15

Zoom in closer to see the individual gray levels.

1. Open lessons/chap9/painter.psd on the CD-ROM that accompanies this book.

2. Choose Image➡Adjust➡Posterize to display the Posterize dialog box (see Figure 9.13).

3. Type 6 into the Levels box to reduce the number of grays in our image from 256 (standard grayscale) to 6.

4. Double-click the Magic Wand tool in the toolbox to display the Magic Wand Options palette (see Figure 9.14).

5. Set the Tolerance to 0 and be sure that Anti-aliased is turned off. We are setting the tolerance to 0 because we want to limit the Magic Wand tool's selection to one gray level. We turn Anti-aliased off because it will expand the selection area to include near gray levels if left on, and we want to select only a single gray level at a time.

6. Choose Window➡Show Layers to display the Layers palette.

7. Find the darkest (blackest) area on the image and click it with the Magic Wand tool. If necessary, zoom in to see the gray level breakdown (see Figure 9.15).

Eyedropper Sample Size

The Eyedropper Options palette contains a setting that controls the area selected when clicking the image. Double-click the Eyedropper tool in the toolbox and set the Sample Size to Point Sample for this exercise. When the Sample Size is set to Point Sample, clicking the image will sample only the data from the single pixel you click. In the case of the Eyedropper tool, the color of a single pixel is sampled to change the foreground color. This setting also controls how other tools work, such as the Magic Wand and Paintbucket. We are setting this option in the Eyedropper Options palette to control how the Magic Wand selects pixel data. If we leave the sample size set to 3×3 average, when we zoom in close and click a pixel that has surrounding pixels with different gray values, the Magic Wand creates a selection containing pixels that are the average color of the pixels within a 3×3 pixel area around the point clicked. We want to be able to select one gray level at a time with the Magic Wand tool; setting this value to Point Sample ensures this.

8. Choose Select➡Similar to select all of the other pixels in the image with the same values as those selected with the Magic Wand tool.

9. Create a new layer by clicking the New Layer icon at the bottom of the Layers palette. Name this layer Gray 1.

10. Be sure the Gray 1 layer is selected in the Layers palette.

11. Type D to set the foreground and background colors to the default black and white, respectively.

12. Press (Option-Delete)[Alt-Backspace] to fill the selected area with the foreground color (black). The Gray 1 layer now contains a solid black area that is representative of the darkest gray in the image (see Figure 9.16).

Figure 9.16

Create layers to hold each of the 6 gray levels in the image.

13. Select the Background layer in the Layers palette.

14. Click the next-darkest level in the image with the Magic Wand tool, and then choose Select➡ Similar to select all of the pixels in the image with that gray level.

15. Create a new layer by clicking the New Layer icon at the bottom of the Layers palette. Name this layer Gray 2.

16. Be sure the Gray 2 layer is selected in the Layers palette.

17. Press (Option-Delete)[Alt-Backspace] to fill the selected area with the foreground color (black).

Repeat steps 12–16 to create separate layers for each of the six gray levels (see Figure 9.17). Remember to select the Background layer before using the Magic Wand each time. Remember to choose Select➡ Similar to select similar pixels before making the new layers.

Now that we have isolated each of the gray levels of the image onto their own layers, we can convert this grayscale file into any of the available color modes and change the color of the contents of each layer.

1. Select the Background layer in the Layers palette and choose Select➡All to select the entire image area on the background layer.

2. Press Delete to fill the selection with the background color (white). We can also opt to keep the background as is and simply make it invisible by clicking the Eye icon next to the layer name in the Layers palette.

3. Convert the grayscale image to a color mode, such as RGB or CMYK. Note that when we convert from grayscale to RGB or CMYK, we are asked if we want to flatten the image. Click the Don't Flatten button to preserve the layers we

TIP

To name the layer, (Option-click)[Alt-click] the New Layer icon at the bottom of the Layers palette to display the New Layer dialog box.

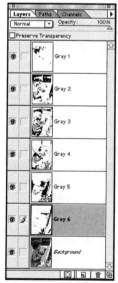

Figure 9.17

We should have six new layers, plus the Background layer.

created in the previous steps. This is also a good time to save the file in Photoshop format so that we don't have to re-create all the layers due to a crash or mistake.

4. Choose the Gray 1 layer and check the Preserve Transparency check box at the top of the Layers palette.

5. Choose a new foreground color (your choice).

6. Make sure the Gray 1 layer is selected and press (Option-Delete)[Alt-Backspace] to fill the non-transparent areas with the foreground color.

7. Perform steps 4–6 for each of the six new layers. Don't forget to turn on Preserve Transparency for the layer before filling. Experiment with the Opacity settings and blending modes in the Layers palette.

8. Be sure to save the file in Photoshop format so that you can make changes in the future. Flatten the image when you have a version you want to use by choosing Flatten Image from the Layers palette menu.

 Open lessons/chap9/painter2.psd on the CD-ROM that accompanies this book to see the completed image. Now that you have all these layers that have been colorized individually, you can flatten the image and convert the image to CMYK mode to print color separated films for offset printing.

Summary

In this chapter you learned some of the basic techniques to colorize grayscale and color images, as well as a special effect technique to create a color illustrated version of a grayscale photograph. In the following chapter we will examine techniques to work with Photoshop's layers.

Working in Layers

In previous versions of Photoshop, you could work with Photoshop and almost never use layers. With the release of Photoshop 4, however, this is no longer the case. Now, when you cut and paste or create text, for example, a new layer is automatically created. In order to use Photoshop effectively and productively, you must become familiar with layers. In this chapter you explore the basic functions of layers as you create an advertisement that requires you to composite images and create some special effects (see Figure 10.1). Chapter 1, "Photoshop Basics," explains the Layers palette.

Compositing Imagery

Creating a Reflection on a Layer

Screening Back an Image Area

Creating Text on Layers

Figure 10.1

The completed advertisement.

Compositing Imagery

In this section, you open two images and composite them using layers. The background image is a lake scene on which you composite a hand holding a bottle of beer. The objective here is to make the hand look like it's coming out of the water. After you achieve this, you create a reflection of the hand holding the bottle.

1. Open lessons/chap10/water.psd and lessons/chap10/beer.psd on the CD-ROM that accompanies this book.

2. Choose Window➧Show Layers to display the Layers palette.

3. Select the Move tool (or type the letter V) and drag the image in beer.psd onto the water.psd image. This automatically creates a new layer named Layer 1 (see Figure 10.2).

Figure 10.2

Drag beer.psd onto water.psd with the Move tool.

4. Double-click Layer 1 in the Layers palette and rename this layer "Beer."

5. The image on the Beer layer is too large, so you must scale it down. Choose Layer➥Transform➥Scale to scale the image to a size that suits your needs (refer to Figure 10.1). Remember to hold down the Shift key while you drag the corners to preserve the aspect ratio of the image. You can click and drag inside the selected area to move the image while scaling. Double-click inside the selected area when you are satisfied with the scaling.

6. Choose Layer➥Transform➥Rotate and rotate the image clockwise until the bottle appears straight. Click and drag along the edges of the selection rectangle. Double-click inside the selected area to make the change permanent.

7. Now would be a good time to save the working file in Photoshop format. Choose File➥Save and save the file to your hard disk.

Now that you have scaled and rotated the bottle, you use a layer mask to eliminate the parts of the image you don't need. By painting on the layer mask with black, you mask out the areas of the Beer layer to silhouette the image. The new layer mask is automatically selected when it is created, so any changes you make affect the mask and not the image. Note that the mask icon is displayed to the left of the layer thumbnail, indicating that you are working on the layer mask. A paintbrush icon appears in the same place when you are working on the actual layer image. You can switch back and forth between the layer and layer mask by clicking the thumbnails in the Layers palette. (Option-Click)[Alt-Click] the layer mask thumbnail in the Layers palette to toggle the view to display the layer mask only.

1. Make sure the Beer layer is selected in the Layers palette and click the Layer Mask icon at the bottom of the Layers palette to create a layer mask for this layer. The layer mask thumbnail appears to the right of the layer thumbnail (see Figure 10.3).

2. Double-click the Paintbrush tool to display the Paintbrush Options palette. Make sure the blending mode is set to Normal and the Opacity to 100%. Be sure that none of the checkboxes in the Paintbrush Options palette are selected.

3. Choose Window➥Show Brushes to display the Brushes palette and choose the 45-pixel brush with a soft edge to begin.

4. Make sure the layer mask for the Beer layer is selected in the Layers palette and the foreground color is set to black.

5. Paint the areas you want to mask on the Beer layer. Avoid getting too close to the part you want to keep because you'll use a smaller brush to fine tune the mask later (see Figure 10.4). Notice that as you paint the layer mask, the layer mask thumbnail displays the mask.

6. Hold down (Command-Spacebar)[Control-Spacebar] to access the Zoom tool and drag a marquee around the image to zoom closer so you can fine-tune the mask. You may also find it helpful to turn off the Background layer. Click the Eye icon to the left of the Background layer to hide the background image.

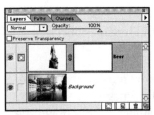

Figure 10.3

The scaled and rotated Beer layer with the layer mask selected in the Layers palette.

Note

To quickly set the foreground color to black, type the letter D to set the default colors followed by the letter X to swap the colors so black is the foreground color.

Figure 10.4

Paint with black on the layer mask to mask out parts of the image.

7. Select a smaller soft brush from the Brushes palette and paint with black on the layer mask to fine tune the mask (see Figure 10.5). If you make a mistake and erase some of the image you want to keep, type the letter X to change the foreground color to white and paint over the missing image area. Painting with white removes the mask.

Figure 10.5

Complete the silhouette using a smaller soft brush to paint the layer mask.

Now that you have silhouetted the hand and bottle, the next step is to create the ripple effect. Make sure the Beer layer is positioned where you want it to be. Dragging with the Move tool moves the layer mask along with the layer.

1. Click the Background layer in the Layers palette to activate it. Use the elliptical Marquee tool to create an oval that radiates out from the wrist on the background layer (see Figure 10.6).

Figure 10.6

Select the water around the wrist with the elliptical Marquee tool.

2. Choose Filter➡ Distort➡ Ocean Ripple to display the Ocean Ripple dialog box. Set the Ripple Size to 15 and the Ripple Magnitude to 20, then click OK.

3. Type (Command-J)[Control-J] to create a new layer of the selected area of the water. Click the layer name and drag this new layer to the top of the Layers palette so it's above the Beer layer. Name this new layer "Highlight" by double-clicking the layer name in the Layers palette.

4. Choose Color Dodge as the blending mode for this layer and set the Opacity for the layer to 65%.

5. Create a layer mask for the Highlight layer by clicking the Mask icon at the bottom of the Layers palette.

6. Set the foreground color to black and paint the mask layer with the Paintbrush tool. Mask out the areas that cover the hand and some of the water so the remaining image covers only the edges around the wrist to create a highlight effect on the water (see Figure 10.7).

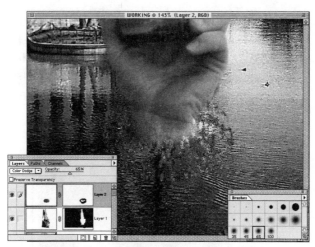

Figure 10.7

Mask out everything but the ripple area close to the wrist.

7. Choose Filter➡Blur➡Motion Blur to display the Motion Blur dialog box and set the Angle to 90° and the Distance to 4 pixels, then click OK.

8. Save what you have done so far.

Creating a Reflection on a Layer

The next step in the beer advertisement is to create the reflection of the hand holding the bottle on the water. Open the file you created in the preceding steps to continue with this exercise. If you did not perform the preceding steps open lessons/chap10/work1.psd on the CD-ROM that accompanies this book.

1. Select the Beer layer in the Layers palette.

2. Choose Layer➡Remove Layer Mask. When the dialog box appears asking you whether you want to apply the mask to the layer before removing, click the Apply button. The layer mask is permanently applied to the Beer layer.

3. Choose Layer➡Duplicate Layer to display the Duplicate Layer dialog box and name the duplicate layer "Reflection."

4. The duplicated layer is inserted in the Layers palette above the Beer layer and directly on top of it in the image window. Choose Layer➡Transform➡Flip Horizontal to reverse the image.

5. Choose Layer➡Transform➡Rotate and rotate the image until it is upside down and angled to the left. Use the Move tool to position the rotated image beneath the original image (see Figure 10.8).

Figure 10.8

Rotate and position the duplicate layer.

6. Click the blending mode drop-down menu in the Layers palette and set the blending mode for the Reflection layer to Hard Light.

7. Set the opacity for the Reflection layer to 60% by dragging the triangle slider in the upper-right corner of the Layers palette or by typing 6 on the numeric keypad.

8. Add a layer mask to the Reflection layer by clicking the Mask icon at the bottom of the Layers palette.

9. Use the Paintbrush tool with a large soft brush to mask out the parts of the image that are overlapping with the underlying layers (see Figure 10.9).

Figure 10.9

Create a layer mask and mask out the overlapping image parts.

10. Save the file and read on to add the other components of this exercise.

Screening Back an Image Area

Many times it is necessary to screen a portion of an image to facilitate placing text over a particularly dark area. By screening a particular area of the image we will reduce the opacity (a rectangular shape in this case) to facilitate placing text that is readable. Usually, the image area is screened in Photoshop and the text added in a page layout application such as QuarkXPress or PageMaker. Small text reproduces best when it is created by the printer fonts on an imagesetting device rather than as a bitmap image in Photoshop. The following steps explain how to screen back a part of the image using layers with the assumption that the text will be added at a later time in some layout application.

1. If it isn't already open, open the file you created following the preceding steps in this chapter. If you did not perform the preceding steps, open lessons/chap10/work2.psd on the CD-ROM that accompanies this book.

2. You are going to screen back a rectangular area of the image that measures 1.75 inches wide and 1.5 inches tall. This rectangle will be positioned 0.25 inches from the top and left side of the image. Select the Background layer in the Layers palette.

3. Create a new layer by clicking the New Layer icon at the bottom of the Layers palette or choose Layer➥New➥Layer and name the new layer "Screen."

4. If the rulers are not currently displayed, type (Command-R) [Control-R] to turn them on. Choose View➥Show Guides and View ➥Snap to Guides to turn on the guides and make your selections snap to the guides.

5. Choose Window➥Show Info to display the Info palette. Use the Info palette to help guide you in placing guide lines precisely. Note that you may have to enlarge the image somewhat to precisely place the guides.

6. Double-click the upper-left corner of the image window where the two rulers meet to set the zero point (0,0 coordinates) to the upper-left corner.

7. Click the horizontal ruler and drag down a guide to 0.25 inches. Drag a second guide down to 1.75 inches.

8. Click the vertical ruler and drag across a guide to 0.25 inches. Drag a second guide across to 2 inches (1.75 inches + 0.25 inches).

9. Choose the rectangular Marquee in the Toolbox or type the letter M and drag a marquee selection to the dimensions of the guides (see Figure 10.10).

10. Set the foreground color to white, then press (Option-Delete)[Alt-Delete] to fill the selected area with white.

11. Type (Command-D)[Control-D] to deselect. Type (Command-;) [Control-;] to hide the guides.

12. Set the Opacity for the Screen layer to 75% by dragging the triangle slider in the upper-right corner of the Layers palette or by typing 75 on the numeric keypad.

13. If you want to add the text, open lessons/chap10/text.psd on the CD-ROM that accompanies this book and drag the text onto the composite working file with the Move tool. Even if the text is going to be set in the page layout application, placing some text to see whether the screened area is light enough to create contrast for the text is often helpful. You can leave off the text layer when saving the final version of the file.

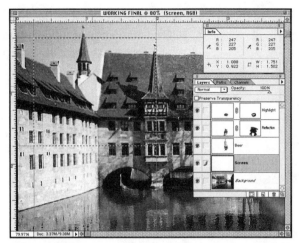

Figure 10.10

Drag a marquee selection to the correct dimensions using the guides.

Creating Text on Layers

In previous versions of Photoshop, the Text tool created text as a floating selection that would be applied to the underlying layer after the text was deselected. In Photoshop 4, the Text tool automatically creates the text on a new layer. You may not have the proper font for the next exercise, but perform the steps using a sans serif font you have, such as Helvetica or Futura.

1. If it isn't already open, open the file you created following the preceding steps in this chapter. If you did not perform the preceding steps, open lessons/chap10/work3.psd on the CD-ROM that accompanies this book.

2. Click the foreground color swatch in the Toolbox to set the foreground color to red. When the Photoshop Color Picker appears, click the Custom button and choose Pantone Red 032 CV from the Pantone Coated color book (see Figure 10.11). You are choosing a foreground color here because text appears in the foreground color.

3. After you create the text, the new text layer will be inserted above the currently selected layer, so be sure the very top layer is selected in the Layers palette.

Figure 10.11

The Custom Colors dialog box.

TIP

You can nudge the image on a layer by selecting the Move tool and pressing the arrow keys on the keyboard.

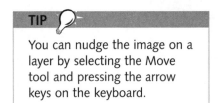

Figure 10.12

The Link icon indicates that the selected layer is linked to the layer with the Link icon.

4. Select the Type tool in the Toolbox or type the letter T and click at the location in the image where you want the text to start (you can always move it later) to display the Type Tool dialog box.

5. Choose a bold sans serif font if you do not have Futura Bold and set the size to 60 points. Leave Anti-Aliased checked so your text will blend smoothly with the background. Click the text box and type the capital letter C. Click OK.

6. Click the image again with the Type tool and set the remainder of the text in 40 point type. Note the lower case "i" in "ARDiNAL."

7. Use the Move tool to position the text on the image.

8. To get the word "CARDiNAL" all on one layer be sure the layer that contains one of the parts is selected, then click the space to the left of the layer thumbnail on the layer that contains the other part. The Link icon is displayed to indicate that the layer is linked to the selected layer (see Figure 10.12).

9. Choose Layer➡Merge Linked or type (Command-E)[Control-E] to merge the two layers into one.

10. Create the script text "at the end of the day . . ." the same way you created the word "CARDiNAL." I used 36-point New Berolina MT, a monotype font, but you can use any typeface you want. Position the text correctly on the image in relation to the word Cardinal.

Now that you have the text created, we will create an embossed effect after combining the two text layers into one layer. We will combine the Emboss filter effect with a layer blending mode to achieve the desired embossed text effect.

1. Link the layer with the words "at the end of the day" to the layer with "CARDiNAL" on it and type (Command-E)[Control-E] to merge the linked layers together into one. All the red text should now be on the same layer. Name the layer with the red type on it "Cardinal."

2. Choose Layer➡Duplicate Layer and name the duplicate layer "Emboss."

3. Set the foreground color to white. Remember, you can type D for default colors followed by X to swap the foreground and background colors.

4. Make sure the Emboss layer is selected, then type (Shift-Option-Delete)[Shift-Alt-Backspace] to change the text color to white.

5. Choose Filter➡Stylize➡Emboss to display the Emboss dialog box (see Figure 10.13).

6. Set the Angle to 135°, the Height to 4 pixels, and the Amount to 80%, then click OK.

7. Drag the Emboss layer underneath the Cardinal layer.

8. Select the Cardinal layer and set the blending mode to Overlay to composite the red type with the embossed layer.

9. Select the Crop tool in the Toolbox or type the letter C. Crop this image so the right side has about ⅛ inch of image to the right of the bottle. Double-click inside the crop rectangle to make the cropping happen.

10. Save the file in Photoshop format to preserve the layers. Choose File➡Save a Copy to save a flattened version of the file in another format, such as TIFF or EPS. Open lessons/chap10/final.psd on the CD-ROM that accompanies this book to view the completed file.

Figure 10.13

The Emboss dialog box.

Summary

In this chapter we created a composite image using layers and layer masks. Working in layers gives you the freedom to experiment and create multiple renditions without changing the original images. We learned how the Blending modes can be used to create powerful special effects like reflections and stylized text on layers. Once you are comfortable working in layers, there is no limit to the imagery you can create. In the next chapter we will examine how to effectively use adjustment layers.

Using Adjustment Layers

Adjustment layers are layers that enable us to make non-destructive changes to our images because the adjustments live on their own layers and can be applied or discarded at will. Using adjustment layers, we can make color adjustments with curves, levels, color balance, hue and saturation, and selective color. We can also adjust brightness and contrast, as well as apply invert, threshold, and posterize effects.

Adjustment layers are actually mask layers, much like a layer mask where we can paint a mask to limit the effect of the adjustment layer—they don't contain pixels that are a part of the image, only adjustments to the existing pixels in the image. Adjustment layers act just like regular layers in every other respect, enabling us to apply blending modes and opacity settings to the layers. In this chapter, we look at a few adjustment layers.

Creating an Adjustment Layer

To create adjustment layers, we must first select the type of adjustment layer, and then make the adjustment on the layer. In the following exercise, we will take an image and apply the Threshold adjustment layer (see Figure 11.1).

Figure 11.1

The original image is a low key color image (left). Using the blending modes, we will create a silhouette of the image retaining some of the detail of the image (right).

1. Open lessons/chap11/park.psd on the CD-ROM that accompanies this book.

2. Choose Window➡Show Layers to display the Layers palette.

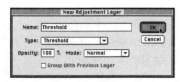

Figure 11.2

The New Adjustment Layer dialog box.

3. Choose Layer➡New➡Adjustment Layer from the menu bar, or select New Adjustment Layer from the Layers palette menu, to display the New Adjustment Layer dialog box (see Figure 11.2).

4. Choose Threshold from the Type drop-down menu in the New Adjustment Layer dialog box, and then click OK to display the Threshold dialog box (see Figure 11.3).

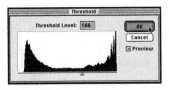

Figure 11.3

The Threshold dialog box.

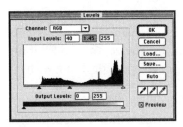

Figure 11.4

Drag the triangle sliders under the histogram to adjust the levels of the image.

5. Drag the triangle slider under the histogram to the right until the Threshold Level reads 166, and then click OK. The Threshold adjustment layer is inserted into the Layers palette above the background image.

6. Choose Multiply from the Blending Modes drop-down menu in the upper-left corner of the Layers palette.

7. Open lessons/chap11/type.psd on the CD-ROM that accompanies this book. Use the Move tool to drag the text onto the park.psd image.

8. Open lessons/chap11/condos.psd on the CD-ROM that accompanies this book. Use the Move tool to drag the condos.psd image onto the park.psd image.

9. Hold down the (Command)[Control] key and click the condos layer in the Layers palette to load the transparency mask for that layer. When you load a layer's transparency mask, a selection is made of the non-transparent pixels on the layer.

10. Choose New Adjustment Layer from the Layers palette menu to display the New Adjustment Layer dialog box, and then select Levels from the Type drop-down menu. Click OK to display the Levels dialog box.

11. Drag the left-most triangle slider under the histogram to the right until the triangle slider is underneath the first black area in the histogram.

12. Drag the center triangle slider under the histogram to the left until the gamma value in the middle Input Levels value box reads 1.45 (see Figure 11.4).

Figure 11.5

The Levels adjustment layer contains a mask in the shape of the picture of the condos and is applied only to the underlying images in the mask shape.

13. Click OK to add the Levels adjustment layer to the Layers palette. The thumbnail preview for the Levels layer contains a mask in the shape of the selection made when we created the adjustment layer. The Levels adjustments apply only to the condos because the mask protects the rest of the underlying images (see Figure 11.5).

To view the finished piece, open lessons/ chap11/condoad.psd on the CD-ROM that accompanies this book.

Editing the Adjustment Layer Mask

As stated in the beginning of this chapter, adjustment layers are mask layers that apply the adjustment specified based on the mask of the layer. When we first create an adjustment layer, the mask is open and the adjustment applies to all of the underlying layers. When you paint on the adjustment layer with black or percentages of black, the painted areas are masked out and the adjustment applies only the non-masked areas of the underlying images. Painting or filling selections with percentages of black on the adjustment layer applies an equivalent opacity to the mask. For example, if you paint on the adjustment layer with 30% black, the adjustment will be applied at a 30% opacity or level of intensity. You can use any of the painting tools or make a selection and fill it to affect the adjustment layer. Painting or filling with 100% black will entirely mask the effect of the ajdustment layer. Painting or filling with 0% black (white) will apply the adjustment at full intensity. If you have an area of the image selected when you create an adjustment layer, a mask is automatically created for the adjustment layer to isolate the selection area.

1. Open lessons/chap11/house.psd on the CD-ROM that accompanies this book.

2. Choose Window➡Show Layers to display the Layers palette.

3. Choose Select➡Load Selection to display the Load Selection dialog box, and then choose #5 from the Channel drop-down menu. Click OK to load the selection.

4. Choose Layer➡New➡Adjustment Layer in the menu bar, or choose New Adjustment Layer from the Layers palette menu, to display the New Adjustment Layer dialog box.

5. Choose Hue/Saturation from the Type drop-down menu, and then click OK to display the Hue/Saturation dialog box.

6. Drag the Hue, Saturation, and Lightness triangle sliders to choose a new color for the house, and then click OK. Because a selection was active when we created the adjustment layer, the adjustment changed the house only—the rest of the image was masked out. The selection is used as the adjustment layer's mask indicated in the adjustment layer thumbnail preview.

7. To change the color of the house again, double-click the words Hue/Saturation of the Adjustment Layer in the Layers palette.

8. To change the name of the layer, double-click the thumbnail icon.

9. Try some of the blending modes on the Hue/Saturation adjustment layer to further adjust the color of the house.

Open lessons/chap11/house2.psd on the CD-ROM that accompanies this book to see the image with the adjustment layer applied.

Using Filters with Adjustment Layers

Some filters can be used on the adjustment layers to achieve special effects. If we fill the adjustment layer with a percentage of black and apply filters to the solid gray area, we can create opacity filters for the adjustment.

1. Open lessons/chap11/blue.psd on the CD-ROM that accompanies this book.

2. Choose Window➡Show Layers to display the Layers palette.

3. Choose Layer➡New➡Adjustment Layer to display the New Adjustment Layer dialog box.

4. Choose Hue/Saturation from the Type drop-down menu in the New Adjustment Layer dialog box, and then click OK to display the Hue/Saturation dialog box.

5. Check the Colorize checkbox in the lower-right corner of the Hue/Saturation dialog box. The Hue and Lightness values are automatically set to 0 and the Saturation value to 180. Drag the triangle slider under Hue to change the hue to 180. Click OK to create the adjustment layer.

6. Be sure the Hue/Saturation adjustment layer is selected in the Layers palette. Choose Filter➡Render➡Clouds.

In these next steps we will open a file that contains a silhouette of some sky divers and add it to the background we created in the previous steps. Using a combination of adjustment layers and filters we will emboss the image and modify the color of the background somewhat.

1. Open lessons/chap11/divers.psd on the CD-ROM that accompanies this book.

2. Select the Move tool in the toolbox and drag the divers onto the blue clouds. Position the image so that the bottom, left, and right bleed off the image area (see Figure 11.6).

Figure 11.6

Position the sky divers at the bottom of the blue.psd file.

3. Hold down the (Command)[Control] key and click the divers layer in the Layers palette to load that layer's transparency mask as a selection.

4. Choose New Adjustment Layer from the Layers palette menu to display the New Adjustment Layer dialog box.

5. Select Invert from the Type drop-down menu in the New Adjustment Layer dialog box, and then click OK. The Invert adjustment layer contains a mask in the shape of the divers and so inverts only the divers layer (see Figure 11.7).

Figure 11.7

The Invert adjustment layer affects only the shapes on the divers layer.

6. Choose Filter➡Stylize➡Emboss to display the Emboss dialog box (see Figure 11.8).

7. Set the Angle to 135°, the Height to 9 pixels, and the Amount to 166%. Click OK to apply the Emboss filter to the Invert adjustment layer.

8. Choose Multiply from the blending modes drop-down menu in the upper-left corner of the Layers palette to multiply the Invert adjustment layer

Figure 11.8

The Emboss dialog box.

with the underlying layers (see Figure 11.9). The multiply blending mode creates darker colors overall, so the background layer will change color as well as the divers layer. See Chapter 7, "Specifying Color," for more information on the Multiply Blending Mode.

Figure 11.9

The Emboss effect of the adjustment layer is multiplied with the divers layer.

In the following steps we will open another file that contains the text "SKY DIVING" and add this text as a new layer to our image. We will then colorize and emboss the text by creating a clipping group with the text layer. When we create a clipping group, the bottommost layer of the clipping group traps the effects of the layers above it.

1. Open lessons/chap11/text.psd on the CD-ROM that accompanies this book.

2. Drag the text onto the blue.psd file using the Move tool.

3. Choose Layer➦New➦Adjustment Layer, or (Command-click)[Control-click] the New Layer icon at the bottom of the Layers palette, to display the New Adjustment Layer dialog box.

4. Choose Hue/Saturation from the Type drop-down menu in the New Adjustment Layer dialog box, and then click OK to display the Hue/Saturation dialog box.

5. Click the Colorize checkbox and set the Hue to 180 and the Saturation to 100. Click OK to create the adjustment layer.

6. Hold down the (Option)[Alt] key and point at the dividing line between the text layer and the Hue/Saturation layer. When the cursor changes to two overlapping circles, click the dividing line (see Figure 11.10).

   The Hue/Saturation layer is now clipped by the non-transparent objects on the text layer. In other words, the Hue/Saturation layer is applied only to the shape of the words "SKY DIVING."

7. Select the Hue/Saturation adjustment layer you just created above the text in the Layers palette.

8. (Command-Click)[Control-Click] the text layer in the Layers palette to load the transparency mask of the text layer creating a selection in the shape of the words "SKY DIVING."

9. Select Layer➡New➡Adjustment Layer to display the New Adjustment Layer dialog box.

10. Select Brightness/Contrast from the Type drop-down menu in the New Adjustment Layer dialog box to display the Brightness/Contrast Layer dialog box (see Figure 11.11).

11. Set the Brightness to –51 and the Contrast to –100. Click OK to create this new adjustment layer above the Hue/Saturation adjustment layer.

12. Choose Filter➡Stylize➡Emboss to display the Emboss dialog box. Set the Angle to 135°, the Height to 9 pixels, and the Amount to 166%. Click OK to emboss the Brightness/Contrast adjustment layer.

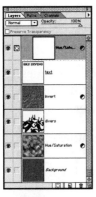

Figure 11.10

(Option-click)[Alt-click] the dividing line between two layers to create a clipping group.

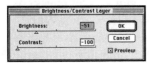

Figure 11.11

The Brightness/Contrast Layer dialog box.

In these final steps, we will apply one of the new filters in Photoshop 4.0 to the Brightness/Contrast layer then use the Multiply blending mode to combine the effect of the filter with underlying layers. We will also activate the Group With Previous Layer option for this layer to add the Brightness/Contrast layer to the existing clipping group.

1. Set the foreground color to black.

2. Choose Filter➡Brush Strokes➡Spatter to display the Spatter dialog box (see Figure 11.12).

3. Set the Spray Radius to 10 and the Smoothness to 5. Click OK to apply the Spatter filter to the Brightness Contrast adjustment layer.

4. Set the blending mode for the Brightness/ Contrast adjustment layer to Multiply by clicking the drop-down menu in the upper-left corner of the Layers palette.

5. Double-click the thumbnail preview of the Brightness/Contrast adjustment layer to display the Layer Options dialog box (see Figure 11.13).

6. Check the Group With Previous Layer checkbox, and then click OK. Checking the Group With Previous Layer checkbox is the same as (Option-clicking)[Alt-clicking] the divider line between the layers to create a clipping group. Note that the word "text" in the text layer is underlined and the Hue/Saturation and Brightness/Contrast layers are indented. This means that the text layer is the clipping path for the two adjustment layers above it (see Figure 11.14).

Figure 11.12

The Spatter dialog box.

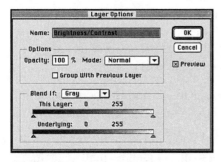

Figure 11.13

The Layer Options dialog box.

Figure 11.14

The text layer is the clipping path for the members of the clipping group.

Open lessons/chap11/skydive.psd on the CD-ROM to view the completed image (see Figure 11.15).

Figure 11.15

The completed image.

Summary

In this chapter we examined the powerful capabilities of the new adjustment layers in Photoshop 4.0. The exercises in this chapter introduced you to the many ways adjustment layers can be used to modify your image. The beauty of adjustment layers is that you can make as many changes and adjusments as you like without altering the original image until you're totally satisfied with the result of the changes. In the next chapter we explore some techniques for creating lighting and shadow effects.

Lighting and Shadows

There are numerous ways to create lighting effects in Photoshop. This chapter explores some of the techniques used to create effective drop shadows and lighting effects. Many of the images used in this chapter are single layer files of images that have been cropped out of their respective backgrounds. See Chapter 4, "Making Selections" and Chapter 6, "Creating Paths" to learn more about silhouetting images.

Creating Drop Shadows

The following exercise takes two objects and overlays them on a textured background, and then creates a drop shadow for the objects (see Figure 12.1). The easiest way to create shadows in Photoshop is using layers to overlay objects and their shadows on backgrounds. Using the blending mode, we can create quite realistic looking shadows.

Figure 12.1

Shadows created using layers and blending modes.

1. Open lessons/chap12/texture.psd and lessons/chap12/cycle.psd on the CD-ROM that accompanies this book.

2. Choose Window➡Show Layers to display the Layers palette.

3. Select the Move tool and drag cycle.psd onto texture.psd. Note that the cycle now resides on its own layer in the texture.psd file. You can close the cycle.psd file after you have moved it into the texture.psd file. Use the Move tool to position the image on the texture (see Figure 12.2).

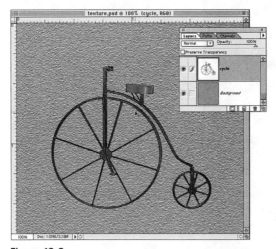

Figure 12.2

Use the Move tool to move the cycle layer onto the texture.

Figure 12.3

The Duplicate Layer dialog box.

Figure 12.4

The Fill dialog box.

Figure 12.5

The Gaussian Blur dialog box.

4. Select the cycle layer in the Layers palette. Choose Layer➡Duplicate Layer to display the Duplicate Layer dialog box (see Figure 12.3). Name the duplicate layer "cycle shadow" and click OK.

5. Turn on Preserve Transparency for the cycle shadow layer by clicking the Preserve Transparency checkbox in the Layers palette.

6. Choose Edit➡Fill or type (Shift-Delete)[Shift-Backspace] to display the Fill dialog box (see Figure 12.4).

7. Choose 50% Gray from the Contents drop-down menu in the Fill dialog box. Set the Blending Opacity to 100% and the Mode to Normal if they are not already set that way. Click OK to fill the non-transparent pixels on the cycle shadow layer with 50% gray.

8. Turn off Preserve Transparency for the cycle shadow layer by clicking the checkbox in the Layers palette.

9. Choose Filter➡Blur➡Gaussian Blur to display the Gaussian Blur dialog box (see Figure 12.5). Set the Radius to 2.0 pixels in the Gaussian Blur dialog box and click OK.

10. Drag the cycle shadow layer below the cycle layer in the Layers palette, and then use the Move tool to offset the shadow (see Figure 12.6).

11. Change the blending mode for the cycle shadow layer to Multiply by clicking the blending mode drop-down menu in the Layers palette (see Figure 12.7). The Multiply blending mode darkens the shadow by combining the luminosity of both layers, creating a realistic looking shadow (see Figure 12.8).

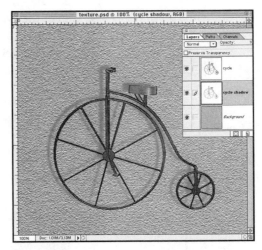

Figure 12.6

Offset the shadow with the Move tool.

Figure 12.7

Choose Multiply from the blending modes in the Layers palette for the cycle shadow layer.

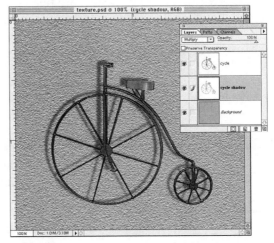

Figure 12.8

The Multiply blending mode creates a realistic looking shadow.

Note

To move both the cycle and the shadow at the same time, select one of the two layers in the Layers palette and click the embossed box to the left of the layer thumbnail of the other one. The link icon appears to indicate that the layer is linked to the selected layer—the one with the paint-brush icon (see Figure 12.9).

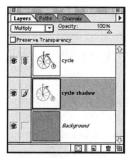

Figure 12.9

Link the two layers together to move them at the same time.

Figure 12.10

Use the Move tool to move the mask image onto the brick image.

12. Open lessons/chap12/dropshdw.psd on the CD-ROM that accompanies this book to see the completed image.

Creating a Bleached Effect

A bleached effect is not necessarily a shadow in the strictest sense of the word, but the properties of this effect are similar to those of a shadow. Bleached "shadows" are present, for example, when an object is backlit or when sunlight is filtered.

1. Open lessons/chap12/bricks.psd and lessons/chap12/mask.psd on the CD-ROM that accompanies this book.

2. Use the Move tool to drag the mask image onto the brick.psd image (see Figure 12.10). A new layer named "mask" is automatically added.

3. Select the mask layer in the Layers palette. Choose Layer➡Duplicate Layer to display the Duplicate Layer dialog box, and then name the duplicate layer "mask shadow." Click OK.

4. Turn on Preserve Transparency for the mask shadow layer by clicking the Preserve Transparency check box in the Layers palette.

5. Choose Edit➡Fill or type (Shift-Delete)[Shift-Backspace] to display the Fill dialog box. Choose 50% Gray from the Contents drop-down menu in the Fill dialog box. Set the Blending Opacity to 100% and the Mode to Normal if they are not already set that way. Click OK.

6. Turn off Preserve Transparency for the mask shadow layer by clicking the checkbox in the Layers palette.

7. Choose Filter➡Blur➡Gaussian Blur to display the Gaussian Blur dialog box, and then set the Radius to 3.0 pixels. Click OK.

Figure 12.11

Offset the shadow with the Move tool.

Figure 12.12

The Color Dodge blending mode creates a realistic looking lighting effect.

8. Drag the mask shadow layer below the mask layer in the Layers palette, and then use the Move tool to offset the shadow (see Figure 12.11).

9. Change the blending mode for the mask shadow layer to Color Dodge by clicking the blending mode drop-down menu in the Layers palette. The Color Dodge blending mode brightens the brick pattern in the shape of the shadow (see Figure 12.12).

10. Open lessons/chap12/bleached.psd on the CD-ROM that accompanies this book to see the completed image.

Casting a Shadow

It is often necessary to create cast shadows when compositing images from different sources. In this exercise, we will take a native of India and place him on a city sidewalk, and then create a cast shadow (see Figure 12.13).

Figure 12.13

The Indian holy man is cropped out of the Himalayan backdrop and placed on a city sidewalk, and then the shadow is added.

1. Open lessons/chap12/street.psd and lessons/chap12/man.psd on the CD-ROM that accompanies this book.

Figure 12.14

Drag the man onto the sidewalk.

2. Use the Move tool to drag the man onto the street image, creating a new layer in street.psd (see Figure 12.14).

3. Choose Duplicate Layer from the Layer menu or palette menu to create a duplicate of the man layer. Name this new layer "man shadow."

4. Turn on Preserve Transparency by clicking the checkbox in the Layers palette.

5. Type (Shift-Delete)[Shift-Backspace] to display the Fill dialog box, and then choose 50% gray for the contents. Set the blending mode to Normal and Opacity to 100%. Click OK to fill the outline of the man with 50% gray.

6. Turn off Preserve Transparency for the man shadow layer by unchecking the checkbox in the Layers palette.

7. Choose Filter➡Blur➡Gaussian Blur to display the Gaussian Blur dialog, and then set the radius to 3.5 pixels. Click OK to blur the edges of the shadow (see Figure 12.15).

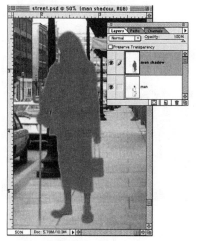

Figure 12.15

Fill the shape of the man with gray and apply a blur filter to soften the edges.

8. Move the man shadow layer underneath the man layer in the Layers palette.

9. Choose Layer➡Transform➡Distort to display the distort rectangle on the man shadow layer. Click the top corner handles of the distort rectangle and drag them down so that the shadow trails behind the man (see Figure 12.16). Double-click inside the distort rectangle to apply the distortion to the man shadow layer.

10. Change the blending mode for the man shadow layer from Normal to Multiply to combine the

Figure 12.16

Distort the shadow so that it appears to be trailing behind the man.

shadow with the sidewalk. Set the opacity of the man shadow layer to about 60% to create a lighter shadow.

11. Open lessons/chap12/castshdw.psd on the CD-ROM that accompanies this book to see the completed image.

Creating a Shadow

The preceding exercises in this chapter have dealt with creating shadows in the shapes of the foreground subjects. In the following exercise, we will have to create the shadow of an F/A-18 jet flying over a beach. Because the shadow will have to somewhat reflect the shape of the underside of the jet and because we do not have a picture of the underside of this jet, we will create the shadow (see Figure 12.17).

Figure 12.17

The shadow for the jet must be invented because it should be in the shape of the underside of the jet.

1. Open lessons/chap12/surf.psd and lessons/chap12/jet.psd on the CD-ROM that accompanies this book.

2. Use the Move tool to drag the jet onto the surf.psd file, and then position it just above the rocks.

3. Use the plane as a starting point to create the drop shadow. Duplicate the jet layer and name the new layer "jet shadow."

4. Turn on Preserve Transparency for the jet layer by clicking the checkbox in the Layers palette.

5. Choose Edit➡Fill to display the Fill dialog box, and then select 50% Gray from the Contents drop-down menu. Set the blending mode to Normal and the Opacity to 100%. Click OK to fill the shape of the jet with 50% gray.

6. Choose Layer➡Add Layer Mask➡Reveal All, or click the Mask icon at the bottom of the Layers palette to create a layer mask (see Figure 12.18). The layer mask is selected automatically for painting in the Layers palette indicated by the mask icon to the left of the layer thumbnail picture.

7. Double-click the Paintbrush tool in the toolbox to display the Paintbrush Options palette and make sure the Blending mode is Normal and the Opacity 100%. Fade and Wet Edges should not be checked.

8. Choose Window➡Show Brushes to display the Brushes palette, and then choose the 65 pixel brush with a soft edge.

9. Set the Foreground color to black.

10. Paint on the layer mask of the jet layer with the Paintbrush tool to remove the fins and cockpit hump from the jet (see Figure 12.19).

11. Choose Layer➡Remove Layer Mask, and then click the Apply button when the dialog box is displayed.

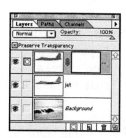

Figure 12.18

The Layers palette showing a layer mask for the jet shadow layer.

Figure 12.19

Paint on the layer mask with black to remove parts of the image.

Now that we have the basic shape of the jet for our shadow, we must create the wings and tail section of the jet as they would appear if we were looking up at the underside of the jet. Because we don't have a picture of the underside of this jet, we'll have to guess what it would look like and create it from scratch.

1. Use the Move tool to move the jet shadow onto the beach in front of the rocks.

2. Turn off Preserve Transparency by unchecking the checkbox in the Layers palette.

3. Select the Paintbrush tool in the toolbox, and then choose the 45 pixel brush with a soft edge in the Brushes palette. (Option-click)[Alt-click] on the gray shadow to load the 50% gray color as the foreground color.

4. Paint on the jet shadow layer to add the wings and tail fins (see Figure 12.20). It does not have to be perfect; we are going to distort the shadow in the following steps.

5. Double-click the Gradient tool in the toolbox to display the Gradient Tool Options palette. Select Foreground to Background as the gradient type from the drop-down menu in the Gradient Tool Options palette. Select Linear as the type of gradient. Make sure the blending mode is set to Normal and the Opacity to 100% in the Gradient Tool Options palette.

Figure 12.20

Add the delta wings and tail fins to the shadow.

6. Turn on Preserve Transparency for the jet shadow layer in the Layers palette.

7. Click and drag a gradient that starts at the bottom of the image at the wing tip and continues up and to the right, ending at the other wing tip (see Figure 12.21).

Figure 12.21

Create a gradient that blends from 50% gray to white.

8. Turn off Preserve Transparency in the Layers palette for the jet shadow layer.

9. Choose Filter➥Blur➥Gaussian Blur, and then enter a radius of 10.0 pixels. Click OK to blur the edges of the shadow.

10. Set the Blending mode for the jet shadow layer to Multiply by clicking the drop-down menu in the Layers palette.

11. Open lessons/chap12/jetcomp.psd to see the completed image.

Using the Lighting Effects Filter

The powerful Lighting Effects filter enables you to create an infinite number of lighting effects—from spotlights to footlights to directional lighting. In the following exercise, we are going to examine the Lighting Effects filter and apply a spotlight effect to an image (see Figure 12.22).

Figure 12.22

Using the Lighting Effects filter, you can create artificial light effects.

1. Open lessons/chap12/director.psd on the CD-ROM that accompanies this book.

2. Choose Filter➡Render➡Lighting Effects to display the Lighting Effects dialog box (see Figure 12.23).

3. If this is the first time you are using the Lighting Effects filter, the default lighting effect is applied to the image in the preview window.

   ► Drag the handles around the lighting effect in the preview window to adjust the amount of light.

   ► Click the handle in the center of the lighting effect to move the lighting effect in the preview window.

   ► Drag the light bulb icon under the preview window onto the preview image to add additional lighting effects. Each of these additional lighting effects can have separate and inepenent settings from each other.

   ► Delete additional lighting effects by clicking the center handle and dragging the lighting

Figure 12.23

The Lighting Effects dialog box.

effect to the trash can under the preview window. Note that one lighting effect must be present at all times.

► Choose a lighting style from the Style drop-down menu. Experiment with some of these lighting effects to see how they work.

► Choose the type of light to use from the drop-down menu for Light Type, and then set the Intensity and Focus of the light using the triangle sliders.

► Set the properties of the light by dragging the triangle sliders in the Properties section.

► Choose a color for the Light Type and Properties by clicking the square outline box in these sections.

► If you include an alpha channel with a texture, choose the alpha channel from the Texture Channel drop-down menu. You can also use the Red, Green, or Blue channels as texture channels.

3. Click the Save button to save your lighting effects settings for future use.

4. Click OK when you have a lighting effect that you like.

5. Open lessons/chap12/spotlite.psd on the CD-ROM that accompanies this book to see the completed image. Your file will be different than the image on the CD-ROM depending on the lighting effects you used.

Summary

In this chapter we explored some of the methods used to create drop shadows and even added a cast shadow to a composite image. You learned the keys to creating convincing shadows by using the Gaussian blur filter and multiply blending mode. We also examined the Lighting Effects filter, a powerful tool with an infinite array of lighting possibilities that you can add to your images. In the next chapter we will explore ways to adjust the focus and tone of our images using the blur and sharpening tools, blur and sharpenging filters and the Dodge, Burn, and Sponge tools.

Adjusting Focus and Tone

You can adjust the focus and tone of Photoshop images with a variety of tools. The focus tools include the Sharpen tool, the Blur tool, the sharpen filters, and the blur filters. The toning tools include the Dodge, Burn, and Sponge tools, as well as commands such as Brightness/Contrast and Hue/Saturation. The sharpening tools and filters are useful for improving the sharpness of images that appear blurred or slightly out of focus. Use the Blur tools and filters to soften edges, eliminate patterns, and for special effects. The toning tools affect the brightness and saturation in the image with precise control. This chapter explores how to use the various focus and tone tools and filters.

Sharpening Images

In this section, you examine the sharpening filters and tools by adjusting the sharpness of a variety of images. When sharpening an image or a portion of an image, it is best to work at the 100% (Actual Pixels) view because sharpening too much can introduce undesirable artifacts into the image by enhancing dust specks and scratches.

It is also worth mentioning here that scanned images you purchase from service bureaus and color houses may appear overly sharp onscreen, but will print fine. In these instances, the Unsharp Mask sharpening filter is usually applied to the image that tends to appear too sharp onscreen. See the following section, "Using Unsharp Mask," for further information.

1. Open lessons/chap13/fall.psd on the CD-ROM that accompanies this book.

2. Zoom to 100% view with the Zoom tool or choose View➡Actual Pixels.

3. The three basic sharpen filters (Sharpen, Sharpen Edges, and Sharpen More) affect almost every pixel in the image, increasing the contrast of the image while sharpening. Choose Filter➡ Sharpen➡Sharpen More to sharpen the image.

4. Choose Filter➡Fade Sharpen More to display the Fade dialog box (see Figure 13.1). Adjust the opacity of the sharpening effect in the Fade dialog box to reduce the sharpening somewhat. You also can select a blending mode from the drop-down menu in the Fade dialog box (though I suggest sticking with the Normal blending mode for simple sharpening). Click OK when the image looks sharp enough, but not too sharp.

5. The Sharpen More filter applies a more sharpening than the Sharpen filter or the Sharpen Edges filter. Type (Command-Z)[Control-Z] to undo the sharpening, and try the Sharpen and Sharpen Edges filters on the same image. For this particular image, the Sharpen Edges filter seems to do

Figure 13.1

The Fade dialog box.

the best job of sharpening without making the image look grainy. Look for grainy or noisy areas in the flat-colored areas of the image, like the sky in this image (see Figure 13.2).

Figure 13.2

The original image.

Sharpen More filter applied one time.

Sharpen More filter applied two times (note graininess).

Using Unsharp Mask

The Unsharp Mask offers the most control over the sharpening process of any of the available sharpening filters. Unsharp Mask is a technique that was used in traditional prepress production to increase sharpness by exaggerating the density along the borders of color change using a negative mask of the image. The Unsharp Mask filter in Photoshop works in much the same way.

There are three values in the Unsharp Mask dialog box that control the amount of sharpening applied:

▶ **Amount** can be a value from 1% to 500% with 1% being the least amount of sharpening and 500% the most. The value you choose for Amount depends largely on the resolution of the image. For most images (150–300 pixels per inch), an Amount setting between 150% and 300% works best. Consider the composition of the image before applying an unsharp mask above 150%, especially if the image contains a lot of small details like faces in a crowd. Setting the Amount value too high can make the image look grainy and too high in contrast.

▶ **Radius** is the number of pixels affected between one color density and another. If you equate unsharp masking to outlining coloring book pictures with a darker edge of the same crayon color, the Radius value is the size of the crayon. A radius between 1 and 2 pixels is recommended for most images.

▶ **Threshold** determines the difference in brightness the edge pixels must be for them to be affected by the unsharp mask. The default value of 0 (zero) includes all of the image pixels when determining the edge pixels to apply the unsharp mask. A number higher than 0 limits the choice to gray levels between the number you specify for Threshold and 255 (white). A threshold of 0 works well for most images; you can set a value between 0 and 50 to eliminate noise in flesh tones and neutral colors.

1. Open lessons/chap13/camel.psd on the CD-ROM that accompanies this book.

2. Choose Filter➡Sharpen➡Unsharp Mask to display the Unsharp Mask dialog box (see Figure 13.3).

Figure 13.3

The Unsharp Mask dialog box.

3. For this image, set the Amount to 300%, the Radius to 2.0 pixels, and the Threshold to 0 (zero). You can view the changes to the image by checking the Preview checkbox or by looking inside the preview window in the Unsharp Mask dialog box. Click inside the preview window to set the sharpening off and on and to see a before and after view. Click OK to apply the Unsharp Mask to the image.

4. Type (Command-Z)[Control-Z] to toggle between undo/redo and to view the overall change to the image (see Figure 13.4).

Figure 13.4

The Unsharp Mask filter applied to the image at right sharpens the image without introducing noise or grain into the image.

Sharpening Individual Channels

You can apply the sharpening filters to any channel in your image. In RGB mode it's usually preferable to sharpen the composite image rather than the individual Red, Green, or Blue channels. In CMYK mode, the sharpening filters can be applied effectively to the black channel to sharpen the contrast areas represented on the black plate and is a method that is especially useful for sharpening grainy images. In the following exercise you will use the Unsharp Mask filter to sharpen the Lightness channel of an image in Lab mode.

The Unsharp Mask filter can introduce bright-colored edges to your image when sharpening the edge between two colors. Sharpening of any sort also can change the color intensity of the image by creating new colors in the image. If your image contains bright colors that are close in proximity to each other, consider sharpening the Lightness channel of the image in Lab Color mode. Sharpening the Lightness channel sharpens the gray values (luminance) of the image without changing the color values. See Chapter 2, "Color and Resolution in Photoshop," for more information on the Lab color mode.

1. Open lessons/chap13/paul.psd on the CD-ROM that accompanies this book.

2. This picture was taken with a Polaroid 1-Step camera, which often produces an out-of-focus print that is also a bit grainy in appearance. To sharpen this image without increasing the graininess and without overly sharpening the colors, first convert the RGB image to Lab mode, then apply the Unsharp Mask filter to the Lightness (L) channel. Choose Image➥Mode➥Lab Color to convert the image to Lab color. The Lab color mode has three channels: Lightness (L), and two color channels (a and b).

3. Choose Window➥Show Channels to display the Channels palette (see Figure 13.5).

Figure 13.5

The Channels Palette showing the Lab channels.

4. Click on the Lightness channel in the Channels palette. Note that the Lightness channel contains most of the detail for the image.

5. Choose Filter➡Sharpen➡Unsharp Mask to display the Unsharp Mask dialog box and set the Amount to 150%, the Radius to 2.0 pixels, and the Threshold to 0 levels. Click OK to apply the Unsharp Mask to the Lightness channel only.

6. Click the composite Lab channel in the Channels palette to view the composite effect of the Unsharp Mask filter. Type (Command-Z) [Control-Z] to toggle between the undo/redo Unsharp Mask to see the before and after views (see Figure 13.6).

original image

sharpened image

Figure 13.6

The Unsharp Mask filter applied to the Lightness channel of the image in Lab Mode (right) sharpens the image while maintaining color integrity.

TIP

Sharpening an image can reveal dust specks and scratches that were not previously apparent. Zoom in and check your image after sharpening it to make sure that there are no artifacts resulting from the sharpening process.

7. Convert this image back to RGB to perform further color corrections; or, convert it to CMYK to prepare it for color separation.

Using the Sharpen and Blur Tools

You can find the Sharpen and Blur tools in the Toolbox. Use these tools to sharpen and blur specific areas of the image by applying the effect with a brush. Press "R" to toggle between the Sharpen tool and the Blur tool in the Toolbox.

1. Open lessons/chap13/squirrel.psd on the CD-ROM that accompanies this book.

2. Double-click the Sharpen tool in the Toolbox to display the Focus Tools Options palette (see Figure 13.7).

3. Choose Window➡Show Brushes to display the Brushes palette; choose a small brush with a soft edge.

Figure 13.7

The Focus Tools Options palette.

4. Set the Pressure to 15% in the Focus Tools Options palette and choose Luminosity for a blending mode. It's always best to apply this effect with a low pressure setting, gradually building the sharpening effect over an area of the image. The Luminosity blending mode sharpens the gray levels of the image without affecting the color values.

5. Paint over the face and tail of the squirrel with the Sharpen tool. Take care not to oversharpen the image by overpainting the same area. Paint using short strokes and work in the 100% view for best results.

6. Select Blur as the tool in the Focus Tool Options palette and set the Pressure to 50%. Set the Blending Mode to Darken to restrict the blurring effect to light pixels, darkening the painted area.

7. Paint over the sharp grass in the foreground of the picture to reduce the bright highlights and to make the squirrel "pop" in the image (see Figure 13.8).

original image   sharpened & blurred image

Figure 13.8

Sharpening the squirrel while blurring the sharp grass in the foreground makes the squirrel appear to "pop."

Using the Blur Filters

Use the Blur filters to decrease the sharpness of a particular area in the image or to create special effects like drop shadows. In cases where you have scanned a previously printed photograph, use the Blur filters to diffuse the halftone dots that were scanned, and apply the Unsharp Mask filter to re-sharpen the image.

In the following exercise you will use a combination of the Gaussian Blur, Motion Blur, and Radial Blur filters to create the appearance of motion in a photograph of a stationary car. Start off by using the Motion Blur filter to blur the image area behind the car.

1. Open lessons/chap13/car.psd on the CD-ROM that accompanies this book.

2. Choose Window➡Show Channels to display the Channels palette.

3. Hold down the (Command)[Control] key and click Channel #4 to load the channel as a selection.

4. Choose Filter➡Blur➡Motion Blur to display the Motion Blur dialog box (see Figure 13.9).

Figure 13.9

The Motion Blur dialog box.

5. Set the Angle to 5° and the Distance to 285 pixels; click OK.

In these next steps you will apply the Gaussian Blur filter to the street in front of the car. The Gaussian Blur filter is a good choice for this effect because you can specify the amount of blur by entering a pixel radius and see the change in the preview window in the Guassian Blur dialog box.

1. Choose Select➡Load Selection to display the Load Selection dialog box and select "#5" in the Channel drop-down menu. Click OK to load channel #5 as a selection.

2. Choose Filter➡Blur➡Gaussian Blur to display the Gaussian Blur dialog box; set the Radius to 10.0 pixels. Click OK to apply a diffused blur to the image.

In these final steps you will use the Radial Blur filter to blur the tires of the car in a circular pattern to create the illusion of the tires moving.

1. (Command-Click)[Control-Click] Channel #6 in the Channels palette to select the front tire of the car.

2. Choose Filter➡Blur➡Radial Blur to display the Radial Blur dialog box (see Figure 13.10).

Figure 13.10

The Radial Blur dialog box.

3. Set the Amount to 12. Choose Spin as the Blur Method and Best as the Quality setting. Click OK to apply the radial blur to the hub cap of the front tire.

4. (Command-Click)[Control-Click] Channel #7 in the Channels palette to select the rear tire of the car.

5. Choose Filter➡Blur➡Radial Blur to display the Radial Blur dialog box; set the Amount to 12; choose Spin as the Blur Method and Best as the

Quality setting. Click OK to apply the radial blur to the hub cap of the rear tire. The exclusive use of blur filters creates the motion effect for this image (see Figure 13.11).

Figure 13.11

The Motion Blur, Gaussian Blur, and Radial Blur filters applied to create motion.

Dodging and Burning

The Dodge and Burn tools emulate the photographic techniques of dodging and burning. When creating photographic prints, the photographic paper is exposed with a light source through the negative film creating a positive image. When dodging, light is withheld in areas of the image, usually by masking areas of the image, to underexpose them—making them appear lighter than the rest of the image. Burning creates a burned-in effect by overexposing parts of the image.

1. Open lessons/chap13/man.psd on the CD-ROM that accompanies this book.

2. Press "O" to select from the Dodge, Burn, and Sponge tools in the Toolbox. Double-click the Dodge tool in the Toolbox to display the Toning Tools Options palette (see Figure 13.12).

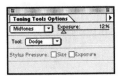

Figure 13.12

The Toning Tools Options palette.

3. Choose Window➡Show Brushes to display the Brushes palette, and select the 35 pixel brush with a soft edge.

4. Choose Midtones from the drop-down menu in the upper left-hand corner of the Toning Tools Options palette, and set the Exposure to 12%. Always use a low Exposure setting to gradually apply the dodge effect. Be sure to select Dodge as the Tool type in the Toning Tools Options palette.

5. Paint over the face and neck of the subject in the photograph to lighten the skin tone somewhat. Go over the areas under the eyes a few times to remove the dark shadows there.

6. Select the Burn tool by pressing "O" to toggle to it, or from the drop-down menu in the Toning Tools Options palette.

7. Choose Shadows from the drop-down menu in the upper left-hand corner of the Toning Tools Options palette, and set the Exposure to 20%.

8. Paint over the beard and mustache area in short strokes to slightly darken the area. Because you chose Shadows in the Toning Tool Options palette, this limits the change to the shadow areas.

9. Select Midtones from the drop-down menu in the upper left-hand corner of the Toning Tools Options palette. Leave the Exposure set to 20% and the Burn tool selected.

10. Select the 65 pixel soft edged brush in the Brushes palette and paint over the shirt area in broad strokes to darken the midtone areas in the creases of the shirt.

11. Use the Dodge tool to lighten the shadow cast behind the subject. Use a low Exposure setting and apply the changes to the midtone area. Remember to select a smaller brush.

12. See Figure 13.13 to compare the original image with the changed image.

Original image

Dodge and Burn applied

Figure 13.13

The Dodge and Burn tools are ideal for making subtle changes to the brightness levels of the image.

Using the Sponge Tool

The Sponge tool makes changes to the saturation levels of the pixels in the image. Each pixel in the image has a specific Hue, Saturation, and Brightness value. The Hue value represents the color of the pixel, the Brightness value is the luminance of the pixel, and the Saturation value represents the intensity of the Hue. See Chapter 2 for a full explanation of Hue, Saturation, and Brightness. The Sponge tool can be used to saturate or desaturate specific areas of the image. It is also an effective tool to pump up the color of a weak image or to reduce the saturation of an image to bring it into gamut for CMYK printing.

1. Open lessons/chap13/family.psd on the CD-ROM that accompanies this book.

2. Double-click the Sponge tool in the Toolbox to display the Toning Tools Options palette.

3. Select the 45 pixel brush in the Brushes palette.

4. Select Saturate from the drop-down menu in the upper left-hand corner of the Toning Tools Options palette; set the pressure to 50%. Paint on the image to increase the saturation of the color. Apply the Sponge tool again to further increase the saturation of the colors in the image.

5. Experiment with different pressure settings and brush sizes. Choose Desaturate to reduce the saturation of color.

Keeping Colors in Gamut with the Sponge Tool

The gamut of colors that can be printed using CMYK inks is significantly smaller than the gamut of colors that can be displayed in RGB on a computer monitor. For this reason, it is possible to convert an image with oversaturated colors in RGB mode to CMYK mode resulting in an image that will produce different printed colors than those displayed on the monitor. When the RGB image is converted to CMYK mode in Photoshop, the out-of-gamut colors will be brought into gamut automatically. If you are editing and color correcting an image in RGB mode, you should bring the out-of-gamut colors in the image into gamut so you have the control over the process rather than trusting this process to Photoshop's conversion algorithms. To bring the out-of-gamut colors into gamut so they will print correctly, use the Gamut Warning feature in concert with the Sponge tool to desaturate oversaturated colors.

1. Open lessons/chap13/leaves.psd on the CD-ROM that accompanies this book.

2. Choose View➡Gamut Warning to turn on the gamut mask. It takes a few seconds for Photoshop to calculate the gamut mask based on the Color Settings specified. Photoshop overlays a gray mask on top of the image, indicating which colors are out of gamut (see Figure 13.14).

3. Double-click on the Sponge tool in the Toolbox to display the Toning Tools Options palette; select Desaturate from the drop-down menu in the upper left-hand corner.

Figure 13.14

The Gamut Warning mask is overlaid on the image.

TIP

If you want to desaturate the entire image or a selected part of the image all the way to grayscale, choose Image➡ Adjust➡Desaturate.

4. Use a low pressure setting (around 10%) to desaturate the color in the image gradually.

5. Paint over the masked areas with the Sponge tool to desaturate the color in the image until the gray mask disappears.

Summary

In this chapter we examined some of the typical methods used to sharpen and blur Photoshop images as well as some practical uses for the Dodge, Burn, and Sponge toning tools. The tools and commands you use to adjust the focus and tone of your images will vary depending on the type of image and level of adjustment needed. In the next chapter you will learn about the Rubber Stamp tool along with methods to retouch and repair Photoshop images.

Retouching and Repairing Images

In this chapter we are going to use the Rubber Stamp tool to fix a photograph that has been torn into two pieces and contains scratches, nicks, stains, and missing pieces (see Figure 14.1). The two parts of the images have been scanned on a flatbed scanner separately and at differing angles to fit the pieces on the scanner bed. We will be working in layers, with a piece on each layer. We will have to rotate the images to align them and use a layer mask to remove the excess parts created in the scanning process. Once we have the pieces where they belong in reference to each other, we will begin the process of repairing the damage by using the Rubber Stamp tool to build the missing sections, repair blemishes, and remove the scratches and stains. The final steps in the process will be to improve the sharpness and contrast of the image using the Unsharp Mask filter along with the Brightness/Contrast command. Our objective is to restore this image to its original state or at least get as close as we can to it. We'll check the dimensions and resolution of the image before we save it to be printed as a limited edition color print on a color inkjet printer (see Figure 14.2).

Figure 14.1

The original portrait in pieces with apparent scratches and stains.

Figure 14.2

The final repaired and retouched portrait.

Combining Two Images

Before we can retouch and repair this image in Photoshop, we must combine the two separately scanned pieces of the photo. In the following steps we will use layers to bring the two parts of this image together and use a layer mask to clean up the edges of the pieces before flattening the image into a single layer.

1. Insert the CD-ROM that accompanies this book and open lessons/chap14/right.psd.

2. Display the Layers palette by choosing Window➡Show Layers. Note that this section of the photograph is on the background layer (see Figure 14.3).

Figure 14.3

The Layers palette indicates that the image is on the Background layer.

3. We will be adding the left section as a layer to this file that contains the right section, so we'll need some extra space on the top and left to accommodate it. The extra space will be added in the background color, so set the background color to white.

4. Choose Image➡Canvas Size to display the Canvas Size dialog box (see Figure 14.4).

TIP

You can set the foreground and background colors back to the default colors of black and white, respectively, by clicking the default colors icon in the Toolbox or by pressing "D" on the keyboard.

5. Change the measurement units to inches if they are not already indicated and change the width to 7 inches and the height to 10 inches.

6. Click in the lower-right corner box of the Anchor grid graphic. This tells Photoshop where to add the extra space, indicated by the arrows in the anchor graphic (see Figure 14.5).

7. Click the OK button. Photoshop will add the extra space to the top and left of the image.

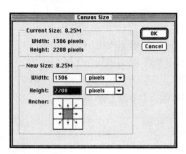

Figure 14.4

The Canvas Size dialog box.

Figure 14.5

Enter a width and height, then click in the grid to position the original image within the new space you are adding.

Figure 14.6

Use the Move tool to drag the left side of the image into the file that contains the right side.

Now would be a good time to save the working file, so choose File➡Save As, select Photoshop as the format, and save this file with the same filename to your hard disk. We're saving the file in Photoshop format because we want the layers we will be creating to be saved with the file. Now that we have the right.psd file prepared with extra space to add the left side of the image, we can bring in the left side as a separate layer.

1. Insert the CD-ROM disc that accompanies this book and open lessons/chap14/left.psd.

2. Select the Move tool from the Toolbox or press V to select the Move tool.

3. Arrange the windows for each image so you can see both at the same time. With the Move tool selected, click and drag the image from left.psd onto right.psd (see Figure 14.6).

4. Because our image does not contain any totally white or black areas, except for the extra space around the image, we can take advantage of the blending range capabilities in the Layer Options dialog box. Double-click Layer 1 in the Layers palette to display the Layer Options dialog box (see Figure 14.7).

5. Select Gray from the drop-down menu next to the words Blend If. Click the Preview checkbox if you want to see the affect of your changes when you make them.

6. Drag the right triangle slider under the This Layer blend bar to the left until the gray value changes from 255 to 200 (see Figure 14.8). This removes the white pixels from the image.

TIP

To make the entire image area fit on the screen, double-click on the Hand tool or choose View➡Fit on Screen or type (Command-0 (zero))[Control-0 (zero)].

7. Drag the left triangle slider under the This Layer blend bar to the right until the gray value changes from 0 to 15 (see Figure 14.9). This removes the black pixels from the image.

8. Click the OK button. If you discover that parts of your image are being clipped because of the adjustments you made to the blending range, double-click the layer again and modify the range. The changes do not become permanent until the layers are merged or flattened.

9. Type (Command-S)[Control-S] to save what you have done so far.

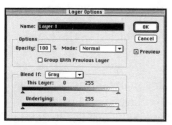

Figure 14.7

The Layer Options dialog box.

Figure 14.8

The white areas of the image on top are clipped (made transparent).

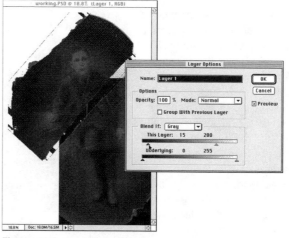

Figure 14.9

The black areas of the image are clipped (made transparent).

Adjusting the Blending Range of a Layer

There are two slider bars in the Blend If section of the Layer Options dialog box that control how the pixels on this layer blend with the underlying pixels. Each pixel in our image has a Red, Green, and Blue component that ranges from 0 to 255. In the drop-down menu next to the words Blend If, you can choose whether you want to affect the range of color (0 to 255) for one of the three RGB channels or Gray, which represents all three channels at once. In RGB mode, a truly white pixel will have the values: 255 Red, 255 Green, 255 Blue. Conversely, a truly black pixel will have the values: 0 Red, 0 Green, 0 Blue. We can change the way the range of color values for this layer interacts with the range of color values for underlying layers by dragging the triangle sliders under the blend bars. If, for example, we drag the right triangle slider under the This Layer blend bar to change the value from 255 to 230, all of the pixels that have values from 230 to 255 will be made transparent (will not blend with the underlying layers). By dragging the right or left triangle sliders we are actually clipping off the pixels that contain those gray values. For the moment we are only concerned with clipping off the white and black areas of our image so we can see the underlying image.

Moving and Rotating Layers

Now that we have both pieces of our image in one file, we can align the pieces by moving and rotating the image on the top layer. In this example, the original photograph was not only torn into two pieces; some of the pieces are missing. Our goal in this next section is to position the pieces so that they are as close as possible to the original position.

1. Make sure that Layer 1 is selected in the Layers palette.

2. The Layer menu contains many of the functions that can be performed on layers, and rotating is one of them. Choose Layer➡Transform➡Rotate to display the rotation rectangle over the image (see Figure 14.10).

Figure 14.10

The rotation rectangle is displayed around the non-transparent areas of the image on Layer 1.

3. Position the cursor inside the rectangle, then click and drag to move the image into position. Get as close as possible without overlapping the two images.

If you have an extended keyboard, you can use the arrow keys to nudge the image in 1-pixel increments. To nudge the image in 10-pixel increments, hold down Shift and press an arrow key.

Figure 14.11

Click any tool in the Toolbox to cancel the rotation and choose whether or not to apply the rotation.

When rotating the layer image, type the escape (Esc) key to cancel the rotation without displaying a dialog box.

Figure 14.12

The Layer mask is positioned to the right of the layer thumbnail in the Layers palette.

4. Click and drag any of the eight handles on the rotation rectangle to rotate the image. You can make as many adjustments as you want before committing to the rotation.

5. When you have the image on Layer 1 positioned and rotated to your satisfaction, double-click inside the rotation rectangle to accept and apply the changes or press Return or Enter. If you want to cancel this rotation and start again, type the Esc key. You can also click any tool in the Toolbox and Photoshop will display a dialog box offering you the choice of applying the rotation or ignoring it (Don't Apply) (see Figure 14.11). The two images do not align exactly and the rip mark is still visible between the two pieces.

6. Type (Command-S)[Control-S] to save what you've done so far.

Retouching with the Layer Mask

We're almost ready to begin retouching and repairing the image. First, we will erase some of the residual lines that our adjustment to the blending range failed to include. In order to erase unwanted parts of the image and still have the option of restoring them, we can create a mask for Layer 1 and mask out the image parts before we actually delete them.

1. Make sure Layer 1 is selected in the Layers palette.

2. Choose Layer➡Add Layer Mask➡Reveal All to create a layer mask for Layer 1. The layer's mask is represented by an additional thumbnail icon for Layer 1 in the Layers palette and is automatically selected (see Figure 14.12).

3. To eliminate the unwanted parts of the image on Layer 1, we are going to make a selection and fill

Note

Layer masks are grayscale masks that affect the transparency of the layer. Painting on the layer mask with solid black results in transparent pixels on the layer (hides the image in that area of the layer). Painting on the layer mask with solid white restores the pixels to their total opacity. Painting on the layer mask with percentages of black (gray) will change the opacity of the image pixels to that of the gray value. Painting the image with 50 percent black, for example, will make the image 50 percent transparent, allowing 50 percent of the underlying image to show through.

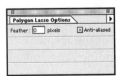

Figure 14.13

The Polygon Lasso Options palette.

 TIP

The default foreground and background colors for the layer mask are the opposite of the standard foreground and background colors. In the cases of layer masks and alpha channels the default foreground color is white (remove mask) and the default background color, black (create mask).

it with black on the layer mask. Click and hold on the Lasso tool in the Toolbox and select the Polygon Lasso tool.

4. Double-click the Polygon Lasso tool in the Toolbox to display the Polygon Lasso Options palette (see Figure 14.13) and make sure the feather radius is set to 0 (zero) pixels. It's OK to leave Anti-aliased checked.

5. The Polygon tool works kind of like a needle and thread: Click once at the point you want to start your selection. Point and click where you want to continue the selection. Continue to point and click until you have surrounded the area of the image you want to mask out. When you return to the first point you clicked, the cursor will contain a loop to indicate that you are about to close a polygonal selection. Click the first point to close the selection.

6. Set the background color to black if it is not already set to black by pressing D for default colors.

7. Press (Delete)[Backspace] to fill the selection with the background color (black). This will paint the mask black in the selected area and make that part of the layer transparent. Note the change to the layer mask thumbnail in the Layers palette (see Figure 14.14).

8. Turn off the selection by choosing Select➡None or by typing (Command-D)[Control-D].

9. Apply the layer mask to the layer by clicking the layer mask thumbnail icon in the Layers palette and clicking the Trash Can icon in the Layers palette. Photoshop will display a dialog box asking you whether you want to apply or discard the layer mask (see Figure 14.15). Click the Apply button to apply the layer mask to the image.

TIP

To view only the layer mask, (Option-Click)[Alt-Click] the layer mask thumbnail in the Layers palette. (Option-Click)[Alt-Click] again to see the layer image. To temporarily turn off and on the effect of the layer mask, Shift-Click the layer mask thumbnail in the Layers palette.

Figure 14.14

The layer mask thumbnail displays the mask and the image pixels are made transparent where the mask is painted with black.

Figure 14.15

The layer mask changes are permanently applied to the layer when you click the Apply button.

10. Choose File➥Save or type (Command-S)[Control-S] to save what you've done so far. We are now ready to begin the restoration process.

Retouching with the Rubber Stamp Tool

We are now ready to begin repairing the photograph. The Rubber Stamp is a cloning tool that enables us to pick up one part of our image and apply it to another. Using the Rubber Stamp tool we will fill in the empty spaces, remove dirt and scratches, and invent some image data to rebuild missing pieces of our image.

1. At this point we can merge our two layers together into one to save processing time. If you want to preserve a copy of the file with the layers intact, choose File➥Save A Copy and save this file in Photoshop format with a new name. Make sure that both of the layers are visible and choose Flatten Image from either the Layer menu or the Layer palette menu.

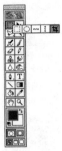

Figure 14.16

Select the Crop tool by clicking and holding on the Marquee tool.

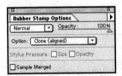

Figure 14.17

The Rubber Stamp Options palette.

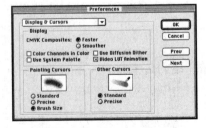

Figure 14.18

Choose Brush Size for the Painting Cursors option to make the cursor display in the brush size when painting.

2. Crop the image to eliminate some of the excess white space to the left of the image. Select the Crop tool from the Toolbox or type the letter C to select the Crop tool (see Figure 14.16) and drag a selection around the part of the image you want to crop. Adjust the cropping area by clicking and dragging the handles around the cropping rectangle.

3. Double-click in the center of the cropping rectangle to crop the image or simply type the Return or Enter key. Type the escape (Esc) key to cancel the cropping without making changes.

4. Choose File➡Save or type (Command-S)[Control-S] to save the image.

5. Double-click the Rubber Stamp tool in the Toolbox to display the Rubber Stamp Options palette (see Figure 14.18).

6. Set the blending mode to Normal, the Opacity to 100%, and the Option to Clone (aligned). You can leave the Sample Merged checkbox unchecked because it only applies to layered files. Turning on Sample Merged would enable you to pick up (sample) part of the image from one layer and apply it to another.

7. Choose File➡Preferences➡Display & Cursors to display the Preferences dialog box and select Brush Size for the Painting Cursors option (see Figure 14.18), then click the OK button. This preference will display the cursor in the size of the brush to help make the correct brush selection.

8. Choose Window➡Show Brushes to display the Brushes palette and select the brush in the middle row above the 100 pixel brush to start off with (see Figure 14.19).

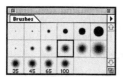

Figure 14.19

The Brushes palette.

TIP

Display the context menu by (Control-clicking)[Clicking with the Right Mouse Button] the image and select from: Next Brush, Previous Brush, First Brush or Last Brush (see Figure 14.20).

Figure 14.20

Use the Context Menu to quickly select a brush size.

9. Zoom in close to the center of the image where the ascot is tied in a bow and position your cursor over the part of the image you want to pick up and use as a replacement for another part of the image.

10. (Option-Click)[Alt-Click] the image to select the point you want to start cloning from. The cursor will change to display the Rubber Stamp cursor with a white triangle.

11. Position your cursor over the part of the image you want to begin cloning and click one time (no keys held down). Note that the place you click is replaced with the part of the image you (Option-clicked)[Alt-clicked]. You can (Option-click)[Alt-click] an origin point and then click and drag with the Rubber Stamp tool, but the dragging often creates a secondary pattern that is undesirable. The most effective way to use the Rubber Stamp tool in this instance is to select the origin point ((Option-Click)[Alt-Click]), then click the destination point, tapping in changes gradually (see Figure 14.21). It's time consuming, but the results are worth it.

Figure 14.21

Tapping in the clone effect, rather than dragging through the image produces the best results.

TIP

Hold down (Command-Spacebar)[Control-Spacebar] to temporarily access the Zoom tool and zoom in. Hold down (Command-Option-Spacebar) [Control-Alt-Spacebar] to Zoom out.

12. Use the above technique to repair the entire image. You will have to invent the parts of the image that are missing by using parts of the image you already have. Note how I chose to handle the missing pieces of the couch in the completed picture at the beginning of the chapter. Concentrate on the larger imperfections, then read on for techniques to repair the specks, dust, and scratches in the image.

Retouching from the Saved Image

If you make mistakes when using the Rubber Stamp tool, you can easily repair them by painting back parts of the image from the last saved version of the file.

1. If you have made changes to the image since the last time you saved the file, you can restore parts of the image from the saved file with the Rubber Stamp tool. Double-click the Rubber Stamp tool to display the Rubber Stamp Options palette.

Figure 14.22

The From Saved Option choice in The Rubber Stamp Options palette.

2. Select From Saved from the Option drop-down menu in the Rubber Stamp Options palette (see Figure 14.22).

3. Position the cursor over the part of the image you want to restore and begin painting. It may take a few seconds for Photoshop to load the saved image, so keep the mouse button held down.

Retouching from a Snapshot

When you take a snapshot of your image, you give yourself another place to undo back to, aside from the saved file.

1. Choose Edit➥Take Snapshot. You won't hear a camera-click noise, but the cursor will probably turn busy for a few seconds while Photoshop stores the snapshot in memory.

2. Make some changes to your image using the Rubber Stamp tool with the Clone Aligned option selected from the Option drop-down menu in the Rubber Stamp Options palette.

3. Select From Snapshot from the Option drop-down menu in the Rubber Stamp Options palette.

4. Position the cursor over the part of the image that has been changed since you took the snapshot and begin painting. It may take a few seconds for Photoshop to load the stored image, so keep the mouse button held down.

Adjusting the Levels

After you have repaired the major damage to the image and can view the entire image in one piece, you can make adjustments to the image's tonal balance. This particular image is rather dark and is heavily weighted in the shadow areas. To adjust the tonal balance of the image, we are going to use the Levels command.

1. If you performed the steps to assemble the image and made the major repairs needed, open the file you created; otherwise, open lessons/chap14/jesse.psd on the CD-ROM that accompanies this book.

2. The first thing we need to do is evaluate the luminosity (brightness) values of our image. The best way to view the distribution of pixels in our image is using the Histogram dialog box. Choose Image➡ Histogram to display the Histogram dialog box (see Figure 14.23). Using the histogram, we can see exactly where all of the pixels in our image fall in regards to brightness level. The gradient bar under the histogram represents the full range of luminance values from 0 (black) to 255 (white). The pixels for our image are all clumped up in the shadow and ¾ tone area, which explains why the image is so dark. The values listed under the gradient bar tell us statistical information about the pixels in our image:

▶ **Mean** represents the average brightness value; in our case 45.29 which is rather dark.

▶ **Std Dev** represents the standard deviation of the pixels or how wide they vary from the mean. In our image, the value of 14.45 indicates that our image pixels are relatively close to the average brightness value.

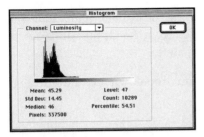

Figure 14.23

The Histogram dialog box before any changes to the brightness and contrast of the image are made.

▶ **Median** represents the middle brightness value of the image. In our image, this value is 46, which means that half the pixels are darker than 46 and half the pixels are brighter than 46.

▶ **Pixels** indicates the total number of pixels in our image.

▶ **Level** displays the brightness level when you drag your cursor over the histogram.

▶ **Count** tells you the exact number of pixels that have a particular brightness value (indicated by Level). In our image, for example, there are 10,289 pixels with a brightness value of 47.

▶ **Percentile** indicates what percentage of the grays in the image are less than or equal to Level value. When the cursor is over the part of the histogram with a Level value of 47, for example, the Percentile value is 54.51. This means that 54.51% of the pixels in our image are equal to or darker than (less than) the 47 gray level.

3. Click OK after you've examined the histogram of our image. We'll come back the Histogram dialog box after we've made some adjustments to the brightness levels of our image.

4. Choose Image➡Adjust➡Levels or type (Command-L)[Control-L] to display the Levels dialog box (see Figure 14.24). The histogram of the image is displayed in the Levels dialog box. The histogram reflects the brightness levels of the pixels in the image. The total number of pixels in the image are distributed in the histogram from darkest (0) to brightest (255). We are going to adjust the overall brightness, so we will be adjusting all three channels (Red, Green, and Blue) at the same time.

5. Be sure RGB is selected in the Channel drop-down menu at the top of the Levels dialog box.

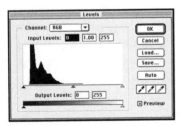

Figure 14.24

The Levels dialog box displays a histogram of the image.

6. Click the black left triangle slider under the histogram and drag to the right until the first Input Levels value is 12. This will cause the shadow areas to darken because we are setting the darkest pixels in the image to 0 (zero).

7. Click the white right triangle slider under the histogram and drag to the left until the third Input Levels value is 154 to increase the contrast (see Figure 14.25). In this case, we are defining the pixels with a brightness value of 154 and mapping them to the Output Level of 255.

8. Drag the gray middle triangle slider to adjust the brightness values of the midtones in the image. Dragging to the right will make the midtones darker, whereas dragging to the left will brighten the midtone pixels. By dragging the gray middle triangle slider, you are setting the midtone of the image (128). Set this level to 1.15 (see Figure 14.25).

9. To decrease the contrast of the image somewhat, drag the left black triangle slider under the Output Levels gradient bar to the right until the shadow output level is 6. Drag the right white triangle slider under the Output Levels gradient bar to the left until the highlight value reads 250. When we adjusted the Input Levels of the image, we defined the darkest and brightest pixels. Adjusting the Output Levels, maps the shadow values so the darkest pixels will have a gray level of 6 and maps the highlight values to a brightest pixel value of 250 (see Figure 14.25).

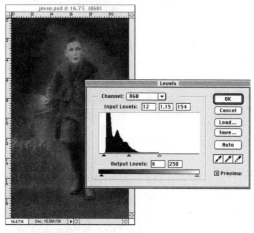

Figure 14.25

Adjust the brightness levels of the image by dragging the triangle sliders in the Levels dialog box.

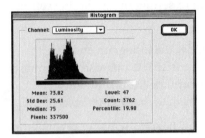

Figure 14.26

The Histogram of our image after adjusting the brightness values using Levels.

Figure 14.27

The Dust & Scratches dialog box.

10. Click OK. Save the file before continuing by choosing File➡Save or typing (Command-S)[Control-S].

11. Let's take a look at the histogram again, now that we have adjusted the brightness values of our image. Choose Image➡Histogram to display the Histogram dialog box (see Figure 14.26). The histogram displays a much wider distribution and indicates that overall our image pixels are significantly brighter.

Using the Dust & Scratches Filter

Now that we have adjusted the brightness values of the pixels in our image, the dust, scratches, and specks are much more apparent. We can use the Dust & Scratches filter to a limited extent to eliminate some of these artifacts. For our image, we are going to concentrate on reducing some of the "dirty-ness" in our image.

1. If you have completed all of the previous stages of correction described in this chapter, open your saved image, otherwise, open lessons/chap14/jesse2.psd on the CD-ROM that accompanies this book.

2. Zoom in to enlarge the top half of the image to fill your screen.

3. Choose Filter➡Noise➡Dust & Scratches to display the Dust & Scratches dialog box (see Figure 14.27). The Dust & Scratches filter blurs the image to some degree, so we'll have to take care not to overdo it.

4. Set the Radius to 2 pixels. Click the Preview checkbox to see the effect of your settings on the image. You may have to wait a few seconds for the screen to redraw. The Threshold value limits the parts of the image affected. We are going to leave the Threshold value at 0 (zero) so all of the pixels in our image are affected.

5. Click outside the Dust & Scratches dialog box on the image to change the picture preview in the dialog box or click inside the preview box and drag with the hand icon. Note that clicking in the preview box with the hand icon toggles a before and after preview. You can also click off the Preview checkbox to see the before and after effect on the whole image.

6. Click OK to apply the Dust & Scratches filter.

Removing Dirt and Dust Specks

The image we are using in this chapter contains a large amount of dirt and dust specks. There are areas of the image that have broken down over time and present a light colored speckle throughout the image. There are also areas of the image that contain very dark specks that are the result of mold and mildew accumulation on the original portrait. Although you can certainly use the Rubber Stamp tool to fix each and every one of these specks and spots, there are two blending modes that will make retouching these specks less time consuming. We are still going to use the Rubber Stamp tool, but this time we're going to use the Lighten and Darken blending modes to limit changes to specific areas.

1. If you have completed all of the previous stages of correction described in this chapter, open your saved image; otherwise, open lessons/chap14/jesse2.psd on the CD-ROM that accompanies this book.

2. Let's start in the upper-right corner of our image which contains an infusion of light colored spots. Double-click the Rubber Stamp tool in the Toolbox to display the Rubber Stamp Options palette and choose Darken from the blending modes drop-down menu (see Figure 14.28).

3. Select a relatively large brush with a soft edge from the Brushes palette.

4. (Option-click)[Alt-click] a dark area of the image next to an area that contains speckling.

5. Click the speckled area. Because we chose Darken as our blending mode, only the pixels with values lighter than the values of the pixels we (Option-clicked)[Alt-clicked] will be changed. Using this method to fix darker areas of the image that contain lighter speckling ensures that the changes to the pixels is limited to lighter colored pixels. Remove as many light colored specks as you can find in the image.

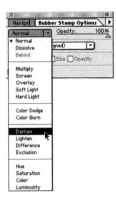

Figure 14.28

The Darken blending mode.

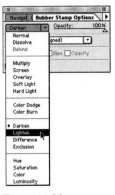

Figure 14.29

The Lighten blending mode.

6. Zoom in close so the middle of the boy's body is displayed in the window. Notice that this part of the image contains many darker specks. Choose Lighten from the blending modes drop down menu in the Rubber Stamp Options palette (see Figure 14.29).

7. Select a medium-sized brush with a soft edge from the Brushes palette.

8. (Option-click)[Alt-click] an area of the image next to an area that contains dark speckling.

9. Click the speckled area. Because we chose Lighten as our blending mode, only the pixels with values darker than the values of the pixels we (Option-clicked)[Alt-clicked] will be changed. Using this method to fix areas of the image that contain dark speckling ensures that the changes to the pixels is limited to darker-colored pixels. Remove as many dark specks as you can find in the image.

Saving the Retouched Image

Saving the image is a somewhat simple process, though we do need to consider the output specifications for our file before we save it. The image we created in this chapter by combining two separate images is currently 12" x 20" at 150 ppi (pixels per inch). As stated in the introduction to this chapter, we want to print this particular image on an inkjet printer to create limited edition prints. The optimum resolution for the color printer you are using may vary, depending on manufacturer, though most color inkjet printers perform optimally with an image resolution of 150 ppi. I printed this portrait on the Iris Inkjet Printer at my service bureau and left the size and resolution as is to support a variety of framing options later on. Most inkjet printers print using CMYK inks or dyes, so the final step in our process before saving the image is to convert it from RGB to CMYK.

1. If you have a completed image that you created by following all of the steps in this chapter, open that file; otherwise open lessons/chap14/jesse3.psd on the CD-ROM that accompanies this book.

2. Before we covert to CMYK we must specify the settings for the conversion process using the color setting options available under the File menu. Choose File➡Color Settings➡Printing Inks Setup to display the Printing Inks Setup dialog box (see Figure 14.30). The Printing Inks Setup dialog box is where we tell Photoshop what inks we'll be printing with, as well as information about expected dot gain.

3. The information for this dialog box must be acquired from the printer or service bureau.

   ▶ **Ink Colors.** This is where you select an ink type or printer in the case of color printers. The Iris Inkjet Printer works best using SWOP (Specifications for Web Offset Publications) inks on coated paper. The SWOP ink colors are the industry standard in the United States and differ from those used in Europe, as well as those used in color wax transfer printers such as the QMS Colorscript and Tektronix Phaser. Ask your printer or service bureau what to specify here.

   ▶ **Dot Gain.** The Dot Gain percentage specifies how much the size of the 50% midtone dot changes when printed and is the result of ink absorbency, paper type, and to some degree press conditions. The only way to accurately determine dot gain is to print a proof with calibration bars and take a reading with a reflective densitometer of the 50% mark on the printed calibration bar. Inkjet printers tend to be around the 20% range for dot gain, so we will leave the dot gain percentage set to 20%. (See Chapter 17, "Printing," for more information on setting the dot gain percentage.)

   ▶ **Gray Balance.** The Gray Balance text boxes contain gamma values to adjust for color cast on the printer. You should rarely have to change these values to print to a well calibrated color printer. Service bureaus and printers generally calibrate their equipment on a regular basis to ensure color consistency, so leave these values at 1.00.

4. Click OK to save the settings illustrated in Figure 14.31.

Figure 14.30

The Printing Inks Setup dialog box.

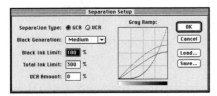

Figure 14.31

The Separation Setup dialog box.

5. Choose File➡Color Settings➡Separation Setup to display the Separation Setup dialog box (see Figure 14.31). The Separation Setup is used to specify precisely how Photoshop converts the RGB data to CMYK data.

6. There are two Separation Type's available: GCR (Gray Component Replacement) and UCR (Undercolor Removal). When you choose UCR, the black plate is used to add depth to the shadow areas and neutral colors and contains much less ink coverage overall than its counterpart, GCR. When you choose GCR, the black ink is used over a much wider range of colors and produces better results for an image that contains dark, saturated color areas. The service bureau or printer can tell you what setting is best to use for Separation Type, though GCR seems to be the most widely specified these days. We are going to use GCR to print the inkjet printer because our image contains some dark saturated areas.

7. When you choose GCR as the Separation Type, you must specify a Black Generation. Medium is the sensible choice for most images because the medium setting will not overtake the color intensity in the image, but will generate enough black to maintain overall contrast.

8. The Total Ink Limit is the maximum ink density your printer or printing press can support. The Black Ink Limit is the proportion of the Total Ink Limit that is generated for the black plate. Photoshop's default settings of 100% for Black Ink Limit and 300% for Total Ink Limit will work fine for us to print to the Iris Inkjet Printer, but check with your printer or service bureau to get these values before changing them. The UCA (undercolor addition) Amount is used to specify how much CMY is added back to the shadow areas. You should leave this value at 0% unless instructed otherwise by your printer.

9. Click OK after you have specified the settings illustrated in Figure 14.31.

10. We are now ready to perform the conversion to CMYK. Choose Image➡Mode➡CMYK Color to convert from RGB to CMYK.

11. Choose File➡Save As and save this file as either a TIFF file or a Photoshop EPS file if you are going to place it in a page layout application such as PageMaker or QuarkXPress. If you want to send the file in Photoshop format, check with your service bureau or printer, because they may prefer another format.

Using Actions

It is now possible to record processes you perform in Photoshop and then play them back later using the Actions palette. Although it would be nice to record everything you do in Photoshop, this isn't necessarily the case with actions. You can access all of the menu commands, although you cannot record some of them; you must add them to an Action script using the Insert Menu Command option. In the Toolbox, the Eyedropper and Crop tools are the only recordable tools. You also can specify foreground and background colors, swap the foreground and background colors and reset them to the default colors. Keystrokes also are not recordable. Choosing Page Setup, for example, and specifying Page Setup parameters are not possible at this time, although you can add the Page Setup command to an action to display the Page Setup dialog box.

In this chapter, you record some actions, play them back and then use the Batch command in the Actions palette to perform recorded actions on a folder full of files. In the first exercise, you record the actions to create a torn edges effect for an image and then apply the effect to another image with the click of a button (see Figure 15.1).

Figure 15.1

The steps to create the torn edges effect are recorded while performed on the first image (left), then played back for subsequent images (right).

Recording Actions

The Actions palette contains some VCR-like buttons at the bottom of the palette to facilitate recording. See Chapter 1, "Photoshop Basics," for more information on the Actions palette. The Record button is represented by a solid black circle, the Stop button a solid square, and the Play button a right pointing triangle. In this palette the icon that looks like an up-turned page is used to define a new action—the first step in creating actions. The Actions palette has two modes: a script mode so you can view and edit the steps in the action, and a Button mode that turns the Actions palette into a palette of clickable buttons. When the Actions palette is in Button mode, you cannot define or record actions.

1. Open lessons/chap15/castle.psd on the CD-ROM that accompanies this book.

Figure 15.2

The Actions palette.

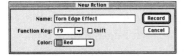

Figure 15.3

The New Action dialog box.

2. Choose Window➡Show Actions to display the Actions palette (see Figure 15.2). The Actions palette contains actions added when you first installed Photoshop. If you want to start out with an empty Actions palette, drag the Actions onto the Trash icon at the bottom of the Actions palette. Chapter 1, "Photoshop Basics," explains the Actions palette in detail.

3. Click the triangle in the upper right-hand corner of the Actions palette and make sure that you have not selected (checked) Button Mode.

4. Choose New Action from the Actions palette menu or click the New Action icon at the bottom of the Actions palette to display the New Action dialog box (see Figure 15.3).

5. Name this action "Torn Edge Effect" and choose a Function key and Color. (The Function Key and Color choices are optional.) If you assign a color to this action, the action displays as a colored button in the Actions palette when it's set to Button Mode. Click on the Record button to begin recording this action. Note that the Record button at the bottom of the Actions palette turns red to indicate recording mode. Photoshop adds the new action you defined to the bottom of the Actions list.

6. Choose Select➡All or type (Command-A) [Control-A]. Note that you record this action in the Actions palette.

7. Choose Select➡Modify➡Border to display the Border dialog box, and then enter a width of 64 pixels. Click OK. This creates a 32-pixel border around our image because the Border command selects 32 pixels inside the original selection and 32 pixels outside. Because our original selection was around the outside edges of the image, only the 32 pixels inside are selected.

8. Choose Select➥Feather or type (Command-Shift-D)[Control-Shift-D] to display the Feather Selection dialog box, and then enter 10 pixels for a feather radius. Click OK.

9. Type the letter D to set the foreground and background colors to the default Black foreground/White background.

10. Press the (Delete)[Backspace] key to fill the selected area with the background color (white).

Figure 15.4

The Torn Edges dialog box.

11. Choose Filter➥Sketch➥Torn Edges to display the Torn Edges dialog box (see Figure 15.4). To view the effect, click and drag the image in the preview window in the Torn Edges dialog box. Note that the Torn Edges filter uses the Foreground color (black) to create the torn edge effect. Set the following parameters: Image Balance, 36; Smoothness, 11; and Contrast, 19; click OK.

12. Type (Command-D)[Control-D] to deselect.

13. Click the Stop Recording icon at the bottom of the Actions palette, or choose Stop Recording from the Palette menu.

14. Close the castle.psd file, or save it to your hard disk.

Photoshop saves the action you just recorded in the Photoshop preferences file. The action now appears in the Actions palette, unless you delete the preferences file from your hard disk. Because it may be necessary at some point to delete the preferences file, save this list of actions by choosing Save Actions from the Actions palette menu. All actions in the Actions palette are saved (including the default actions), so you may want to delete the default actions before saving to facilitate appending the saved action to the Actions palette at a future date. Now that you have created an action, let's open another file and employ the action.

1. Open lessons/chap15/alps.psd on the CD-ROM that accompanies this book.

2. Select the Torn Edge Effect action in the Actions palette.

3. Click the Play Action icon at the bottom of the Actions palette, or choose PlayTorn Edge Effect from the Actions palette menu.

Editing Actions

Once you have recorded an action in the Action palette, you can edit the individual steps, remove action steps, or insert action steps into the action. You also can annotate an action by inserting stops that display a dialog box that contains instructions you specify.

1. To display the steps in the Torn Edge Effect action, click the triangle to the left of the action in the Actions palette so it points downward. Each step in the action displays in an expandable list (see Figure 15.5).

   ► If the action's step has parameters, it will have a triangle to its left. Click these triangles to view the parameters (settings) for the step.

   ► Click the check marks to the left of the action and the action steps to toggle the items on and off. If an action or command is toggled off (no check mark), it won't be executed when you play the action.

   ► Click inside the embossed boxes to the left of the action and action steps to toggle dialog boxes on and off. If you turn on dialog boxes for the entire action, the action pauses playback and waits for user input at every dialog box. If you want to specify the dialog boxes that wait for user input, click in the embossed box to the left of the individual step. When dialog boxes are turned on for the entire action, the dialog box icon displays in black; it displays in red if dialog boxes are turned on for some, but not all of the steps in the action.

2. Select the Delete step in the "Torn Edge Effect" action by clicking its name to highlight it.

3. Choose Delete from the Actions palette menu and click OK when the confirmation dialog box appears.

Figure 15.5

The Actions palette with actions and steps expanded.

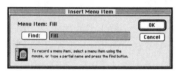

Figure 15.6

The Insert Menu Item dialog box.

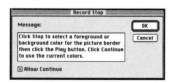

Figure 15.7

The Record Stop dialog box.

4. Instead of filling the background color, give the user the choice of fill color by displaying the Fill dialog box. Photoshop will insert the new step you are about to record directly below the step selected in the Actions palette; so, select the Reset step to insert the new step between Reset and Torn Edges.

5. Choose Insert Menu Item from the Actions palette menu to display the Insert Menu Item dialog box (see Figure 15.6).

   You can specify the command you want to insert in one of three ways:

   ► Choose Edit➡Fill from the menu bar.

   ► Type the word Fill in the text box.

   ► Type a partial command like Fi in the text box; click the Find button to locate the command that contains the entered text.

6. Click OK to add the Fill command as a step in the Torn Edge Effect action. Note that with the Fill command, you do not have the option of turning the dialog box on or off because this command requires user input every time.

7. Give the user the option of specifying the border and feather radius. Click in the embossed box to the left of the Border and Feather steps to turn on the dialog box for these steps.

8. Choose Delete Reset from the Action palette menu or drag the Reset step onto the Trash icon at the bottom of the Actions palette.

9. Select the Feather step in the Actions palette to highlight it; choose Insert Stop from the Actions palette menu to display the Record Stop dialog box (see Figure 15.7).

10. Type *Click Stop to select a foreground or background for the picture border then click the Play button. Click Continue to use the current colors.* Check the Allow Continue checkbox to include a Continue button in the dialog box that appears. Click OK.

11. Open lessons/chap15/wall.psd on the CD-ROM that accompanies this book.

12. Choose Button Mode from the Actions palette menu to display the actions as buttons.

13. Click the Torn Edge Effect button in the Actions palette. The action pauses at the dialog boxes you indicated and displays a dialog box with the message you entered in Step 9 for the Stop item. If you click the Stop button to define the foreground and background colors, click the Torn Edge Effect button again to continue playing back the action. Keep in mind that the Torn Edges filter uses the foreground color you specify to create the torn edge effect.

Batch Processing

Batch processing is probably the most exciting addition to Photoshop 4.0, especially if you're routinely converting scanned images into indexed color Web graphics. You can perform batch processing on a folder full of files, on the fly as you scan images into Photoshop with your desktop scanner or import them from a digital camera. In this section we're going to define an action that converts an RGB image into an Indexed color image conforming to the Web specific 216 color palette and save the file in GIF format. Once we've defined the action, a few simple steps enables us to batch process a folder full of files using the action.

Using the Batch Command to Make Web Graphics

The Action palette contains the batch command that enables you to apply an action to a folder full of files or to files that you have imported using a scanner or digital camera. The batch command is helpful if you want to apply the same effects to a number of images on disk or if you want to make color and sharpening adjustments automatically while scanning. In the following exercise you will learn the steps to batch process files to create GIF files for the Web. You can use the same techniques outlined below to create other Web graphic format files such as PNG and JPEG as well.

1. Open lessons/chap15/tower.psd on the CD-ROM that accompanies this book.

2. Choose Window➡Show Actions to display the Actions palette (if it isn't already onscreen).

3. Before you can use the batch option, you must first create an action. Choose New Action from the Actions palette menu or click the New Action icon at the bottom of the Actions palette to display the New Action dialog box.

4. Name the new action "Make Web Ready" and click on the Record button to begin recording this action.

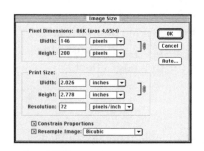

Figure 15.8

The Image Size dialog box.

5. Choose Image➡Image Size to display the Image Size dialog box (see Figure 15.8).

6. Make sure that you have checked the Constrain Proportions and Resample Image (Bicubic) checkboxes.

7. Change the Resolution to 72 pixels/inch.

8. For purposes of this example, limit your Web graphics to no more than 200 pixels in height. Enter 200 in the Height text box. Click OK to resize the image.

Figure 15.9

The Indexed Color dialog box.

9. Choose Image➡Mode➡Indexed Color to display the Indexed Color dialog box (see Figure 15.9).

10. Choose Web as the palette type from the Palette drop-down menu. The Color Depth and Colors values automatically change to Other and 216 respectively. Choose Diffusion as the Dither type, if it's not already selected. Click OK to convert the RGB image to Indexed Color.

Figure 15.10

Create a new directory on your hard disk before saving the GIF file.

11. Navigate to your hard disk and create a new (folder)[directory] called "gifs," and choose Compuserve GIF from the Format drop-down menu (see Figure 15.10). Click Save to display the

Note

MacOS users only: Choose File➥Preferences➥Saving Files to display the Preferences dialog box and choose Always from the drop-down menu to the right of Append File Extension. Set this preference so the file extension changes when you save your file. Choose File➥Save As to display the Save As dialog box.

Figure 15.11

Select Interlaced from the GIF Options dialog box.

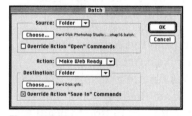

Figure 15.12

The Batch dialog box.

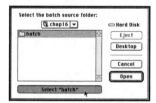

Figure 15.13

Select batch as the source folder.

GIF Options dialog box. Click the Interlaced radio button, and then click OK to save the file as a GIF file (see Figure 15.11). This new directory will be the target directory when you perform the batch in the next steps. Don't worry that the action will create a new directory each time it is run because this step is not recorded as an action.

12. Click the Stop Recording icon at the bottom of the Actions palette, or choose Stop Recording from the Actions palette menu.

13. Close the open file without saving changes.

Now that you have recorded the actions you want to perform on a bunch of files, the next steps detail the process of performing the batch process.

1. Choose Batch from the Actions palette menu to display the Batch dialog box (see Figure 15.12).

2. Choose Folder from the Source drop-down menu.

3. Click the Choose button to select a source directory. On the CD-ROM that accompanies this book, navigate to lessons/chap15/batch, and then click the button below the file list window that says Select "batch" (see Figure 15.13).

4. The checkbox for Override Action Open Commands can remain unchecked because the Make Web Ready action does not include any open commands.

5. Choose Make Web Ready from the Action drop-down list to select the action that will be performed on your batch of files.

6. Choose Folder from the Destination drop-down menu and click the Choose button to select the target directory for your batched files. Navigate to your hard disk to the gifs directory you created earlier and click the button that says Select "gifs" (see Figure 15.14).

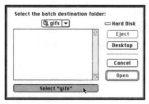

Figure 15.14

Select a destination directory for your batched files.

Using GIF89a Export for Batch Processing

You may be wondering why I used the CompuServe GIF format instead of exporting to the GIF89a format. If you want to use the GIF89a Export plug-in to save your GIF files, you must turn on the dialog box for the Export step in the action. This is necessary because Photoshop saves the files with the same name you used to create the action originally. You can avoid this naming problem by using the Insert Menu Item option in the Actions palette menu and inserting the GIF89a Export menu item—in which case you have to manually save the files anyway. You end up with twice as many files because the batch creates new files in the original format as well as the GIF89a format, even if you turn on the dialog box to save the GIF files. This seems like a glitch with the GIF89a plug-in and may be corrected in future updates. For more information on the GIF89a Export filter see Chapter 16, "Creating Web Graphics."

7. Check the checkbox for Override Action Save In Commands (to make sure that the files are saved in the directory you specified in the Batch dialog box, and not the directory specified in the action). In this example, they are both the same directory so it doesn't matter if you check this box or not.

8. Click OK to begin batch processing the files. Once the batch is complete, you will find the new GIF files in the gifs directory on your hard disk.

Recording Batch Commands

You can record the batch command as a separate action. This enables you to quickly batch files from one folder to another, or to batch files from an input device like a scanner or digital camera.

1. If you did not perform the steps previously outlined to create the Make Web Ready action, perform them before continuing.

2. Choose New Action from the Actions palette menu or click on the New Action icon at the bottom of the Actions palette to display the New Action dialog box. Name the new action Batch Web Ready. Click the Record button to begin recording this action.

3. Choose Batch from the Actions palette menu to display the Batch dialog box.

4. Choose Folder from the Source drop-down menu.

5. Click the Choose button to select a source directory. On the CD-ROM that accompanies this book, navigate to lessons/chap15/batch and click the button below the file list window that says Select batch.

6. The checkbox for Override Action Open Command can remain unchecked because the Make Web Ready action does not include any open commands.

7. Choose Make Web Ready from the Action drop-down list to select the action you want performed on your batch of files.

8. Choose Folder from the Destination drop-down menu and click the Choose button to select the target directory for your batched files. Navigate to your hard disk to the gifs directory you created earlier; click the button that says Select gifs.

9. Check the checkbox for Override Action Save In Commands to make sure that the files are saved in the directory you specified in the Batch dialog box, and not the directory specified in the action. In this example, they are both the same directory so it doesn't matter if you check this box or not.

10. Click OK to begin batch processing the files. Once the batch is complete, click the Stop Recording icon in the Actions palette, or choose Stop Recording from the Actions palette menu. You now have an action that opens files in one location (batch) and saves the changed files in another location (gifs). You can use this method of recording batches to process files for your Web site, for example—assuming you do not rename the directories or move them.

Record multiple batch commands and include them in one action to perform multiple transformations with different source and target directories. For example, you may want to have one batch save scanned RGB images to a directory on your hard disk; a second batch to convert those RGB files to CMYK and save them into another folder; a third batch to convert the RGB files into indexed color and save them to a directory on your Web site. Remember to save the actions you create, in case the Photoshop preferences file becomes corrupt and must be thrown away.

Summary

In this chapter you learned how to define actions and record processes to later apply to other images. Even though the recordable functions are limited in some respects, actions can still save you tons of time and increase your productivity. The last part of this chapter deals specifically with batch processing files for the Web, though the batch processing function lends itself nicely to many situations where a number of files must have the same changes made to them. If you find yourself performing the same functions over and over again, ask yourself if these processes can be recorded in an action and perhaps used in a batch processing scenario. In the next chapter you'll learn much more about Web graphics and how to create and save them.

Creating Web Graphics

Photoshop is a great tool for creating graphics to be used on Internet Web pages. Creating custom graphic elements and saving photographic images in the correct format is a breeze once you learn the basics of Web graphics. If you are not currently creating graphics for Web pages, chances are pretty good that you will be in the near future because the trend in publishing of late is to repurpose print graphics for Web pages.

Web graphics have some very specific requirements as far as resolution and color depth go. They are generally rendered at 72 pixels per inch (ppi) on Web pages designed in HTML (HyperText Markup Language) and are indexed color images that can contain a maximum of 256 colors.

Because Web pages are viewed on a variety of platforms, most notably MacOS and Windows, color specification for Web graphics is very important. There are 40 of the 256 colors that do not display the same way on both the MacOS and Windows platforms. For this reason, Photoshop now supports a 216-color Web palette (same as the Netscape non-dithering palette) when converting color images to indexed color.

Currently, the most popular file formats for Web graphics are GIF (Graphics Interchange Format) and JPEG (Joint Photographic Experts Group), though I expect the relatively new PNG (Portable Network Graphics) format will continue to gain popularity and acceptance. Before we begin the exercises for this chapter, let's take a look at the file formats we need to keep in mind when designing Web graphics.

GIF Files

The GIF file format was originally developed by CompuServe as a platform-independent graphic format. GIF files are compressed using LZW compression, a lossless compression scheme. This means the GIF file can be compressed, uncompressed, and recompressed any number of times without loss of image quality. GIF images are indexed color images that should be indexed to the lowest possible number of colors to a maximum of 256 colors.

Photoshop 4 comes with the GIF89a plug-in, which enables you to export indexed color images to the GIF format. The GIF89a format supports a single transparency color that you define when saving the file and has the option of creating an interlaced GIF file. Interlaced GIF's are rendered onscreen in stages, enabling the person browsing a Web page that contains the GIF to see the full image at a low resolution right away so he or she can decide whether or not to wait for the graphic to complete (see Figure 16.1). For more information on GIF transparency see the section "Transparency in GIF Files," later in this chapter.

GIF files are primarily used as design elements such as buttons, divider lines, banners, and stylized text on Web pages and can also be used as hypertext links to another part of the Web page, another URL address, or a higher resolution JPEG file of the same image. GIF files are best for graphics that contain flat color as opposed to photographic images that display best in the JPEG format. For information on saving GIF files, see the section "Exporting the GIF File" later in this chapter.

Figure 16.1

Interlacing renders the image onscreen in stages, each successive stage making the image clearer and sharper.

JPEG Files

JPEG files are used on Web pages when high-resolution, full-color images are needed because JPEG files are RGB images that can contain millions of colors. Because JPEG files are 24-bit RGB color images, they lend themselves well to transference over the Internet and across platforms when you want to transfer a high-resolution image. JPEG files are compressed using a "lossy" compression scheme that deletes color data from the file. Most software packages that generate JPEG files, Photoshop included, provide a method to specify the amount of compression to use based on the image quality desired. When the compression setting is set too high, the image quality suffers (see Figure 16.2). This is the drawback to JPEG files; once the color data is thrown away to compress the file, uncompressing the file does not restore the data. Amazingly enough, even the highest compression setting (largest loss of color data) can produce a decent image for use on Web pages, though I wouldn't recommend printing with the same file.

Figure 16.2

The image on the left is the original image with no compression applied; the image at right is a JPEG image with the maximum compression applied (enlarged view).

PNG Files

The Portable Network Graphics (PNG) format (pronounced ping) was designed to replace the GIF format for some applications. Though not supported by the most popular Web browsers at this writing, full support seems like it's right around the corner and a lot of people are really excited about this new format. The PNG format has three distinct advantages over the more common GIF format.

► Supports alpha channels, so it is capable of saving images with variable transparency such as vignettes and fades.

► Contains algorithms for gamma correction so images display properly on different platforms.

► Supports two-dimensional interlacing to progressively display color images.

For the most part, PNG files compress better than GIF files and can contain 48-bit RGB color or 16-bit grayscale—GIF's can contain only 8 bits. RGB images contain 24 bits of data and grayscale images contain 8 bits of data to describe the pixel's color. A 48-bit RGB image contains the standard 24 bits of RGB data plus an additional 24 bits to support alpha channels with variable transparency and gamma correction. 16-bit grayscale images contain the standard 8 bits of grayscale data plus an additional 8 bits to support an alpha channel with variable transparency and gamma correction. The compression method is lossless, like the GIF file, so compressing and uncompressing does not degrade the image. PNG files also compress 10 to 30 percent smaller than GIF files. In Photoshop you can choose from five different filters that prepare a file for compression: Sub, Up, Average, Paeth, and Adaptive (see Figure 16.3).

Which filter to use is pretty much up in the air at this point because there isn't a lot of information out there about which ones to use and when. I find that I generally get the best compression with the Adaptive filter, though the difference in file size is not significant and varies from image to image. The interlace method used for PNG files is called Adam7 and is the method supported in Photoshop 4 as well. The PNG format also contains code that detects some forms of file corruption and performs data integrity checking to help the image display properly on the user's computer platform.

As of this writing the PNG format is not widely implemented, so the exercise we perform in this chapter deals primarily with the GIF and JPEG formats.

Figure 16.3

The PNG Options dialog box.

Resolution and Dimensions

When designing a Web page, it is best to design for the lowest common denominator in regards to monitor size. The rule of thumb is to design for a 13-inch monitor (640×480 pixels) and a resolution of 72 ppi. Keep in mind that the browser software takes up some of the space, so you probably want to keep the width around 600 pixels and the height around 400 pixels.

Note

When choosing color schemes or photographic images, it helps to keep in mind that some folks on the Web only have a grayscale monitor so images that are heavily weighted in the shadows or highlights will lack adequate contrast. There isn't anything we can do about the people with non-graphical mono-chrome monitors, though alternate text is usually provided by the Web designer to substitute for the lack of graphics in this case.

When creating graphics for Web pages in Photoshop, change the measurement units to pixels and work in the 100% view to see an accurate representation of the graphics you're creating. You should also keep in mind that many users will be connecting to the Internet at less than optimum speed, some as slow as 2,400 bits per second. Keeping the graphic elements small (around 150–200 pixels on a side) greatly reduces the amount of time a browser takes to draw a Web page compared to a graphic that covers half or more of the screen area.

Creating a Background Image

You no doubt noticed that a fair amount of Web pages contain background images instead of the plain gray background of the browser. HTML documents (Web pages) display images in the background based on the image size. If the image size is small enough, the image is tiled to fill the background area. When the image size is large enough to cover the entire background area, the image is displayed as a backdrop for the Web page.

In this exercise we create a backdrop for a fictitious Web page for a ski resort (see Figure 16.4). We will include some rectangular elements that serve as buttons on our Web page. In order for these buttons to be implemented, the Web designer and Web master must work together to determine X and Y coordinates of the buttons' "hot spots" to create an imagemap that will be handled by a CGI (Common Gateway Interface) script on the Web server. Check with your service provider or Webmaster (system administrator) before including imagemap graphics on your Web page because access to a CGI inter-preter on the file server, as well as a knowledgeable person to write a CGI script, is necessary.

Figure 16.4

A graphic image as a backdrop for a Web page.

To start off with, we will open the background image and take advantage of Photoshop 4.0's new ruler guides to help us align things on our Web graphic.

1. Open lessons/chap16/village.psd on the CD-ROM that accompanies this book.

2. Choose Window➡Show Layers to display the Layers palette.

3. If the rulers are not visible, type (Command-R) [Control-R] to turn them on.

4. Set the ruler units to inches by double-clicking the ruler and selecting inches from the drop-down menu in the Units & Rulers Preferences dialog box, then click OK.

5. Make sure the 0,0 coordinates are in the upper-left corner by double-clicking in the upper-left corner where the horizontal and vertical rulers meet.

6. Choose View➡Show Guides or type (Command-;) [Control-;].

7. Click the horizontal ruler and drag a guide to the
0.5-inch mark on the ruler and another to the
6-inch mark.

8. Click the vertical ruler and drag a guide to 9.75
and another to 7.

Now that we have some guides to follow, we will
create a new layer and draw a semi-transparent box,
using the Snap To Guides function to draw the box to
the dimension within the guides.

1. Create a new layer in the Layers palette by
clicking the New Layer icon at the bottom of the
Layers palette or by choosing
Layer➡New➡Layer. Name the new layer "box."

2. Choose View➡Snap to Guides from the menu
bar.

3. Select the rectangular Marquee tool in the
Toolbox and drag a rectangular marquee to the
dimension of the guides.

4. Choose Edit➡Fill to display the Fill dialog box
and choose White for the contents. Leave the
Opacity slider at 100% and the Blending mode
pull-down menu at Normal. Click OK to fill the
selected area with solid white (see Figure 16.5).

Figure 16.5

*Drag a marquee to the dimensions
of the guides and fill the area with
solid white.*

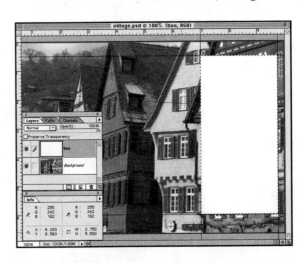

5. The solid white box should be on the "box" layer in the Layers palette, though it won't show up in the layer thumbnail because it's white. Type (Command-D)[Control-D] to deselect.

6. Choose Dissolve from the Blending Modes pull-down menu in the Layers palette and set the Opacity to 50% (see Figure 16.6).

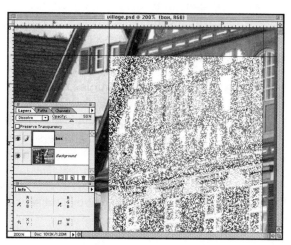

Figure 16.6

Use the Dissolve blending mode at a 50% opacity to create a snow effect.

In these next steps we will add some more guides to aid in creating some tabs that will serve as buttons on our Web page.

1. Hold down the (Command)[Control] key and drag the vertical guide at 7 to 8.5. Drag another vertical guide from the ruler to 5.5.

2. Drag ten horizontal guides 1/2-inch apart starting at 1 inch.

3. Choose Window➥Show Swatches to display the Swatches palette.

4. Create a new layer in the Layers palette.

5. Use the rectangular Marquee tool to drag a marquee starting 1 inch down and 5.5 inches across to 1.5 inches down and 8.5 inches across using the guides you made.

6. Select a bright color from the Swatches palette and type (Option-Delete)[Alt-Backspace] to fill the selected area with the new foreground color (see Figure 16.7). We will be adding white text on top of this box, so the color should be dark enough to provide contrast.

Figure 16.7

Use the guides to drag a selection and fill it with a dark bright color.

 TIP

Instead of dragging a new selection for each of the colored tabs, click inside the selection area with the Marquee tool and drag the selection marquee to the next position.

Figure 16.8

Create five tabs, each colored a different bright color.

7. Create four more rectangles 1/2-inch apart, coloring each a different bright color (see Figure 16.8). Create all five tabs on the same layer as the first tab and name the layer "Tabs."

The tabs are nice looking, but we really want the person browsing our Web page to get the idea that they should click these for information. In the next steps we will use a combination of layers and filters to make the tabs look more like buttons.

1. To make the tabs look like buttons, duplicate the Tabs layer. Choose Layer➡Duplicate Layer or drag the Tabs layer onto the New Layer icon at the bottom of the Layers palette. The new duplicate layer is inserted above the Tabs layer.

2. Choose Filter➡Stylize➡Emboss to display the Emboss dialog box and set the following parameters (see Figure 16.9):

   ▶ Angle: 135 degrees

   ▶ Height: 4 pixels

   ▶ Amount: 80%

3. Choose Multiply from the Blending Modes pull-down menu in the Layers palette to combine the embossed effect with the underlying tabs. Drag the Opacity slider on the Tabs copy layer to lessen the effect of the emboss and brighten up the buttons. I chose 80%.

4. To combine the embossed layer with the Tabs layer type (Command-E)[Control-E] or choose Layer➡Merge Down. This step is optional because you may want to change the opacity of the embossed layer later on.

In these next steps, we will add some text to our buttons using the Text tool, employing additional

Figure 16.9

The Emboss dialog box.

guides to help us position the text uniformly in all the buttons. We'll use the Emboss filter and the Difference blending mode to make the text stand out on the button tabs.

1. Drag a new vertical guide to 5.75 to help line up the text for the buttons.

2. Create a new layer for the text and name the layer "Text."

3. Set the Foreground color to White.

4. Select the Type tool in the Toolbox and click the first button you created in the image window to display the Type dialog box. Use a bold sans serif typeface at around 24 point and type the word "LODGING" in the text box. Click OK.

5. Use the Move tool to position the text in the button, aligning the left side with the guide at 5.75 inches. Turn off the Snap to Guides option in the View menu if your text is jumping to the guides. Use the arrow keys on your keyboard to nudge the text into position.

6. Create the text for the rest of the buttons (SKI TRAILS, DINING, EVENTS, and NIGHT LIFE). Each time you create new text a new layer is automatically created. Type (Command-E)[Control-E] or choose Layer➡Merge Down to merge the new layers with the Text layer (see Figure 16.10).

7. Be sure all of the text is on the Text layer and the Text layer is selected in the Layers palette.

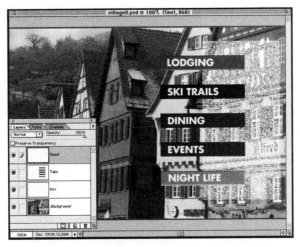

Figure 16.10

Create all the text for the buttons on one layer.

8. Choose Filter➡Stylize➡Emboss to display the Emboss dialog box and set the following parameters:

   ► Angle: 135°

   ► Height: 2 pixels

   ► Amount 100%

9. Choose Difference from the Blending Modes menu to create raised text in complementary colors.

Now that we have our button tabs created, let's add the title to this Web page using vertically aligned text.

1. Set the Foreground color to a bright red.

2. Use the Type tool to create the "ALPINE VILLAGE" text. Select a bold sans serif typeface and set the size to 30 points. Choose centered vertical alignment from the Alignment choices in the Type Tool dialog box by clicking the radio button in the center of the right column of choices (see Figure 16.11).

3. Position the text ½ inch in from the left side of the image and visually center it top and bottom.

Figure 16.11

The Type Tool dialog box with centered vertical alignment selected.

4. Set the Foreground color to White and use the Type tool to create the words "Ski Resort" in a script typeface at about 60 points. Don't forget to set the alignment back to left-aligned in the Type Tool dialog box.

5. Duplicate the layer with the words "Ski Resort" on it and move the duplicate layer below the original layer in the Layers palette.

6. Make sure the Preserve Transparency checkbox in the Layers palette is not checked. Choose Filter➡Blur➡Gaussian Blur and in the dialog box that appears set the Radius to 2.5 pixels. Click OK.

7. Set the Blending mode for the duplicate layer to Dissolve to create the snow effect behind the text (see Figure 16.12).

Figure 16.12

Use the Dissolve blending mode on the blurred text to create a snow effect behind the text.

Exporting the GIF File

Now that you have created the backdrop for our fictitious Web page, it's time to save the file in a format that works for the Web. Because this image is intended to be a backdrop for a Web page, we must save the file in GIF format. We could also save the file in JPEG format, but the JPEG file would take too long to display for most Web users.

1. If you performed the steps in this chapter to create the Alpine Village Ski Resort image, open that image in Photoshop. If you did not perform the steps in this chapter prior to this section, open lessons/chap16/village0.psd on the CD-ROM that accompanies this book.

2. Before we can export this file as a GIF file we must convert it to an Indexed Color image. Choose Image➡Mode➡Indexed Color and click OK when the dialog box appears asking if you want to flatten the layers. Choose the following settings in the Indexed Color dialog box (see Figure 16.13).

   ► Choose Web as the palette to create an indexed color file containing colors that will display correctly on both the Macintosh and Windows platforms.

   ► When you choose Web as the palette, the color depth is automatically set to Other and the colors to 216. There are 216 colors that the Macintosh and Windows platforms have in common.

   ► Diffusion is the best choice for indexed color images when you choose the Web palette. The Diffusion dither creates smoother transitions between the colors in the indexed color file creating the illusion of more colors than are actually present.

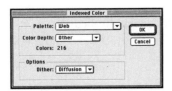

Figure 16.13

The Indexed Color dialog box with the Web palette choices.

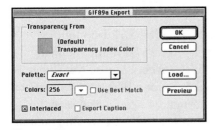

Figure 16.14

The GIF89a Export dialog box.

3. Choose File➡Export➡GIF89a Export to display the GIF89a Export dialog box (see Figure 16.14).

4. Do not click in the preview window of the GIF89a Export dialog box with the Eyedropper icon because this selects a color to be saved as transparent. This particular image does not require any transparency. Check the Interlace checkbox so the image displays in stages on the Web page. Click OK and name this file "village.gif."

Transparency in GIF Files

When saving GIF files you have the option of assigning transparency by selecting a color or series of colors in the image to convert to transparency. It's important when specifying the transparency color to be sure there are no other parts of the image with the same color.

1. Open lessons/chap16/logo.psd on the CD-ROM that accompanies this book.

2. Convert this image to Indexed Color mode (Image➡Mode➡Indexed Color). GIF files cannot save grayscale images, but converting the grayscale image to indexed color produces RGB equivalents for the grays. Also note that when you convert from grayscale to indexed color, the conversion is done without presenting any dialog boxes because the image is automatically converted to a 256 color indexed image.

3. Choose File➡Export➡GIF89a Export to display the GIF89a Export dialog box.

4. Select the Eyedropper tool in the GIF89a Export dialog box and click the white background in the preview window to make the white color the transparency color.

5. Click the color swatch above the tools in the GIF89a Export dialog box to change the transparency color to a color that is more visible.

6. Notice that the color box that corresponds with the color you chose as the transparency is outlined in black in the palette color. You can click these little boxes with the Eyedropper tool to add to the transparency color range.

7. To remove colors from the transparency color selection, hold down the (Command)[Control] key and click either the image in the preview window or the colors in the color palette.

8. Click OK and give the file a name. Photoshop automatically appends the GIF extension to your file's name.

Saving JPEG Files

JPEG files are usually RGB color images that contain a relatively wide dynamic range. Many Web pages use a low resolution GIF file as a thumbnail image that when clicked links to a higher resolution JPEG file.

1. Open lessons/chap16/girl.psd on the CD-ROM that accompanies this book. This is a 300 ppi RGB color file.

2. Choose File➡Save As and choose JPEG from the Format pull-down menu in the dialog box that appears.

3. Change the name of the file to "girl.jpg" and click the Save button to display the JPEG Options dialog box (see Figure 16.15).

4. Choose a quality setting from 1 to 10 by typing a number in the Quality box, dragging the slider, or selecting from the pull-down menu. The higher the quality of the image, the larger the file is. A quality setting between Medium and Maximum produces the best results, though the composition of the image affects how apparent the color loss is.

5. There are three choices in the Format Options section of the JPEG Options dialog box:

   ▶ **Baseline ("Standard")**—The standard color format for JPEG files.

   ▶ **Baseline Optimized**—Optimizes the color of the image and produces a better resulting image than Baseline ("Standard").

   ▶ **Progressive**—Similar to interlacing and downloads the JPEG image to Web browsers in multiple passes. When you choose

Figure 16.15

The JPEG Options dialog box.

progressive you can specify the number of scans (3, 4, or 5) that it takes to build the file on the Web browser. Progressive JPEG files are not currently supported by all Web browsers and require a significant amount of RAM to create and view in a browser.

6. Click OK to save the JPEG file.

Summary

In this chapter you learned about the different file formats supported by Photoshop for use on Web pages as well as instructions on how to save them. The tutorial in this chapter represents a typical Web graphic that would be used as an image incorporating an imagemap. You can, of course create Web graphics of any size for use on your Web pages by applying the same principle steps used to create the graphic in the tutorial and even apply some of the steps detailed to create button graphics for your pages. To learn more about creating Web graphics in Photoshop, I suggest *Photoshop Web Magic* from Hayden Books. Check out the many books on the Internet and creating Web pages on Hayden's Web site: http://www.mcp.com/hayden.

Printing

For the majority of us, printing from Photoshop usually involves printing to a desktop laser printer or color printer. Photoshop can print to any output device as long as its printer driver resides on your computer system. Like most desktop publishing software, printing in Photoshop is set up through the Page Setup and Print dialog boxes.

Specifying Page Setup

The Page Setup dialog box is where you specify the paper size, orientation, and scaling percentage for the printed file (see Figure 17.1). The printer driver you have installed on your computer determines the Paper Size choices, as well as the options available when you click the Options button. Select a scaling percentage to reduce the size of the image to fit the desired paper size. Click one of two Orientation buttons to specify whether your image prints landscape or portrait.

Figure 17.1

The Page Setup dialog box.

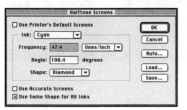

Figure 17.2

The Halftone Screens dialog box.

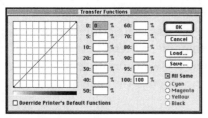

Figure 17.3

The Transfer Functions dialog box.

Specifying Halftone Screens

Click the Screen button in the Page Setup dialog box to specify the Halftone Screen information for your image (see Figure 17.2). You should always check with your service bureau or printer before specifying your halftone screen information. If you are printing to a PostScript Level 1 printer, check the Use Printer's Default Screens checkbox. If you are printing to a PostScript Level 2 printer, check the Use Accurate Screens checkbox. Click the Auto button to display the Auto Screens dialog box where you can specify a printer resolution and halftone screen frequency to set the screen angles automatically in the Halftone Screens dialog box.

Adjusting Transfer Functions

Click on the Transfer button in the Page Setup dialog box to display the Transfer Functions dialog box (see Figure 17.3). You can use the Transfer Functions dialog box to correct for a printer's calibration errors. Before you can enter any values in the Transfer Functions dialog box, you must perform some printed tests using calibration bars and a color densitometer. Enter the values from the color densitometer in the corresponding slots in the Transfer Functions dialog box to compensate for calibration problems. Most color printers come with calibration software or have ways to set the calibration on the device itself, so it's unlikely you will specify Transfer Functions in Photoshop.

Setting Background Color and Border

Click the Background button in the Page Setup dialog box to specify a background color using the Color Picker. When you select a background color, the rest of the page area outside the image area fills with the background color. This option is useful if you are printing slides to a film recorder for example, because you can fill the background of the slide with

When to Specify a Bleed

The only time you'll have to specify a bleed in Photoshop is when the image will be printed to film directly from Photoshop. A bleed is necessary when an image goes right to the edge of a printed page to accommodate trimming and binding after the page is printed. For example: If you create an image that is to cover an entire 8.5"×11" page when printed, you must create the image larger to facilitate a bleed on all sides (typically 1/8"). This means the Photoshop image will be 8.75"×11.25" with a .125" bleed specified in the Page Setup dialog box. When the page is printed and ready to be trimmed, the person cutting the page down to size uses the inset crop marks to trim the page to its correct size of 8.5"×11".

black or another dark color. If you would like your image to print with a black border, click the Border button in the Page Setup dialog box to display the Border dialog box; specify a width for the border in points, millimeters, or inches.

Setting the Bleed Option

Click the Bleed button in the Page Setup dialog box to display the Bleed dialog box; enter a width for the bleed in inches, millimeters, or points. The bleed amount insets the crop marks by the amount specified to trim your image. The image size does not increase to accommodate the bleed amount.

Printing a Caption with the File

Check the Caption checkbox in the Page Setup dialog box to print the caption you specified in the File Info dialog box. Choose File➡File Info to display the File Info dialog box; enter the caption text before choosing Page Setup (see Figure 17.4). Click the Labels checkbox to print the name of the file above the image.

Printing Registration Marks

Check the appropriate boxes to print registration marks with your image. If you are printing to a film imagesetting device, check Negative to print negative film and select the emulsion setting (usually down for offset printing). Use the Interpolation checkbox when printing to a PostScript Level 2 printer that supports interpolation to resample a low resolution image while printing (see Figure 17.5). The registration options available are as follows:

Figure 17.4

The File Info dialog box.

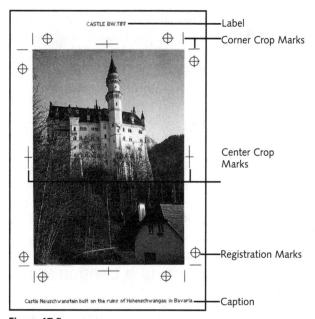

CASTLE BW.TIFF ———————— Label
————— Corner Crop Marks

Center Crop
Marks

Registration Marks

Castle Neuschwanstein built on the ruins of Hohenschwangau in Bavaria ——— Caption

Figure 17.5

Registration Marks and Page Setup options.

► **Registration Marks:** Prints bullseye and star-target registration marks on all four sides of the image to help when registering color plates for proofing and offset printing.

► **Corner Crop Marks:** Photoshop inserts crop marks at the four corners of the image.

► **Center Crop Marks:** Photoshop centers crop marks on each side of the image.

► **Calibration Bars:** When the printer driver supports this feature, you can print calibration bars to check the dot percentages and density of the image using a densitometer.

Printing the Image

Before you print your image, click and hold on the left corner of the Image window to preview how the image will fit the specified paper size you selected in the Page Setup dialog box (see Figure 17.6). You should make sure that the image area fits on the page. Choose File➡Print to display the Print dialog box (see Figure 17.7).

Figure 17.6

A preview image of how the file will print with the current page setup.

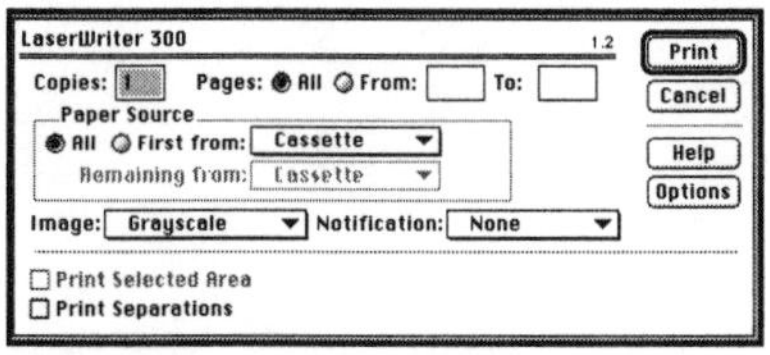

Figure 17.7

The Print dialog box.

If you are printing color separations of a CMYK file, click on the Print Separations checkbox.

When printing an RGB file, you can select from three radio buttons to print the image in Gray, RGB, or CMYK. You also can select and print a portion of your image with the selection tools and by checking the Print Selected Area checkbox in the Print dialog box.

Summary

This chapter covered the basic setup and printing procedures that are most typical when you want to print a file directly out of Photoshop. Your particular printer may include other options not mentioned here, though the basic options will remain the same from one printer to the next. If you're working with a lot of small images and do not need crop marks for each image, you can save paper and printing time by placing the images in a page layout application such as QuarkXPress or PageMaker and printing them ganged up on pages. Consult your printer manual for the specifics about your particular printing device.

File Formats

Photoshop images can be saved in a large variety of file formats including the most popular formats for desktop publishing and Web graphics. In most cases, the file format options are available in the Save As dialog box under the File menu, or in the Export submenu under the File menu. This chapter discusses the determining factors when deciding the correct file format for a particular image.

Save As File Formats

Each file format available in Photoshop has limitations to how you can use the file after you save it. In many cases, there are specific settings that you must set when saving the file to achieve a particular result. Open any file and choose File➡Save As to display the Save As dialog box (see Figure A.1).

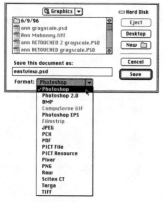

Figure A.1

The Save As dialog box.

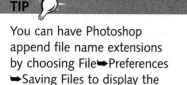

You can have Photoshop
append file name extensions
by choosing File➡Preferences
➡Saving Files to display the
Preferences dialog box and
selecting an Append File
Extension option.

Figure A.2

The BMP Options dialog box.

Each file format also has a corresponding three-character extension, which is a necessary part of the filename for the Windows platform. Windows 95 supports long filenames, but you should conform to the DOS-naming convention of an eight-character filename with a three-character extension when creating files for use on platforms other than Macintosh.

▶ **Photoshop.** This is the native format for files created in the current version of Photoshop (4.0 at this writing). You can open these files with only the current version of Photoshop. Saving files in this format preserves all Layers and Channels for later modification. Photoshop's Erase to Saved and Fill from Saved features can only be used if the file you're working in has been saved in this format.

▶ **Photoshop 2.0.** This is the native format for files created in Adobe Photoshop 2.0. If you share files with other Photoshop users who have not upgraded to the latest version of Photoshop, this is the format that is most likely to work, assuming they're using version 2 or later.

▶ **BMP.** Windows Bitmap Format. This is the native format for Microsoft Paint on the IBM PC and compatible platforms. Supported by a number of MS Windows and OS/2 software applications, this bitmapped file format can save up to 16 million colors. The BMP Options dialog box presents options for File Format and Bit Depth (see Figure A.2).

▶ **CompuServe GIF (Graphics Interchange Format).** Originally created by CompuServe (an online service) to save screen oriented low-file-size graphics, the GIF file format is widely used by Internet Web sites. The GIF format supports a maximum of 256 colors and must be in Indexed

Figure A.3

The GIF Options dialog box.

Color Mode or Grayscale. Small file size and the capability to render onscreen using a method called interlacing, make this format highly portable and desirable for online services. The GIF Options dialog box offers two choices for Row Order, Normal and Interlaced (see Figure A.3).

▶ **Photoshop EPS (Encapsulated PostScript).** This format can include both PostScript data (vector graphics) and bitmap data. Because it can save PostScript code, EPS is the format of choice for files that contain clipping paths. The EPS format is supported by all high-end desktop page layout programs including QuarkXPress and PageMaker. When you save a bitmap (1 bit per pixel) image, you have the choice to make the whites transparent. The EPS Format dialog box offers format options before saving the file (see Figure A.4). Choose a Preview option from the drop-down menu in the EPS Format dialog box. Choose TIFF preview for EPS files that will ultimately be placed in page layout programs in Windows. The 1-bit per pixel preview is a black-and-white preview that does not contain gray levels. If the EPS file is in color, you should choose the 8-bit per pixel option to see the image in color in layout applications. If you have defined a Path in Photoshop, choose the path to use as the clipping path from the Path drop-down menu. See Chapter 6, "Creating Paths," for more information about creating and saving paths. Do not check the two checkboxes in the lower left-hand corner of the EPS Format dialog box unless you really know what you're doing. Checking these two boxes can sometimes cause more harm than good, especially when sending files to service bureaus or printers.

▶ **EPS-DCS (Encapsulated PostScript File for Desktop Color Separations).** When you save a CMYK image as an EPS file, the EPS Format

Figure A.4

The EPS Format dialog box when saving a CMYK image.

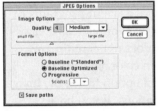

Figure A.5

The JPEG Options dialog box.

dialog box includes a choice for DCS (see Figure A.4). Saving an EPS file with the DCS option produces five separate files that include a controlling EPS composite file along with separate files for cyan, magenta, yellow, and black. Only applications that perform color separations support this format. Check with your service bureau or printer before using this file format option.

► **Filmstrip.** Adobe Premiere (a movie and QuickTime editing application) creates the filmstrip format first. A filmstrip can include multiple frames from a segment of a movie. Once modified in Photoshop, you can export the movie as a Filmstrip format file and then import it back into Premiere. You should not crop or resize the Filmstrip format file in Photoshop if you intend to return the file to Premiere. Refer to the *Premiere Users Manual* for information on saving Filmstrip files.

► **JPEG (Joint Photographic Experts Group).** This format is most commonly used to display images on Web pages. JPEG files are RGB images that are saved with a compression algorithm that discards data not essential to the display of the image (see Figure A.5). This method of compression, referred to as "lossy," permanently removes some data from the file each time the compression is applied. See Chapter 6, "Creating Paths," for more information on saving JPEG files.

► **PCX (Paintbrush Color eXchange format).** This format was developed by Zsoft for PC Paintbrush, an IBM DOS and MS Windows application. Photoshop can open and save PCX files that contain up to 16 million colors (32 bits per pixel). Most IBM PC applications that support importing graphics support version 5 of the PCX format. The PCX format does not offer a dialog box when saving the file.

▶ **PDF (Portable Document Format).** The PDF
format was created by Adobe Systems. Adobe
Acrobat, a software application for electronic
publishing created by Adobe, uses the PDF
format. An Acrobat file can be read on
Macintosh, Windows, Unix, and DOS platforms
using the Acrobat Reader software (available
from Adobe Systems and also included on the
CD-ROM that comes with Adobe Photoshop).
See the "Electronic Publishing Guide" on the
Photoshop Tutorial CD-ROM for more information
about the PDF format.

Figure A.6

The PICT File Options dialog box.

▶ **PICT File (PICTure file format).** This format is the
MacOS's native graphics format. The PICT format
supports both object (vector) graphics and
bitmapped graphics. It also supports every bit
depth, size, and resolution. The PICT file format is
most often used for onscreen presentations and
screen captures. When saving an RGB image, the
PICT format offers either a 16-bit or 32-bit per
pixel resolution (see Figure A.6). When saving
grayscale images you can choose from 2, 4, or 8
bits per pixel. The compression options depicted
in Figure A.6 are only available if you have
QuickTime installed on your MacOS system.

Figure A.7

*The PICT Resource Options
dialog box.*

▶ **PICT Resource:** MacOS systems uses resource
files to display icons and pictures within applications. You can open these hidden PICT resources
in Photoshop by choosing File➡Import➡Pict
Resource. Generally, the PICT Resource file
format is used to save StartupScreen files on
MacOS systems. If you save a file as a PICT
resource, name it "StartupScreen", and place it in
the System Folder, the picture displays onscreen
at startup time. The PICT Resource Options
dialog box allows you to give the resource an ID
number and a name. Specify resolution and
compression settings by clicking the appropriate
radio buttons (see Figure A.7).

▶ **PIXAR.** Pixar Corporation's 3D rendering applications use this format exclusively. The PIXAR format supports RGB color and grayscale images and offers no options when saving the file.

▶ **PixelPaint.** PixelPaint versions 1.0 and 2.0 for the Macintosh use the PixelPaint format exclusively. Your image can be either indexed color or grayscale. PixelPaint Professional version 3.0 or higher does not support this format; use a PICT or TIFF file instead of the PixelPaint format if you're using a newer version of the program.

▶ **RAW.** This format is a flexible file format for transferring documents between applications and computer systems. The RAW format consists of a stream of bytes that describe the color information in the file. You must have a firm grip on file formats and file specifications to use this format. Please consult the Photoshop documentation for a rather lengthy explanation of each of the parameters that you must set to use this format properly.

▶ **Scitex CT (Scitex Continuous Tone format).** Scitex Color Workstations and peripherals use this format most often. There are no options available for this format in Photoshop and files can be in Grayscale, RGB, or CMYK mode. Scitex CT is the default and proprietary format that Scitex drum scanners create.

▶ **Targa.** This format was developed by TrueVision Corp. to facilitate the use of 32-bit images that contain an 8-bit alpha channel to display live video. Use this format to combine graphics with live video; however, only systems that include a Truevision® video card support this format. MS-DOS color applications often support this format. When you save an RGB image in this format you choose the color bit depth from the Targa Options dialog box (see Figure A.8).

▶ **TIFF (Tag Image File Format).** If you create alpha channels for an image, use either the TIFF format or the default Photoshop format to make sure they're saved with the image. MacOS and IBM PC and compatible computers use different "bit orders" for the TIFF file. You can specify the correct bit order for the TIFF file by clicking the checkboxes for either Macintosh or IBM PC when saving the file (see Figure A.9). The LZW compression option is a lossless compression scheme that does not throw data away when compressing. Adobe Photoshop reads and saves captions in TIFF files, used

Figure A.8

The Targa Options dialog box

Figure A.9

The Tiff Options dialog box

primarily by the Associated Press Picture Desk System. To enter caption information, choose the File Info command in the File menu.

Export Formats

Some file formats are only available in the Export submenu under the File menu. The export formats are actually external plug-ins, which Photoshop stores in the Plug-Ins directory. There are three export plug-ins that ship with Photoshop: GIF89a Export, Paths to Illustrator, and Quick Edit Save. Chapter 16, "Creating Web Graphics," covers the GIF89a Export option in greater detail, while Chapter 6, "Creating Paths," discusses the Paths to Illustrator option. Use the Quick Edit Save option to save files opened using the Quick Edit import option. Choose File➡Input➡Quick Edit to open a portion of a Photoshop, Scitex, or uncompressed TIFF file. Edit the file and put it back in the original file using Quick Edit Save.

Using Save a Copy

When working in Photoshop, you most likely will create alpha channels and layers at some point. When you need to save the file, but want to retain a working copy of the file with alpha channels and layers intact, choose File➡Save a Copy to display the Save a Copy dialog box (see Figure A.10). Check the checkboxes at the bottom of the dialog box to flatten the image and/or ignore alpha channels when saving the file.

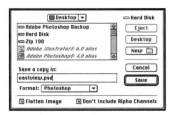

Figure A.10

The Save A Copy dialog box.

index

Hard Light blending mode, 87
histograms (grayscale images),
 181
HSB color, 169-170
Hue blending mode, 87
hues (colorizing), 203-204

I

Illustrator (paths, exporting to),
 165
Image Cache preferences, 11
image modes
  Bitmap mode, 53-56
  CMYK mode, 58-59
  Duotone mode, 61-64
  Grayscale mode, 56-58
  Indexed Color mode, 68
    color tables, 71-72
    converting, 68
    palettes, 69
  Lab mode, 60
  monotones, 65
  Multichannel mode, 73
  RGB mode, 58
image previews, 6
image window, 15-16
  document sizes, 15
  efficiency, 16
  scratch sizes, 16
  timing, 16
imagemaps (WWW), 304
images
  background (WWW), 304-311
  CMYK
    adjusting, 189-192
    *Selective Color dialog box,
     193-194*
  combining, 267-269
  compositing, 210-215
  converting
    bitmap to grayscale, 57
    color to grayscale, 57-58
    grayscale to color, 58
  down-sampling, 52-53
  edge effects, 145-150
    layers, 150-151
  enlarging, 51-52

erasing, 271
file formats, 328
flattening, 32
grayscale
  adjusting, 180-185
  histograms, 181
imperfections, removing,
 281-282
levels, 277-280
reducing, 52-53
resampling, 51-52
retouched (output specifications), 282
RGB
  adjusting, 185-189
  gamma, 188
screening, 217-219
sharpening, 249-251
  channels, 253-255
  Sharpen tool, 256-257
  Unsharp Mask, 252-253
indexed color (resolution), 50-51
Indexed Color mode, 68
  color tables, 71-72
  converting, 68
  palettes, 69
Info palette, 21-22
ink limit (Color Settings), 82
interface, 11-13
  image window, 15-16
  tool cursors, 14-15
  Toolbox, 12-16
interpolation (preferences), 5
intersections, selecting, 110-111

J

JPEG (Joint Photographic
 Experts Group), 326
  batch processing, 293
  saving, 314-315
  WWW, 301-302

L

Lab color, 168-169
Lab mode, 60
Lasso tools

Freehand, 112-114
Polygon, 112-114
layers
  adjustment, 32-33
  adjustment layers, 32-33, 223
    creating, 224-226
    filters, 227-233
    masks, editing, 226-227
  blending modes, 29
  compositing images, 210-215
  drop shadows, 235-239
  edge effects, 150-151
  masks, 29
    permanently applying, 145
    retouching, 271-273
  merging, 31
  moving, 270-271
  opacity, 29
  palette, 27-32
  reflections, 215-217
  retaining with Save As Copy
   command, 329
  rotating, 216, 270-271
  screening images, 217-219
  selections, 130
  text, 219-221
    embossing, 220
  vignettes, 140-152
Layers palette, 27-32
levels, adjusting, 277-280
Lighten blending mode, 87
lighting
  bleached effect, 239-240
  Burn tool, 259
  Dodge tool, 259
Lighting Effects filter, 246-247
Line tool, 91-92
loading selections, 125-131
LPI (Lines Per Inch), 44-45
Luminosity blending mode, 88

M

Macintosh monitor calibration,
 76-77
Magic Wand tool, 114-118
  selecting color ranges,
   118-120

MACMILLAN COMPUTER PUBLISHING USA

A VIACOM COMPANY

Technical ---- **Support:**

If you need assistance with the information in this book or with a CD/Disk
accompanying the book, please access the Knowledge Base on our Web
site at **http://www.superlibrary.com/general/support**. Our most
Frequently Asked Questions are answered there. If you do not find the
answer to your questions on our Web site, you may contact Macmillan
Technical Support **(317) 581-3833** or e-mail us at **support@mcp.com**.